The Marriage Paradox

EMERGING ADULTHOOD SERIES

Series Editor

Larry J. Nelson

Advisory Board

Elisabetta Crocetti
Shagufa Kapadia
Koen Luyckx
Laura Padilla-Walker
Jennifer L. Tanner

Books in the Series

Emerging Adults' Religiousness and Spirituality: Meaning-Making in an Age of Transition
Edited by Carolyn McNamara Barry and Mona M. Abo-Zena

Flourishing in Emerging Adulthood: Positive Development During the Third Decade of Life
Edited by Laura M. Padilla-Walker and Larry J. Nelson

The Marriage Paradox: Why Emerging Adults Love Marriage yet Push It Aside
Brian J. Willoughby and Spencer L. James

Forthcoming Books in the Series

The Developing Self in Emerging Adulthood: Comparing Narrative and Traditional Approaches
Michael W. Pratt and M. Kyle Matsuba

The Experience of Emerging Adulthood Among Street-Involved Youth
Doug Magnuson, Mikael Jansson, and Cecilia Benoit

The Romantic Lives of Emerging Adults: Expanding the Narrative
Varda Konstam

Leaving Care and the Transition to Adulthood: International Contributions to Theory, Research, and Practice
Edited by Varda Mann-Feder and Martin Goyette

Pathways to Adulthood: Emerging Adults in Contemporary America
Patricia Snell Herzog

In Pursuit of Love and Work: A New Lens for Understanding Development During Emerging Adulthood
Shmuel Shulman

Developing Mental Health in Emerging Adulthood
Edited by Jennifer L. Tanner

The Marriage Paradox ▲

Why Emerging Adults Love Marriage yet Push It Aside

Brian J. Willoughby
Spencer L. James

OXFORD
UNIVERSITY PRESS

Oxford University Press is a department of the University of Oxford. It furthers
the University's objective of excellence in research, scholarship, and education
by publishing worldwide. Oxford is a registered trade mark of Oxford University
Press in the UK and certain other countries.

Published in the United States of America by Oxford University Press
198 Madison Avenue, New York, NY 10016, United States of America.

CIP data is on file at the Library of Congress
ISBN 978-0-19-029665-0

9 8 7 6 5 4 3 2 1
Printed by WebCom, Inc., Canada

CONTENTS ▲

SERIES FOREWORD ▲

The *Emerging Adulthood Series* examines the period of life starting at age 18 and continuing into and through the third decade of life, now commonly referred to as emerging adulthood. The specific focus of the series is on flourishing (i.e., factors that lead to positive, adaptive development during emerging adulthood and the successful transition into adult roles) and floundering (i.e., factors that lead to maladaptive behaviors and negative development during emerging adulthood as well as delay and difficulty in transitioning into adult roles) in the diverse paths young people take into and through the third decade of life.

There is a need to examine the successes and struggles in a variety of domains experienced by young people as they take complex and multiple paths in leaving adolescence and moving into and through their 20s. Too often the diversity of individual experiences is forgotten in our academic attempts to categorize a time period. For example, in proposing his theory of Emerging Adulthood, Arnett (2000, 2004) identified features of the development of young people, including *feeling in-between* (emerging adults do not see themselves as either adolescents or adults), *identity exploration* (especially in the areas of work, love, and world views), *focus on the self* (not self-centered, but simply lacking obligations to others), *instability* (evidenced by changes of direction in residential status, relationships, work, and education), and *possibilities* (optimism in the potential to steer their lives in any number of desired directions). Although this is a nice summary of characteristics of the time period, the scholarly examination of emerging adulthood has not always attempted to capture and explain the within-group variation that exists among emerging adults, often making the broad generalization that they are a relatively homogenous group. For example, emerging adults have been categorically referred to as "narcissistic," "refusing to grow up," and "failed adults." Although there certainly are emerging adults who fit the profile of selfish, struggling, and directionless, there are others who are using this period of time for good. Indeed, there is great diversity of individual experiences in emerging adulthood. Hence, there is a need to better examine various beliefs/attitudes, attributes, behaviors, and relationships during this period of time that appear to reflect positive adjustment, or a sense of flourishing, or conversely those that lead to floundering.

For example, recent research (Nelson & Padilla-Walker, 2013) shows that young people who appear to be successfully navigating emerging adulthood tend to engage in identity exploration, develop internalization of positive values, participate in positive media use, engage in pro-social behaviors, report healthy relationships with parents, and engage in romantic relationships that are characterized by higher levels of companionship, worth, affection, and emotional support. For others who appear to be floundering, emerging adulthood appears to include anxiety and depression, poor self-perceptions, greater participation in risk behaviors, and poorer relationship quality with parents, best friends, and romantic partners. Thus, although various profiles of flourishing and floundering are starting to be identified, the current work in the field has simply provided cursory overviews of findings. This series provides a platform for an in-depth, comprehensive examination into some of these key factors that seem to be influencing, positively or negatively, young people as they enter into and progress through the third decade of life and the multiple ways in which they may flourish or flounder. Furthermore, the series attempts to examine how these factors may function differently within various populations (e.g., cultures and religious and ethnic subcultures, students vs. nonstudents, men vs. women). Finally, the series provides for a multidisciplinary (e.g., fields ranging from developmental psychology, neurobiology, education, sociology, criminology) and multi-method (i.e., information garnered from both quantitative and qualitative methodologies) examination of issues related to flourishing and floundering in emerging adulthood.

It is important to make one final note about this series. The choice to employ the term "emerging adulthood" was not meant to imply that the series will include books that are limited in their scope to viewing the third decade of life only through the lens of emerging adulthood theory (Arnett, 2000). Indeed, the notion of "emerging adulthood" as a universal developmental period has been met with controversy and skepticism because of the complex and numerous paths young people take out of adolescence and into adulthood. It is that exact diversity in the experiences of young people in a variety of contexts and circumstances (e.g., cultural, financial, familial) that calls for a book series such as this one. It is unfortunate that disagreement about emerging adulthood theory has led to a fragmentation of scholars and scholarship devoted to better understanding the third decade of life. Hence, although the term "emerging adulthood" is employed for parsimony and for its growing familiarity as a term for the age period, this series is devoted to examining broadly the complexity of pathways into and through the third decade of life from a variety of perspectives and disciplines. In doing so, it is my hope that the series will help scholars, practitioners, students, and others better understand, and thereby potentially foster, flourishing and floundering in the lives of young people in the various paths they may take to adulthood.

▲ The Marriage Paradox

As noted, one of the problems that exists in both scholarly and media approaches to understanding and depicting the third decade of life is the failure to capture the diversity of individual experience. One of the areas in which this mistake is made is in the examination of the role of marriage in the lives of young people. It may be argued that the diversity in and complexities of navigating the 20s might be due to the delay in marriage more than any other single factor. Compared with past decades when young people married in their early 20s (or younger), the delay in marriage now leaves the 20s as a period of time for many young people to engage in a number of other recreational, academic/vocational, and personal pursuits. Because of this, broad generalizations are made regarding the complete lack of importance of marriage to emerging adults. This completely ignores the actual diversity that exists related to both beliefs and behaviors associated with marriage in emerging adulthood.

This sweeping generalization might likewise be responsible for a trend we see of researchers not treating marriage as a viable area of scholarly inquiry during the third decade of life. Again, this fails to capture the diversity of paths through the third decade of life. Focusing solely on the average age at marriage as a potential starting point of when marriage might become a worthy target of scholarly interest, researchers are missing out on the potential fruitful area of examining how cognitions about marriage may play important roles in guiding the behaviors of young people throughout their 20s. And, lastly, a failure to examine the diversity in how young people think about and approach marriage dismisses the very real and personal inner struggle that many young people experience as they grapple with very personal and meaningful aspects of their lives related to marriage (i.e., How can I avoid/replicate what I saw in my parents' marriage? Do I want to marry? Will I marry and, if so, when? How will it fit within my career plans? How does my current romantic relationship play into my plans for my life—now and in the future?). These are real issues for young people, and as such they should be of significant interest to scholars as we attempt to unpack the multiplicity of factors that account for the diversity of individual experience in the third decade of life.

It is for these very reasons that "The Marriage Paradox: Why Emerging Adults Love Marriage yet Push It Aside" by Drs. Brian J. Willoughby and Spencer L. James is such an important contribution to this book series with its goal to better understand how various beliefs/attitude, attributes, behaviors, and relationships are associated with flourishing or floundering in emerging adulthood. Although the authors make it very clear in the book what the shifts have been during the emerging adulthood period (e.g., rise in the average age of marriage, disconnecting childbearing from marriage) that have changed the marriage landscape during and past the third decade of life, they also make it clear why a discussion focused solely on those aggregate trends across all segments of the population masks the underlying complexity and reality of marriage for many emerging adults.

The foundation for their book is found in the examination of what they refer to as the marriage paradox, which is the apparent contradiction of two key findings related to marriage in emerging adulthood—(1) that modern-day emerging adults largely value, respect, and plan for marriage; and (2) that modern-day emerging adults are marrying later and less often than previous generations. Through the use of both quantitative methods and extensive interviews with a diverse cross-section of young people, the authors help us understand at a scholarly level the effect that this paradox has in accounting for within-group differences related to views about and approaches to marriage in emerging adulthood and also help us feel at the personal level the lived experiences of individuals as they grapple with this paradox in their own lives. The book shows how modern emerging adults think about and orient their lives either around or away from marriage. The authors articulate how emerging adults' beliefs, values, and choices of behavior affect their lives now and in the future. In doing so, the authors provide valuable information to both scholars and the general public that illuminates the internal struggles about marriage that many emerging adults feel, and how that intrapersonal grappling with these issues can help account for the diversity in approaches to marriage, specifically, and individual differences in flourishing and floundering, more generally, during the third decade of life.

Larry J. Nelson
Series Editor

ACKNOWLEDGMENTS ▲

The authors would like to thank the many people who helped collect, analyze, and clean the data used in this book. This volume represents hundreds of hours from faculty colleagues, graduate students, and undergraduate volunteers. We would like to thank the participants of the Marital Paradigm Study, who were willing to share with us their personal thoughts on marriage and allow us to enrich this volume with the real voices of emerging adults. We especially thank Dr. Larry Nelson as editor of the Emerging Adulthood Series for his guidance and feedback throughout the process and Andrea Zekus, our editor at Oxford, for her patience and direction. The authors would also like to thank the anonymous peer reviewers whose feedback was pivotal and greatly improved the quality of the book.

Of course, we would be remiss if we did not specifically acknowledge the many students who helped with various aspects of this book. Although their names may not be on the cover, the long hours spent contacting participants, cleaning data, coding interviews, and checking citations were critical to the overall integrity and quality of the study that forms the backbone of this exploration of emerging adults and marriage. The authors would specifically like to thank Kyle Bartholomew, Melissa Medaris, Lizette Larned, Ian Marsee, Miranda Marsee, Amanda Terry, Logan Dicus, Jenna Cassinat, Daye Son, Samuel Ruckus, Raechel Flowers, Christina Rosa, Saige Goff, McKenzie Vance, Lora Tomlinson,

Monica Stebbing, Elizabeth Hendrickson, Andy Thompson, and Keri Bloxham for their excellent work on various aspects of the Marital Paradigm Project and this book.

Finally, Brian would like to thank his wife Cassi for putting up with his long hours both writing and talking about this book as well as showing him personally the transformative power of marriage. Spencer, too, would like to thank his wife Alyssa for the support, love, and patience she's shown during this process and the truly selfless way she's helped him become a better person.

INTRODUCTION ▲

▲ The Marriage Paradox

Is marriage dead? Is it merely changing? Has it been replaced by alternatives such as cohabitation or serial dating and singlehood? These questions, and others like them, have been the subject of debate across American and Western societies for decades. Journalists, media personalities, scholars, and policy makers have all argued over the role marriage plays in modern life, and it has been the topic of myriad casual discussions around office water coolers and family dinner tables. In fact, perhaps no other question has been as enduring across the past 50 years of American history as whether marriage is relevant in modern society. Over the past several decades, marriage rates have declined, divorce and age at marriage have increased, and single parenthood has become more widely accepted. To the casual observer, it may seem that marriage, the primary mechanism for bearing and raising children and regulating the sexual behavior of adults for thousands of years, has become obsolete, a relic of the past.

But such a declaration about the death of marriage seems premature at best. If marriage were dead, people in the typical marriageable age range—emerging adults in their 20s and early 30s—would report that marriage no longer matters to them. In reality, emerging adults, those individuals typically between the ages of 18 and 30, continue to tell scholars and pollsters, and anyone else who asks, that marriage is important and is one of the most important milestones of life.

According to the Monitoring the Future data, in the late 1970s, 69% of high school senior boys and 80% of high school senior girls said that having a good marriage and family life was extremely important to them. By the early 2010s, virtually the exact same percentage of girls stated the same thing. The boys? The percentage actually increased slightly to about 72%. These results, perhaps startling when considering the monumental changes that have shaped the contemporary American family, reveal a nuanced and complex picture of where marriage fits. How can marriage be dying if so many emerging adults still value it and plan to marry someday? Paradoxically, why are emerging adults seemingly abandoning an institution they seem to value so much?

This dichotomy, whereby emerging adults value and plan for marriage while simultaneously relegating it to the back shelf, is the key question of this book. To state it more succinctly, we seek to answer one of the more puzzling questions facing those who study emerging adults: Why do modern emerging adults behave in ways that move against marriage when they say marriage is so important to them?

Data have consistently suggested two trends among modern-day emerging adults:

1. *Modern-day emerging adults largely value, respect, and plan for marriage, perhaps even more so than previous generations.*
2. *Modern-day emerging adults are marrying later and less often than previous generations.*

This is what we refer to as the *marriage paradox*. This is the question mystifying so many who study and seek to understand both family formation trends and the emerging adulthood period itself. Understanding this paradox requires not just an examination of national trends, although that is certainly essential, but also an understanding of the lived experience of emerging adults themselves. That is, to understand the marriage paradox we must first understand how marriage has become a paradox in the minds of emerging adults. We must understand how an institution that represents stability, perceived happiness, and "adulthood" can also exemplify fears of divorce, a loss of independence, and, potentially, the end of the best years of their lives. By natural extension, we must also explore the implications a shift away from marriage has on emerging adults' behaviors. How do changing attitudes toward marriage translate into their conduct and demeanor, as well as the activities in which they choose to engage?

We divide this book into three separate sections. The first section comprises Chapters 1, 2, and 3. This section provides a contextual and foundational discussion of the setting in which emerging adults live. After all, values, ideas, and beliefs are both creations and expressions of the wider context in which they are immersed. For this reason, we first discuss the cultural context of the developmental period of emerging adulthood (Chapter 1) before discussing the unique relationship context of the 20s (Chapter 2) and scholarship on marital beliefs generally (Chapter 3).

Our second section describes and articulates emerging adults' views of themselves in relation to marriage (Chapters 4, 5, and 6). This section seeks to understand how emerging adults think about marriage and how they value and measure it against their other goals and aspirations.

The remainder of the book examines the influences and consequences of emerging adults' beliefs about marriage (Chapters 7–11). It is here that we attempt to understand where the marital paradox of emerging adulthood might come. We explore how influences such as parents, religion, and peers—along with larger cultural contexts such as the media—contribute to contemporary emerging adults' understanding of the costs and benefits of marriage. In doing so, we hope the reader might appreciate how modern emerging adults' beliefs about marriage are both complex in their nature and complex in how they are created and maintained.

THE MARRIAGE PARADOX ▲

1 ▲

Modern Marriage and Emerging Adulthood in the United States

▲ Understanding Emerging Adulthood

Despite ongoing debates about whether emerging adulthood is a new developmental period or the result of middle- and upper-class privilege (Arnett, 2000; Arnett, Kloep, Hendry, & Tanner, 2011), there is no denying that the third decade of life in the twenty-first century is a very different experience than it was even a generation or two ago. Emerging adults' views and behaviors toward marriage are not divorced (pun intended) from this fact. Societal changes—including shifting norms, attitudes, and behaviors surrounding marriage and family life during this period—have paved the way for many of the paradoxical findings we detail later in this book. Here, we briefly discuss the unique cultural environment that many emerging adults currently find themselves in, before we tackle the specific issue of the marriage paradox.

Most discussions of the emerging adulthood period begin with the simple fact that fewer than half of emerging adults believe they have reached adulthood, but most do not feel that they are youths or teens either (Arnett, 2000). Rather, they occupy an ambiguous period rife with decisions about relationships, education, sexuality, and occupations, but often without the direction of norms that guided previous generations. Although many elements of emerging adult culture have been discussed elsewhere, we focus on several of the most salient elements for how emerging adults think about marriage and family formation. Numerous potential explanations for emerging adults' perceived lack of adulthood exist, from biological and genetic factors to large-scale shifts in how society is organized. We argue that the increased *variation* in how emerging adults experience their 20s is perhaps the most important factor in the shifting marriage and family formation trends currently seen among emerging adults. In this chapter, we explore what this variation is and examine its historical roots. In chapter 2, we will explore how economic uncertainties have led some young people to make very different choices regarding relationships than their parents or grandparents made, and why this matters for marriage in America in the twenty-first century.

▲ The Age of Choice

Nearly all scholars agree that emerging adults today have more socially acceptable choices and possibilities upon leaving the parental home than previous generations. One prominent scholar noted that emerging adulthood could partially be described as the "age of possibilities" and suggested that modern emerging adults' life trajectories are often more varied than in previous generations (Arnett, 2000, 2007). In previous generations, emerging adults often encountered fairly normalized and institutional guidelines for the pathway to adulthood, even if these pathways tended to vary by social class and were somewhat restrictive. Just a few generations ago, this path was clear for the majority of emerging adults: Upon leaving one's family of origin, one either entered the labor force or, for a lucky minority, attended post-secondary education. Either way, marriage was expected to come fairly soon after leaving home, with children quickly nipping at the heels. This sequence was fairly straightforward and simple: job, marriage, and finally children. Deviations and variations certainly existed but were generally frowned on, and emerging adults of the time experienced strong cultural pressure to conform to this sequence of life transitions.

Much has changed in the last 70-odd years since the *Leave-It-to-Beaver* stereotype of the American family was firmly rooted into the psyche of most emerging adults. From the 1960s forward, cultural changes meant that the stability of family life began to erode and even evaporate for many. Variations from the normative family life sequencing became both more acceptable and common. The sexual revolution of the 1960s and 1970s brought with it structural shifts in the form of legalized abortion, widespread availability of affordable birth control, and more liberal cultural attitudes surrounding sex.

One result of greater sexual freedom outside of marriage has been an increase in nonmarital childbirth (both planned and unplanned). From 1940 to 2013, the nonmarital birth rate in the United States increased more than tenfold, from 3.8% of all births in 1940 to 40.6% of all births in 2013 (Hamilton, Martin, Osterman, & Curtin, 2014; Ventura & Bachrach, 2000). Although this increase in nonmarital childbearing has affected nearly all socioeconomic groups, the disconnect between marriage and childbearing is especially stark among the disadvantaged. In 2010, 65% of births to families with a household income of less than $25,000 were outside of a marital context (U.S. Census Bureau, 2010). The difference is even more striking when considering racial and ethnic differences. In 2013, for example, 71% of births to black women were nonmarital, which was almost twice that of white women (35.8%). Hispanics were right in the middle at 53.2% (Martin, Hamilton, Osterman, Curtin, & Mathews, 2015).

Beyond the increase in nonmarital childbearing, changes in divorce laws have also contributed to the remaking of the American family. Perhaps most notably, the advent of *no-fault divorce* (Adams & Coltrane, 2007; Stevenson & Wolfers, 2007) helped usher in a divorce boom during which divorce rates sharply spiked, peaking around the early 1980s. Since that time, the divorce rate has decreased, from a high of 22.8 divorces per 1,000 married couples in 1979 to 16.7 divorces per 1,000 married couples in 2005 (Stevenson & Wolfers, 2007). Despite the divorce rate itself decreasing, the proportion of the population that is divorced has continued to increase. The percentage of women in the United States who had ever divorced almost doubled from 1980 to 2011, from 6.6% to 11% (U.S. Census Bureau, 2011). Rates of marriage and divorce from 1900 to 2012 are shown in Figure 1.1. At marriage's high point in 1940, there were about twelve marriages per 1,000 people. This number has now dropped to fewer than seven marriages per 1,000 people. The divorce rate, on the other hand, rose to five divorces per 1,000 people in the 1980s, but has recently dropped to less than four divorces (see Figure 1.1).

Despite these changes, many of today's emerging adults, as children of the baby boomers, grew up in the economic prosperity that was the norm in the 1980s and 1990s ("The Economy in the 1980s and 1990s," 2012), which provided families with resources for their children that were unheard of even 20 years before. Consequently, the baby boomers' children (the Gen X and Gen Y crowd) grew up in a time when vacations became standard practice for many middle-class American families, when home sizes dramatically increased, and when access to newly available electronic devices, such as cell phones

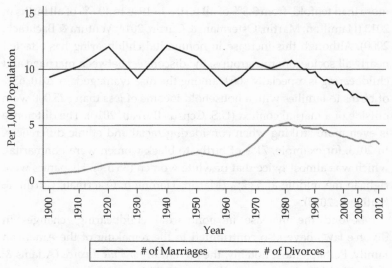

FIGURE 1.1 Historical marriage and divorce rates, 1900–2012.

Source: Centers for Disease Control and Prevention: National Vital Statistics System.

and the Internet, began to change interpersonal communication on a large scale.

▲ A Changing Economic and Educational Reality

Along with shifts in the institutional norms regarding family life, economic and educational shifts have also contributed to the day-to-day lives of modern emerging adults. One of the most prominent shifts of the past several generations has been the dramatic rise in postsecondary enrollment. Although college or university attendance was traditionally a privilege of the elite, the Servicemen's Readjustment Act, or "GI Bill," instituted in 1944 made college education a realistic possibility for an increasing number of Americans. This trend has continued throughout the twentieth century and into the twenty-first century. In 2012, 20.6 million people were enrolled at a degree-granting institution in the United States, an increase of 24% compared with the previous decade (U.S. Department of Education, 2015). The trends of obtaining a college education versus other levels of education are seen in Figure 1.2. A bachelor's degree has gone from the least common

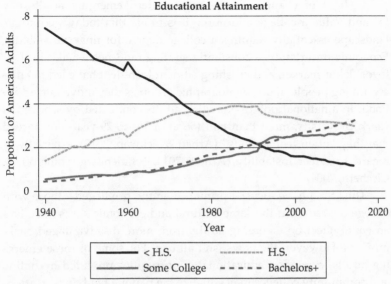

FIGURE 1.2 Educational attainment in the United States.
Source: US Census Bureau.

to the most common level of attainment, whereas the reverse is true of having less than a high school education. It is also interesting that the spread of educational attainment was previously very polarized, whereas now the levels have converged.

Although increases in college education have been beneficial to both the individual and society, they have had a more problematic effect as well. As the number of people with college degrees grew, the societal value of those degrees began to decline, leading to higher unemployment rates among college graduates. In recent times, the Great Recession of 2007–2009 saw many companies cut back on entry-level positions for newly minted college graduates. Subsequently, only 46.1% of 16- to 24-year-olds were employed, the smallest portion recorded since data collection began in 1948 (Pew Research Center, 2009). In turn, the lack of employment opportunities pushed more people back into school, creating a continued influx of college graduates seeking employment in a tepid job market. The lackluster job market, coupled with increasing student loan debt (the average college graduate has $24,000 in loans; Cheng & Reed, 2010), has resulted in difficult economic circumstances for many of today's emerging adults (see Figure 1.2).

In light of changes in the way modern emerging adults pay for and value a college education, it is ironic that today's economic landscape essentially requires a college degree for financial stability. Economic uncertainty, a constantly shifting (and not usually in their favor) labor market, and crushing student loan debt have led to anxiety among people in this demographic group as they move into adulthood. In a national poll of emerging adults conducted by scholars at Clark University, more than half (56%) of 18- to 29-year-olds agreed that they "often feel anxious" (Arnett & Schwab, 2013), especially in regard to career instability (Arnett, 2014; Schulenberg, Sameroff, & Cicchetti, 2004).

Thus far, I have focused primarily on the privileged—those with college degrees. But the same cultural and economic shifts have had an equal effect on emerging adults from more disadvantaged backgrounds. However, the news isn't all bad. For some of these emerging adults, expanded educational opportunities provided by online and community colleges may equalize the playing field. In fact, attendance at community colleges rose to an all-time high of 3.4 million emerging adult students in 2008 (Pew Research Center, 2009). Still, for many other disadvantaged emerging adults, restrictive labor markets and the general decline of traditional blue-collar jobs have meant an increase in residential and employment instability (Michaelides & Mueser, 2012; U.S. Bureau of Labor Statistics, 2009). Thus, emerging adults from impoverished backgrounds also have experienced increased instability in their lives, although often for very different reasons than emerging adults from a middle-class or upper-class background. To illustrate this, Figure 1.3 shows trends of six different categories of the labor force.

▲ The Rise of Individualism

Accompanying changing norms and behavioral expectations regarding relationships, education, employment, and sexuality, there has been a general cultural shift toward individualism—a trend that goes hand-in-hand with the number of choices available to modern emerging adults. Individualism is not a new characteristic, especially in the modern West, yet the rigor and strength with which it has gripped the public

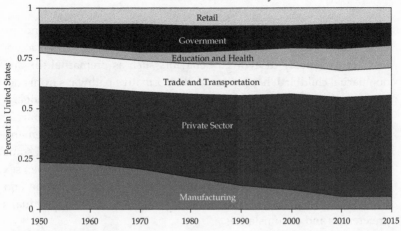

Labor Force Historically

FIGURE 1.3 Labor force areas historically.
Source: US Bureau of Labor Statistics.

psyche has been staggering. Although much of Western thought and culture are founded on principles of individual prosperity and freedom, prevailing social structures and norms in the United States historically structured what was considered proper behavior in almost all facets of life. As outlined previously, however, these norms have shifted toward valuing an individual's right to choose his or her own path regardless of whether those choices conform to "normative" behavior.

For example, the Monitoring the Future Study, which began in 1970, has been asking high school seniors a battery of questions about social norms and behaviors for decades. One of these questions is whether students agree or disagree with the following statement: "Having a child without being married is experimenting with a worthwhile lifestyle or not affecting anyone else." As recently as the late 1970s, only about one third of girls agreed with this statement. By the early 2000s, that percentage had almost doubled to more than half, hovering around 55%. This increase in acceptance of previously non-normative behavior suggests another, related shift: moral relativism. *Moral relativism* suggests that emerging adults believe that their own behavior should be unencumbered by social norms and, additionally, that they should not be judged for their actions as long as those action don't "affect others."

▲ An Age of Paradox

What is the net effect of these cultural changes? Sociologist Andrew Cherlin (2004) calls it *deinstitutionalization*. Simply put, as societal acceptance of previously disavowed behaviors such as premarital sex and nonmarital childbirth has increased, the normative pathways from adolescence to adulthood have become more volatile. There is no longer a clear right answer for how to live life or for the order in which to pursue romantic relationships, education, sexuality, or a career. Instead, emerging adults confront conflicting messages about each aspect, with some people proclaiming the supremacy of tradition (marriage first, then sex and career) and others declaring that the ordering of family life and educational or career pursuits ultimately depends on an individual's preferences and circumstances.

What was once a clear and straight path is now a splintered and winding road (Arnett, 2000) toward adulthood, a pathway that may or may not include an eventual marriage. That is, what was once clear and straight has become opaque and convoluted. Modern emerging adults now see a blank slate on which to carve out their place in life according to their goals, preferences, and opportunities. At the same time, new economic and educational realities have put constraints on these choices. Emerging adults feel the freedom to choose but also the burden of realizing that such choices may have long-lasting implications for their personal satisfaction and prosperity. This prospect induces both excitement and anxiety for many emerging adults. It is this dichotomy of emotions that has given rise to many paradoxes in the lives of emerging adults. On the one hand, emerging adults feel free to (re)make the world according to their choosing, to explore and experiment with people, places, and behaviors. On the other hand, they live in a world of largely dwindling job prospects and instability. In addition, modern emerging adults exist within a culture that values their individual choice, often withholding any clear guidance on these issues while emphasizing an ability to shape one's life as one desires.

The remainder of this book explores what this means for modern marriage, specifically its place and value in a society mostly untethered from previous generations' normative beliefs in it. Most norms surrounding traditional family formation have receded. In their place, we now have strong beliefs about the value of individual choice and agency. Although such a circumstance certainly has some benefits, this uncertainty in emerging adulthood has also created conflict, anxiety, and ultimately paradoxes around marriage and family formation that are vexing many modern emerging adults.

2 ▲
Dating, Hooking Up, and Love
Relationships During Emerging Adulthood

Unlike in past generations when adults married comparatively early in life, emerging adults in the twenty-first century often do not marry until their late 20s at least. These later marriages do not mean, however, that emerging adults postpone entry into committed romantic relationships. Marriage is, after all, only one type of long-term committed relationship. As we will show throughout this book, emerging adults often view marriage as an eventual final destination rather than the first stop. In many ways, marriage is still perceived to be the culmination of romantic relationship experiences during the life course. Despite a growing cultural nomenclature around *marriage redos, beta marriages,* or *starter marriages,* most emerging adults still see marriage to one partner for life as the end result of searching through a sea of potential partners. To many, marriage remains the relationship light at the end of a tunnel filled with first dates, breakups, cohabitation, and personal anxieties.

In this chapter, we explore the central role that romantic relationships play in how emerging adults view marriage. After all, it is during emerging adulthood that individuals gain vital experience with love, sex, and other relational encounters that shape and mold thinking about relationships. Despite the importance of situating emerging adults in a relational context, this chapter is not intended as an exhaustive discussion or study of relationships during emerging adulthood. We encourage interested readers to explore some of the many books dedicated exclusively to this topic (the excellent edited volume by Fincham and Cui, 2011 is a good place to start). In the remainder of the chapter, we briefly touch on several important relationship elements relevant to emerging adulthood, focusing on dating and the dominant hookup culture. We also describe trends related to sexual intimacy and cohabitation, two areas in which emerging adults have forged a drastically different pathway than previous generations.

Before moving forward, a quick note is in order regarding some of the data that will be presented in this chapter and in all subsequent chapters. At this point, we will begin to introduce the stories of real emerging adults. These stories and quotes were obtained through a longitudinal research study of emerging adulthood that took place over the course of 4 years in the Midwest and Mountain West areas of the United States. The study was aimed at understanding how emerging adults in middle America think about marriage and relationships. As part of this study, emerging adults were interviewed regarding their thoughts, beliefs, and values pertaining to marriage and relationships. Most of these emerging adults were at an important transition point in their lives: Many had recently graduated from college and were seeking their place in the world, both relationally and in terms of their careers. We provide their words throughout the remainder of this book in hopes that their stories may enhance, illustrate, and deepen the other content and statistics that are discussed. Full details on the methodology and sampling of this study and coding information for interviews can been found in the Appendix. Names and other identifying details have been changed to maintain the confidentiality of the participants of the study.

▲ The Death of Dating

For anyone who has recently talked to or interacted with an emerging adult—or viewed just about any program airing on MTV or a similar channel—it is obvious that the dating scene has experienced a dramatic upheaval over the past several decades. This upheaval is well illustrated by a recent story from *Vanity Fair* magazine announcing the "dating apocalypse" brought on by the rise of Tinder and similar social media apps (Sales, 2015). Running through this apocalypse are debates about whether dating is truly dead or whether shifting cultural norms about dating (or the lack thereof) signal a transition to more gender-neutral forms of intimacy, making dating an often ambiguous process. Although gaining relational experience (Snyder, 2006) and establishing a "relational identity" are key tasks of the emerging adult period (see Arnett, 2004; Montgomery, 2005), the logistics of dating itself for individuals in their 20s have radically altered.

Perhaps because of this increased ambiguity around dating during emerging adulthood, an increasing proportion of emerging adults are forgoing committed relationships and living alone for larger portions of their 20s. Compared with the 1950s, when only 5% of unmarried young adults in their 20s lived on their own, today's generation of unwedded emerging adults are much more likely to head their own households, with 36% of women and 28% of men doing so in 2000 (Rosenfeld, 2007). In fact, the majority of emerging adults remain single into their late 20s (Kreider, 2005), as fewer emerging adults marry before age 25 than previous generations (Cherlin, 2010).

Singlehood has become a dominant part of the emerging-adulthood landscape. A 2014 Gallup poll documented this increase in singlehood. Although a little more than one half (52%) of all 18- to 29-year-olds were single and never married in 2004, a similar poll in 2014 showed this percentage had increased to 64%, an almost 25% increase in 10 years (Saad, 2015). Even though some of these emerging adults are likely dating, these numbers suggest that many emerging adults are at least postponing formalized relationship commitments. When emerging adults do form romantic relationships, their relationships tend to be more casual than in previous generations. Although previous generations could draw on normative scripts involving clear dating how-tos and lists of dos and don'ts, today's emerging adults form relationships in a world where social networks can make traditional dating seem archaic. For example, today's emerging adults infrequently pair off for traditional dates, favoring group social settings—hanging out—and social media interactions instead (Fauth & Marganski, 2013; Kalkan & Odaci, 2010).

The emerging adults we interviewed had first-hand experiences with this shift. Isabelle, a 22-year-old white woman, had recently broken up with her boyfriend of 9 months when we interviewed her. She commented that she loved the single life but also expressed some frustration with the casual dating scene around her:

> I think our generation's kind of sad, personally, but that's just me. The first thing that comes to my mind—it's more trashy. There are no real virtues when people are dating anymore, and it's just kind of sad. You know sometimes people don't even know how to ask people out on a date. It's just more like just hanging out or talking. Everything is just twisted into something a lot more casual. That is okay for some situations and sometimes it's just not. It [dating] needs to be taken to a higher level of maturity.[1]

1. All interviews have been lightly edited for grammar, punctuation, and clarity.

Isabelle's frustrations are tied, in some ways, to emerging adulthood itself. Emerging adults often lead lives in which transitions in residency, employment, and social circles are common, so it is no wonder that their romantic relationships follow a similar pattern. This chaos and uncertainty may lead some emerging adults to the conclusion that intertwining their lives with another person's may be overwhelming and fraught with anxiety. Furthermore, many emerging adults may feel that dating should be fun, something to reduce stress, not increase it. Such a mentality may turn some emerging adults toward casual relationships that they perceive to be less burdened with interpersonal commitment and others toward avoiding relationships altogether. Is it any wonder, then, that traditional dating has become a relic of the past for many emerging adults?

Take Brianna, a Hispanic woman in her early 20s, as a case study. Similar to Isabelle, Brianna ended a long-term relationship shortly after the first data collection of our study. However, Brianna's relationship dated back to her early teens and had lasted 8 years. Brianna had spent the year before our interview moving in and out of a series of casual relationships, relationships she described as never fully committed. When we asked Brianna why she was no longer seeking a long-term partner, her answer was simple: She was just too busy. She wanted the men she dated to be stress relievers, people who could distract her from the other obligations in her life. As Brianna explained,

> I don't think I'm going to go into a relationship anymore expecting
> this is the one or that anything has to go anywhere. I just think
> that you start something thinking that it might be fun or it
> might be something that you just generally enjoy. And if it keeps
> happening then that's okay, and if it doesn't, then that's okay too.

That is to say, when life is filled with multiple pursuits, the result is often conflict between pursuits that are considered valuable; for most emerging adults, it is the educational/career and relational domains that are consistently in tension with each other. Shulman and Connelly (2013) commented on this interconnection by saying, "While on one hand they [emerging adults] might be psychologically ready to become committed to a relationship (likely attained through adolescent romantic experiences), they have to cope simultaneously with economic and financial demands." (p. 33). The net result? Long-term relationships often get put on the back burner.

Devon, a 23-year-old white man who identified as gay, had been dating the same partner for a little over a year when we spoke to him. Despite the seeming stability of his relationship and that he and his partner hold steady jobs and college degrees, when asked to comment about the long-term prospects of his current relationship, Devon suggested, "For me, I'm just not really ready to think about that portion of our relationship, and so I guess the answer is, for me, no. But for him—I think he does think about it a lot. I just don't think about it a lot." When asked to elaborate on why he avoids thinking about the long-term possibilities of his current relationship, Devon continued,

> I think that it makes me anxious just because of the idea that when you're with [someone]—whether it is marriage or [something else]—you're with them for life. That just makes me nervous, you know? Because if you think about your life 3 months ago, or 6 months ago, or 10 months ago, you normally didn't plan out where you are right now, and so I think it's really hard to plan out past a couple of months 'cause you never know what could change or what could happen. I just get nervous . . . it's just long term that makes me nervous. It's more of the future makes me a little bit anxious to think about.

Devon's views are not unique. By the time emerging adults reach their mid-20s, they have learned to expect chaos in their lives. Years of unique demands from both educational institutions and work environments have taken on a variety of forms. Whether it is trying to make a good impression at work or trying to piece together part-time employment to pay rent, emerging adults face a seemingly large opportunity cost by prioritizing relationships over career decisions. Faced with such dilemmas, emerging adults, particularly those in the middle to upper-middle class, are increasingly putting career and educational priorities first, which makes dating only a fun distraction.

In addition to serving as a source of personal entertainment, dating has also become a means for many emerging adults to explore and develop their personal identities, to explore likes and dislikes, and to refine characteristics and life goals. In some ways, relationships may have become more about personal than relational benefits. One of the men in our study put it quite bluntly: He ends any relationship if he's

"becoming negatively affected by it compared to gain[ing] from it."
Perhaps more telling is the experience of Alexis, a 22-year-old white
woman with a Sociology degree from a small Midwestern university.
After dating the same man for most of her time in college, she found
herself at a crossroad. On the one hand, she enjoyed dating him. The
flip side was that career pursuits were likely to drive them apart unless
she prioritized the relationship. "I sat on my mom's couch for a while
after graduation that summer," she said. "I didn't know what to do with
myself." Eventually, Alexis decided to join a nonprofit agency in the
southern United States. She explained,

> I moved in August. At the time, I was dating my boyfriend of
> 4 years ... well, we hit 4 years in January. So we were going
> really well. He came to visit me in November of last year, right
> after I moved basically. We had a great time. Everything was
> going really well. When January came around, he moved from
> Indiana to Illinois for an internship, and his schedule and my
> schedule were very different, so we started to drift a little bit.
> There was a lot of stuff going on, and I was kind of freaking out
> because I'm like, "Wow. I've been with this person for 4 years,
> but I'm only 22 years old," you know? "What am I doing?"

She worried that this long-term relationship was interfering with
her other goals and experiences. Therefore, she ended the relationship,
claiming she was "in a new place where I'm thriving and meeting all
these new people." For Alexis, the decision to end the relationship had
little to do with her boyfriend or their relationship, nor was it due to
conflict or underlying tension. Alexis simply made a personal decision
to prioritize her career options, which first created physical and then
emotional distance in her relationship. Eventually, Alexis did not see
any sense in pursuing the relationship. David, a 23-year-old who was
divorced and trying to support his music career by playing at local bars,
had decided to avoid relationships altogether so that they would not
interfere with his other goals. He said, "I've come to realize that there
are a lot of things in life that I want to do. That being in a relationship
would definitely hinder. In a sense that not that I couldn't make it work,
but it would just make it harder financially and stuff like that. . ... I look
at it as like if you get yourself into a relationship, you're giving away a
lot of your freedoms."

Alexis's and David's words represent the thinking of many emerging adults. Relationships serve the emerging adult; emerging adults are no longer willing to make many sacrifices for the benefit of a relationship partner, although they certainly wish their partners well. Put another way, relationships for emerging adults are about shaping emerging adults' future selves, not making long-term plans with a current partner. A recent study of emerging adults bore out this mentality when researchers Zimmer-Gembeck and Petherick (2006) found that having more and stronger individually focused dating goals was associated with increased dating satisfaction during emerging adulthood. In other words, in addition to good communication and healthy conflict resolution, emerging adults' relationship satisfaction is also tied to what they learn about themselves during the process.

In addition to changes in the ways emerging adults think about dating, the time between launching from their families of origin and forming new families through marriage is increasing, creating longer periods of independent living where emerging adults can experiment. This increased time span is resulting in greater opportunities for emerging adults to pursue both committed relationships and sexual relations with more partners. The average age at marriage has been steadily increasing from the 1950s, when men married at 22.8 years on average and women married at 20.3 years on average. In 2015, that average age increased to 29.3 years for men and 27 years for women. Figure 2.1 shows the average ages at marriage from 1890 to 2015. This elongated time spent in the dating market has drastically increased the relationship history of emerging adults in their 20s. Today, the average number of sexual partners before marriage among millennials is five, with at least one fourth of 18- to 29-year-olds reporting two or more partners in the past year alone (Civic, 1999; Critelli & Suire, 1998). Further, about 25% of college-aged adults are expected to have five to ten sexual partners during their lifetime (Harris et al., 2009). The effects of emerging adults having multiple sexual partners before marriage is up for debate, although recent research suggests an increase in the number of sexual partners throughout a person's lifetime may undermine long-term relationship success (Busby, Willoughby, & Carroll, 2013). Regardless of the specific effects of having multiple sexual partners before marriage, these shifting patterns have suggested that dating and relationships during emerging

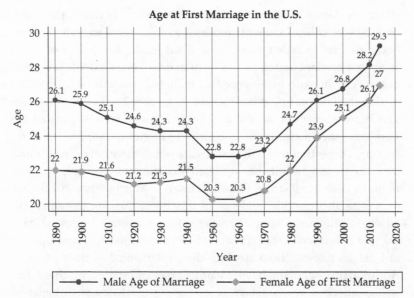

Age at First Marriage in the U.S.

FIGURE 2.1 Age at first marriage in the United States.
Source: US Census Bureau.

adulthood have become a largely individual and varied process, one that parallels the increasingly fluid state of adults' many transitions within their 20s.

▲ The Birth of the Hookup

As the markers of traditional dating have dissipated and traditional dating increasingly has become a thing of the past, a wave of casual romantic relationships has begun to fill the relational void. Where stability and exclusivity once reigned supreme, modern emerging adults live in a romantic world of multiple partnerships and ambiguously defined partners. In such a world, romantic and sexual partners may come and go and are sometimes held at a distance so as not to interfere with educational or career trajectories.

One of the best indicators of this rise in casual relationships is the advent of the hookup culture, particularly among college students. Hookups are usually defined as any sexual act between partners that involves no expectation of prior or future commitment

(Paul, McManus, & Hayes, 2000). In 2000, one study found that more than 30% of college students reported at least some experience with hookups that included intercourse (Paul et al., 2000). Eleven years later, that number had risen to 45% of male college students reporting at least one hookup experience that included penetrative intercourse during the last year (Owen, Fincham, & Moore, 2011)—data that suggest hookups may be on the rise. Some scholars have suggested the numbers may, in reality, be dramatically higher because of underreporting. One estimate put the true figure somewhere between 60% and 80% of emerging adults having likely experienced a hookup at some point in their life (Garcia, Reiber, Massey, & Merriwether, 2012). Our own data also provide evidence of this trend. Among the emerging adults in our initial sample, participants, on average, reported having just two intercourse partners within committed relationships yet at least four casual hookups including intercourse in their lifetime. Additionally, scholars have identified several types of these no-strings-attached relationships (e.g., hookups, friends with benefits, and one-night stands) that are becoming increasingly common during emerging adulthood (Claxton & van Dulmen, 2013). The increased popularity of cultural phrases for hooking-up (think "Netflix and chill") has also pointed to the increasingly normative role of casual sexual experiences among emerging adults. Casual relationships have become a central component of emerging adulthood. As one emerging adult man told us, "[This] generation . . . we have shown that sleepin' with different people is like, that's how you find love."

Engagement in these types of casual behaviors makes it clear that such behaviors are central to the relational experiences and lives of many emerging adults. In the words of Shulman and Connolly (2013), "we cannot overlook the reality that growing numbers of young people are not in stable and committed relationships" (p. 30). The story of one of our participants illustrates the power and allure of the casual sexual culture for some emerging adults. When we first met Jadyn, she was fresh out of high school, was in a committed relationship (her fourth), had generally conservative views about marriage and sexuality, and had no sexual experience outside of a serious relationship. In short, Jadyn was well within normal bounds of sexual and dating behavior for her age group. Yet over the 3 years we followed her, Jadyn's views and behaviors changed dramatically. Three years later, Jadyn was still enrolled at the same university but was in a polyamorous relationship with a male and a female partner. She reported six relationship partners over her lifetime and nine sexual partners from casual relationships.

Jadyn described what happened this way: "I was just coming into college and I still believe that serious dating is a preview to marriage, but I'm coming into college, I need to have fun. . . .. I'll go out, do this, do that, whatever." Jadyn embraced the casual culture regarding relationships and sexuality around her. As we talked to Jadyn about relationships and her changing views, she proudly described her latest sexual adventure from the previous weekend:

> I had a foursome with a couple and another girl over the
> weekend. That was . . . fun and hilariously awkward, because the
> couple has been together for 6 years. And it was his birthday, and
> actually I had been her present back in September. We're all good;
> we're all friendly. The other girl and I hadn't seen each other in
> a year and didn't know each other very well. But it's fine, you
> know, just go with it. But I'm not serious with any of them. Like,
> we're just good friends that happen to be sexual with each other.
> And that's been the most major change. I [used to] not even hug
> anyone who wasn't family or [who I wasn't] dating, and now I've
> loosened up a bit.

Although Jadyn's experience may be extreme (most emerging adults are not engaging in regular hookups with multiple partners simultaneously), her transformation captures how many emerging adults respond when casual sex becomes not only acceptable but also normative.

▲ Is Anyone Dating Anymore?

Despite the prevailing hookup and casual culture of emerging adulthood regarding relationships and sex, not all emerging adults forgo dating and committed relationships. Although it is true that hookups often grab media headlines, this focus on only one type of relationship during emerging adulthood masks other important truths. Indeed, many emerging adults continue to form and dissolve committed romantic relationships. More important, evidence suggests that when emerging adults do form committed relationships, they put effort and energy into keeping them intact. More than 40% of emerging adults report that their current or most recent relationship went through a breakup and reconciliation, suggesting that young adults both seek out romantic relationships and try to repair them (Dailey, Pfiester, Jin, Beck, & Clark, 2009; Halpern-Meekin, Manning, Giordano, & Longmore, 2012). Similarly, another study reported that, among a small sample of students at a southeastern university, respondents averaged 2.5 breakups, often with the same partner.

In fact, some emerging adults expressed outright disdain for the prevailing casual culture surrounding relationships. Blake, a 22-year-old in a serious committed relationship, stated, "I myself am incredibly uncomfortable with casual relationships. I've never had one. I don't like the ideas behind them. I don't like the methods through which you find casual relationships. I have only had long-term, serious relationships in the past." Even if some emerging adults do not share Blake's frustration with casual relationships, many join him in actively pursuing serious and committed relationships. Although marriage may not commonly be considered a part of relationships in emerging adulthood, in many ways these relationships resemble marriage, as though modern emerging adults seek the echoes of marital relationships while rejecting the need to legally tie themselves down to one person. Evidence of these marriage-like relationships can be seen in two prevalent relational patterns among emerging adults: the sexual behaviors of these committed couples and the explosion of cohabitation as the dominant relationship form among emerging adults who do seek committed partnerships during their 20s.

Sexual Intimacy Within Committed Relationships

Emerging adults may delay marriage and often parenting, but their transition to becoming sexual in their relationships has remained fairly consistent with past generations. Although some may view the current relational patterns of emerging adults regarding sexual intimacy and think that modern emerging adults are more sexually experienced than previous generations (and much evidence certainly points to that fact), in other ways, emerging adults are engaging in sexual intimacy just as they have in the past. The difference is that today, first sexual experiences normatively occur before marriage.

Despite claims that emerging adults simply seek sexual gratification in any way possible (some certainly do), many emerging adults use sexual intimacy to connect physically, emotionally, and perhaps even spiritually with their partners. For example, feelings of love toward their partner are significantly related to engagement in sexual intimacy among emerging adults (Kaestle & Halpern, 2007). Adolescents and emerging adults (aged 15 to 21 years) also report that about 70% of their sexual experiences are motivated by a desire for intimacy (such as, "we are in love"; Dawson, Shih, de Moor, & Shrier, 2008). The vast majority (92%) of emerging adults also report that romance and love preceded sex in their relationships (Harris et al., 2009). In fact, most sex that emerging adults are engaging in still occurs in romantic relationships (Regnerus & Uecker, 2010), although many men report knowing their partner for between less than 2 weeks (36%) and less than 6 months (70%) when such intimacy begins.

Thus, although the casual hookup culture is prevalent, this does not mean that most sex is happening in casual relationships. Indeed, the highest frequency of sex is still reported by those in stable, romantic relationships: One study found that 63% of emerging adults in relationships that had lasted more than 4 months reported sex at least twice weekly (Harris et al., 2009).

The stability and sexual frequency a committed relationship offers may partly explain the increase in the amount of time between when adolescents and emerging adults become sexually active and when they marry. The median age at first sex in the United States for both men and women is about 17 years old (Centers for Disease Control and Prevention, 2013). As noted previously, the median age at marriage, which has been climbing for several decades now, is 27 years for women and 29 years for men (U.S. Census Bureau, 2014). As a result, premarital sex is nearly universal, with one estimate suggesting that only 3% of people report not have sex before marriage (Finer, 2007).

Although such findings only scratch the surface of the sexual lives of emerging adults, they suggest that, in the minds of emerging adults, relationships are often inseparable from sex. Within both casual and committed relationships, sexual markers, such as exclusivity and chemistry, influence and shape how emerging adults think about intimacy and marriage throughout life. As Ryan, a 23-year-old, explained,

> I think that's [sex exclusivity] actually really meaningful in that
> the natural tendency of just a human being, sexual being, is to
> have sex with others that we find attractive, and I think that's why
> sex is important as a marker. It's like if you can withstand the urge
> to have sex with everyone you're attracted to and only have sex

with me, that shows that you actually really care, 'cause that's a hard commitment to make.

Many emerging adults also equated sexual intimacy as a necessary step before marriage. As David explained, "Not to be crude or anything. If you don't like having sex with that person, then why would you want to be married? Like. Not that it's that big of a deal, but it's a pretty big deal."

The Rise of Cohabitation

The premarital sex most emerging adults engage in often takes place when the couple lives together, a trend that is rapidly going from unheard of to normative. Perhaps no other trend in romantic relationships during emerging adulthood has been as dramatic as the increase in cohabitation. Trends in cohabitation over the past 100 years illustrate many of the shifting cultural and familial trends witnessed across many industrialized countries. Before the widespread cultural shifts seen in the United States during the 1970s and 1980s with the sexual revolution, the widespread availability of contraception, divorce reform, and the women's rights movement, cohabitation was largely the purview of the social elite, often occurring at private universities scattered across the country. However, with increased cultural acceptance of premarital sex and increased fear of divorce came a strong desire among many young couples to test the waters of marriage before actually jumping into such a commitment. From 1970 to 2000, cohabitation rates in the United States increased tenfold (Jose, O'Leary, & Moyer 2010), with roughly 4 million cohabiting couples reported in the United States in 2000 (U.S. Census Bureau, 2015a). In the past 50 years, the number of cohabiting couples has risen from 500,000 to 7.6 million (The National Marriage Project, 2012). The biggest jump was between 2005 and 2010, going from less than 5 million couples to more than 7.5 million couples cohabiting. Full results from 1960 through 2014 are shown in Figure 2.2.

During the time cohabitation became popular in the 1980s, such relationships were seen as a test run for marriage, one that many scholars at the time agreed would likely strengthen marriages by weeding out the bad relationships before they could become another divorce statistic. However, scholarship during the later part of the

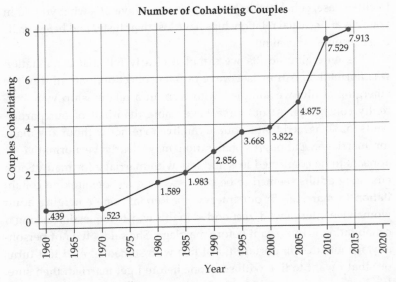

Number of Cohabiting Couples

Numbers are in millions

FIGURE 2.2 Number of cohabitating couples in the United States.
Source: US Census Bureau.

twentieth century suggested a troubling trend: Cohabiting couples who went on to marry were not more stable or happy. Quite the opposite, cohabiting couples were found to be at a higher risk for divorce and unhappy marriages than those who choose to forgo a trial period and jump straight into matrimony (Hall, 1997; Hall & Zhao, 1995; Smock, 2000), although recent scholarship suggests the higher risk for divorce in cohabitating couples is likely shrinking over time (Manning & Cohen, 2012).

Despite such findings, not only did cohabitation continue to become more popular, the rates of cohabitation also increased exponentially over the next decade. This trend is especially striking among emerging adults. One recent report noted that the majority (65%) of all women between the ages of 18 and 24 years in a committed relationship were cohabiting (Manning & Stykes, 2015). Many scholars have attributed this phenomenon to a different way of viewing cohabitation among modern emerging adults. Rather than being a means of testing a relationship prior to marriage, cohabitation may have become an alternative to being single (Heuveline & Timberlake, 2004). Cohabiting is simply the next step many emerging adults take after committing to a dating partner and is disconnected from anything related to marriage.

In either case, cohabitation has become normative: It's what you do in your 20s after casual relationships have lost their luster and before marriage becomes appealing.

The emerging adults we sampled clearly felt that cohabitation was normative. At our last wave of data collection, one third of the emerging adults we sampled who were in a relationship were currently cohabiting. At our first wave, more than half of our participants (55%) agreed that a couple can live together without any plans for marriage. Although cohabitation may clearly be normative, it appears to be connected less and less with marriage for many. Some emerging adults seemed to be confused by questions linking cohabitation to marriage in our interviews. Kendall, one emerging adult woman we interviewed, responded in this way to a question asking if cohabitation is important before marriage. She said, "It's not personally, for me, that important that I live with someone. And if it turns out that I want to live with someone before I get married, then sure. It's just what feels right with that person at the time." Like many things, cohabitation, to Kendall, was tied to individualistic and relativistic beliefs that leave relational decisions up to the couple. There is no right or wrong way to utilize cohabitation. Cohabitation does not, in her mind, automatically lead to anything, including marriage. It is a tool that some couples may use, whereas others may not. Hayley, another woman we interviewed, put it more simply: "I never really thought about it [cohabitation being linked to marriage] until I took the survey and never thought about it being a necessary precursor." Although cohabitating has become an important part of the relational lives of emerging adults, it has an ambiguous, at best, connection to eventual marriage.

Despite disconnects between cohabitation and marriage for some, other emerging adults continue to use cohabitation as a trial run for marriage. Blake, a 22-year-old college student in a committed relationship, is one such emerging adult. He has what he refers to as a 3-year rule. He explained,

> I won't ask someone to marry me unless I've lived with them for 3 years minimum. That's kind of a rule. I feel that it's important to live with someone before you get married to them because there's just so many things that can go wrong in any relationship and cause it to become messy and legal and just a terrible idea.

Of course, treating cohabitation as either a trial or alternative to marriage is not the only option. After all, this mindset presumes a long-term orientation to relationships, an approach that is not necessarily taken by all emerging adults. Indeed, many cohabiting couples live together simply out of convenience (Manning & Smock, 2005). Whether it is because a lease ran out for one partner or because of the realization that the couple was spending most nights together anyway, living with a romantic partner is simply what happens for the majority of committed couples in their 20s. The exact nature of how emerging adults utilize cohabitation in the selection of potential marital partners will come up again in chapter 6.

Taken together, relationships among emerging adults are more complex than in previous generations. Societal shifts in the acceptability of nonmarital sex and cohabitation have created a space where emerging adults can engage in long-term serial monogamy (Andersson, 2015; de la Croix & Mariani, 2015; Mulder, 2009). Brooke, a 22-year-old, recognized the relational space of emerging adulthood as an opportunity to learn and grow as a person and partner. Having recently graduated from college and working as an intern, Brooke explained her dating life in this way:

> I am that serial monogamist. I've been in a relationship for 2 years, we broke up for 3 months, and I'm in another 2-year relationship now. So I guess, for me, I've just kind of learned from those things. There are things I find acceptable and unacceptable.

Relationships, then, provide an important illustration of the principles outlined in chapter 1. As social norms surrounding sexuality and dating have shifted and eroded, emerging adults must blaze their own relational pathway. Emerging adults, confronted with a period of time that may or may not include commitment, casual sex, cohabitation, or any semblance of a formal courtship period, face confusion amid the bewildering number of ways to form, maintain, and dissolve romantic and sexual relationships. They are granted almost ultimate relationship flexibility based on their own preferences and life situations. Emerging adults must navigate this complex world of relationships through which they alter, frame, and develop their views on what marriage means for them—although they often undertake this without explicitly thinking about marriage.

3 ▲

Why Marriage Still Matters

Understanding Marital Paradigms
During Emerging Adulthood

At some point, you have likely asked yourself a perfectly reasonable question, one that may have been lurking in the back of your mind as you read the opening chapters of this book: Why should you (or anyone else) care about marriage at all? After all, marriage has been rumored to be ill (perhaps terminally!) and has even been pronounced dead dozens of times over the past several decades. As far back as the 1970s, papers in the United States began sounding the warning cry of family breakdown with such headlines as "Marriage and Family Face Stormy Future" and "Broken Marriages on Rise" (*The Hartford Courant*, 1975b, 1975a). More recently, several outlets have suggested that marriage may be on the way out. Such headlines have sported titles such as "The Death of Marriage" (Phillips, 2007), "Is There Hope for the American Marriage?" (Flanagan, 2009) and "It's Official: To Be Married Means to Be Outnumbered" (Roberts, 2006).

Popular media has also trumpeted the end of marriage, although perhaps more subtly. For example, many modern television shows over the past decade now obsess over questions such as, will they move in together? Or, will they ever sleep together? Marriage, once at the center of relationships across many popular television shows and films, has often now taken a back seat. While we remain focused on whether couples enter long-term, romantic relationships (i.e., coupling), the question of whether the two will marry seems irrelevant, perhaps even quaint. Consequently, marriage may come off feeling old and outdated, a relic of the past we are simply moving beyond toward greener and more enlightened pastures.

This idea, that marriage is unnecessary or something you could leave behind, much like that picture of your high school crush buried in your top dresser drawer, occurred often among the emerging adults we interviewed. For example, Alec, a 22-year-old single man we interviewed, said:

I mean marriage is, it's a piece of paper, it can be a piece of paper, and I think there are a lot of people that are able to form healthy relationships and maintain them without being married and feeling like you're restricted because you have to be with someone. I think there are plenty of people that are able to be with someone their entire life without being married and still be happy.

Similarly, Elizabeth, a 21-year-old who had previously been engaged, put it this way:

I don't know so much that it's [marriage] needed as just it's nice to have. I mean, I certainly think from a historical perspective it's definitely something that was needed to continue on societies and to continue on blood lines and everything, but presently with all the different options and the more socially acceptable ways of having kids, or adopting and all those these different things, I don't know that there's as much of a necessity of marriage as there once was.

Perhaps Candice, a 23-year-old about to move in with her boyfriend, put it best when she succinctly said:

I think it's more wanted than needed in today's world. Because people want that romantic connection, people want that status of being married, but I don't think they necessarily need it since there's been a shift to being more independent as a person rather than having to be a couple. I don't think it's really needed. It's just something people strive for.

Despite this apparent apathy or even animosity toward marriage, we argue that marriage still matters—to emerging adults themselves and to our society at large. This is not based on a political argument, religious bias, or any empirical data regarding the real or perceived benefits of marriage, although there is evidence for that (see "The Case for Marriage" by Linda Waite & Maggie Gallagher, 2000). Instead, our argument is far simpler and, we hope, more convincing: when you talk to people and ask them whether marriage means something *to them* instead of *to everyone*, the response is usually positive. The vast majority of individuals, including emerging adults, continue to report a high personal importance placed on the institution of marriage (Willoughby &

Carroll, 2015). Most emerging adults also still expect to marry someday (Carroll et al., 2007; Willoughby & Dworkin, 2009). In a recent review of the literature on marital beliefs among emerging adults, Willoughby and Carroll (2015) concluded that "perhaps the clearest implication of the recent research linking marriage, marital beliefs, and emerging adulthood is that emerging adults in general have not rejected marriage as an important and hoped for institution" (p. 292). And after talking with the emerging adults from our own sample, we are even more convinced of this somewhat perplexing reality. Indeed, 79% of all the emerging adults with whom we spoke agreed that marriage was an important goal for them.

As mentioned in the Introduction to this book, understanding this paradox is at the heart of our exploration of emerging adults and marriage. Having covered the developmental, cultural, and relational context of emerging adulthood, we now turn to a discussion of how emerging adults think about marriage. In the chapters that remain, we explore marital beliefs, how they are generated, and what their consequences may be. The remainder of this chapter, however, covers how emerging adults generally conceptualize the institution of marriage itself and how they think about marriage in a culture that bombards them with messages of its irrelevance.

▲ Overview of Marital Paradigm Theory

We begin with an overview of why we predominantly focus on beliefs, values, and attitudes[1] as opposed to behavior (although we will get into a discussion of emerging adults who actually marry in chapter 10). In particular, some may ask why we should focus on the internal and personal realm of values or attitudes. Do they even matter in the grand scope of emerging adulthood? Why not focus on more tangible things like employment rates, drug use, or actual relationship behavior? Certainly, rates and behaviors are important (that is why we have devoted the first two chapters to highlighting these types of trends), but a body of research is emerging that clearly shows that how people think

---

1. In this book, we use terms like *beliefs* and *attitudes* interchangeably. Although some have differentiated between these terms, for our purposes, we treat them equivalently.

about marriage is central to understanding the very nature of emerging adulthood during and after this period in life.

First, if you'll indulge us, let's take a quick (and hopefully painless) detour to delve into the theoretical thinking among scholars in this area. Let us start with a fairly uncontroversial observation: Thought precedes action. Despite being self-evident, this simple observation forms the backbone of some of the most powerful social science thinking in history. When applied to marriage, the idea is simple: People think about marriage before they take their marriage vows. This thinking about marriage takes many forms: People think about potential marriage partners, their wedding, or how a marriage fits with their other goals. Research shows that even people who have no interest in marrying still think about marriage! For example, they think about why they do not want to marry, why being single will make them happier, or perhaps all the unhappy married people they know. Thus, it is not much of a stretch to assume that thoughts about marriage inform marriage-related decisions (whether, whom, when, and where to marry).

Importantly, scholars have noted that such beliefs about marriage extend beyond decisions explicitly about marriage. In a recent article, Willoughby, Hall, and Luscak (2015) outlined a theory, called *Marital Paradigm Theory*, which can help us understand how emerging adults think about marriage. Marital Paradigm Theory starts with an assumption: Every person has a "marital paradigm," which consists of his or her collective thoughts, values, and beliefs about marriage. Perhaps this can best be illustrated by an example. Let's think about basketball for just a moment. You likely have an opinion on how hard the sport is, if and when children should start playing it, how much time is too much time spent practicing it, which professional or college team is best, and perhaps hundreds of other specific attitudes that encompass as much or as little as you actually know or care about basketball. Collectively, these thoughts, beliefs, attitudes, and opinions form what we might call your basketball paradigm. You will use this paradigm every time basketball comes up in conversation or in life, which will occur in a variety of contexts. For example, if a friend asks you to come play basketball at a local gym, you will rely on your basketball paradigm to make a decision. Likewise, if one of your children is invited to play on a competitive basketball team, you will again turn to your paradigm as you consider your decision. Additionally, your basketball paradigm will likely inform decisions that have nothing to do with actually playing or watching basketball. When choosing a pair of sneakers to buy, for example, your basketball paradigm could be invoked based on a favorite player. That is, you will rely on the set of beliefs, values, and attitudes you have developed over the years when making decisions about basketball-related things.

Our marital paradigms work the same way. When the topic of marriage (or something related to it) comes up, we turn to our paradigm to inform our decision. Unlike basketball, however, which you can spend your life avoiding (except perhaps during March Madness), almost everything in an emerging adult's life invokes this marital paradigm to some degree because marriage is often so central to emerging adults and their future. Because marriage remains a central element of modern society (as seen by heated societal debates over its definition) and a major expected transition for emerging adults, virtually all the decisions they make have at least some bearing on a future marriage. Decisions about college majors, employment locations, dating partners, and even friendships are connected in many emerging adults' minds to marriage. In this way, emerging adults' marital paradigms are central to almost every major decision they make as they move through their 20s.

According to Marital Paradigm Theory, paradigms inform *intentions* (see Ajzen, 1991). The formation of intentions happens when we draw on our marital paradigm to shift our intended behaviors to conform to the paradigm. These intentions then constitute a major factor in decisions about whether to follow through with a given action. Take, for example, the link between positive beliefs about marriage during emerging adulthood and fewer instances of risk-taking behavior (Carroll et al., 2007; Willoughby & Dworkin, 2009; Willoughby, Medaris, James, & Bartholomew, 2015). In a sample of emerging adults at several universities, those who held positive views of marriage engaged in significantly less drug use and binge drinking (Carroll et al., 2007). Seen through the lens of Marital Paradigm Theory, the decision to drink or not likely has quite a bit to do with a person's paradigm about marriage (Willoughby & Carroll, 2015). If some fictional female emerging adult has been thinking about marriage frequently and has recently decided to think more seriously about finding a committed partner, she may shift her intention to drink less at the party, especially because such drinking may be more likely to lead to a casual hookup rather than a committed relationship. Subsequently, her likelihood of drinking may also decrease. Of course, marital paradigms are only one of several factors in the previous example that would determine the actual action taken, but marital beliefs do seem to play a part in determining emerging adults' actions across a wide variety of behaviors.

This type of influence can occur even when emerging adults are not completely aware of it. Take Carli as an example. Carli was 21 years old and about to get married when we interviewed her. During a portion of the interview, she discussed how she would often find herself avoiding "risky situations" because of her wedding plans. She explained:

> I wouldn't go out to the bar and have an excessive amount to drink if he [her fiancé] wasn't around or I wouldn't go to hang out with a big group of dudes without him there. I don't know, or maybe just the fact that I don't talk to people that I feel might have ulterior motives. I don't want to put our relationship at risk, and so I think about him in those situations.

Carli recognized that her actions may have consequences for her relationship and approaching marriage. She realized that a transition to marriage meant she needed to alter her behavior around both alcohol and opposite-sex peers. In other words, through her own personal marital paradigm, she realized her marriage plans were a driving force in the individual decisions she was making.

Taking this idea further, other scholars (Carroll et al., 2007, 2009) have introduced the idea of *marital horizons* during emerging adulthood. The idea, although slightly more narrow in scope than Marital Paradigm Theory, adds one important idea: The collective marital beliefs of emerging adults (marital paradigms) help each single person place marriage on the horizon at some particular point in the future. The relative length of that horizon is key to emerging adulthood because how far out on the horizon emerging adults place marriage helps determine the length and nature of emerging adulthood itself. If an emerging adult places marriage close, he or she may take education more seriously or engage in fewer risk behaviors than someone whose marital paradigm places his or her marital horizon farther in the distance.

As we talked to various emerging adults, these differing placements and priorities on marriage were clearly influencing how they looked at their future. Consider these contrasting stories from some of the emerging adults we interviewed, each with a very different marital horizon. The first comes from Adam, a 23-year-old man who was engaged when we interviewed him. For Adam, marriage is clearly on the near horizon. When describing what marriage means to him, Adam noted, "Marriage is important to me. It's something that I really want to do, to be married, that's always been a goal of mine and one of my top goals." Adam identified marriage as one of his top goals in life, a goal that factored into his decisions about education, work, and dating partners. At the time of our interview, Adam was an underemployed comparative literature graduate working at Dunkin' Donuts but was actively making plans to propose to his girlfriend of 3 years. To him, the desire to marry soon was directing and motivating almost all aspects of his life. Similarly, Allison, a 24-year-old woman who was already married when we interviewed her, experienced a change in her marital horizons when she met her now husband:

> I probably noticed the most how important marriage was to me. Because I think at the time it kind of was, but it wasn't very high on my priority list, and I think that's changed as I got older because, and especially having known now my husband, because it turned into—as I was planning my future and my career, I couldn't really imagine part of that future without involving him. So I think that changed my views a little bit on getting married.

For both Adam and Allison, a near marital horizon shaped their trajectory through emerging adulthood, leading both of them toward a quick (and comparatively early) transition into marriage. In contrast, Chelsea, a 24-year-old woman, strikes a very different tone when it comes to marriage:

> I think for me I've, since graduating college, I have been focused on sort of traveling as much as I can and doing what I want to do and to me marriage right now feels like settling down in a big way, like really not being able to do what I want to do all the time anymore. I'm slowly feeling like that's what I want to do, but it's still kind of a scary thing at the moment.

Interestingly, Chelsea was in a serious relationship at the time we spoke to her. Marriage, the "scary thing" she mentioned, had become a potential reality in her life. She noted the family pressure she has been getting recently, explaining,

My sisters ask me this all the time. "Is he [her boyfriend] going to propose when you go back to Denver?" I don't know. I really don't think he would. But I probably would say yes, but I think I would delay marriage a little bit.

Like Chelsea, Samantha and Shaina had later marital horizons, and both talked about marriage as part of a still somewhat hazy future. Samantha, a 21-year-old student in a committed relationship, noted when discussing her future plans with her current boyfriend that marriage was a very ambiguous entity for her, saying:

We haven't really set any plans in stone at all. We know that we're both in a really transitional period of our lives where things change unexpectedly and we're graduating and going off into the real world and doing all kinds of things that we might not expect that we would and we don't really have plans for that [marriage]. Like I said, we do, we've discussed it and, you know, toyed around with the idea of getting married in the future and sort of what that would mean, what our lives would be like hypothetically, but we don't have any solid plans, we've never really sat down and said, "Okay, so what are we doing next?"

She noted that marriage might be in the future for her, but her horizon was clearly more distant.

Shaina, a 25-year-old actuary, was more direct in her discussion of her future plans. She indicated that her distant marital horizon was at odds with her current boyfriend. She explained:

It's a personal decision. I love my boyfriend, and I know he wants to get married, but I'm just not ready, and I think that that's my biggest hurdle to get over—I'm still very selfish. I want to live on my own for a while, I want to find out more about myself before giving myself to somebody else.

Such illustrations are only a sample of the many marital horizons expressed to us during the interviews, but these examples make it clear that where emerging adults place marriage generally and how they think about marriage globally start to influence the very structure of emerging adulthood and their trajectory through it.

▲ What Does Marriage Mean to Emerging Adults?

Now that we've (hopefully) established the theoretical importance of marital beliefs during emerging adulthood, let's now turn toward what marriage means to emerging adults today. Specifically, let us discuss how emerging adults think about marriage as an institution and how it fits broadly into their lives. When we introduced this book, we mentioned the essence of the marital paradox—that although emerging adults still say they value marriage, their behavior indicates otherwise. As seen in the Figure 3.1, the goal of having a good marriage has been rated as "very important" for most emerging adults for several decades and has stayed consistent from the mid-1970s to 2014. However, the graph in Figure 3.1 also shows the proportion of emerging adults who planned to get married in the next 3 years. More than 30% of young adults in the 1970s planned to get married in the next 3 years, which dropped to just over 10% in 2014. Clearly, something is changing for these emerging adults. Although marriage remains important, fewer and fewer emerging adults actually plan to marry. To understand why,

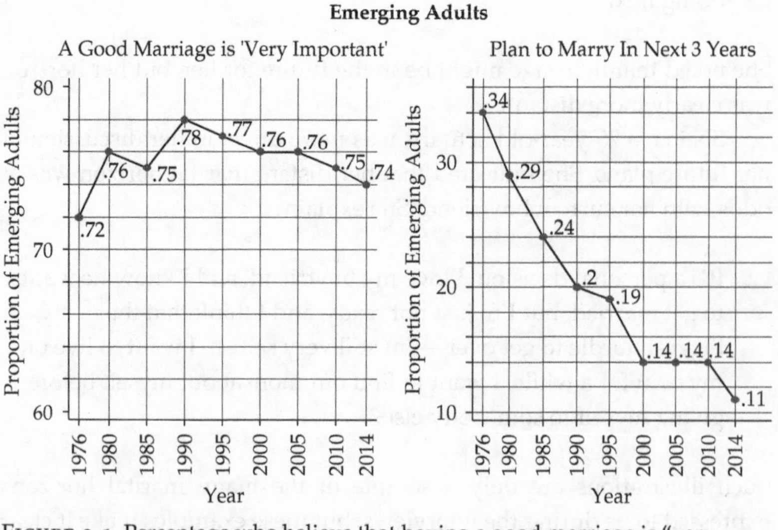

Emerging Adults

FIGURE 3.1 Percentage who believe that having a good marriage is "very important" and who plan to marry.

Source: Monitoring the Future Survey.

we must delve deeper into the specific meaning of marriage for those in their 20s.

When we set out to interview emerging adults, one of the first questions we asked was simply, "What does marriage mean to you?" Although responses varied from person to person, with each person adding his or her own anecdotes and life experiences, three themes emerged in nearly every interview we conducted. First, marriage entails commitment. Second, marriage has lost meaning and can be equated to a legal piece of paper. Third, marriage is first and foremost about romantic love. These themes provide valuable insight into understanding the changing climate modern emerging adults roam as they consider the decision to marry. Below, we explore each of these themes in more detail to help illustrate what these broad beliefs mean and the influence they have during emerging adulthood.

Marriage as Proof of Commitment

Perhaps the most consistent theme across the interviews was that of commitment. Commitment was mentioned 339 separate times in our interviews, with the average emerging adult mentioning it more than five times as they discussed their thoughts on marriage. Furthermore, 82% of the emerging adults we interviewed identified commitment as a key component of marriage, and only 17% never mentioned it at all. Time and time again, emerging adults spoke of how important commitment is to the marriage relationship in order for it to endure for the long haul. Take the following quotes as a small sampling of the responses from our interviews that included the idea of commitment:

> Hayley: I think it's sort of a commitment that people make. I think marriage is a good thing for people cause they can make that definition for themselves—this is the person I'm going to be with for the rest of my life. Even if it doesn't work out that way, that's the intent when they do it.
> Kimberly: I think it [marriage] means that . . . you plan on being with them for a really long time and that it's the two of you in a relationship and whoever else in your family that it would be with them as well.

Parker: I think that's the biggest part of what marriage should
be—that it's a new level of commitment, a solid steel beam to
make sure that you stay up.
Ashlyn: Marriage is commitment.

These quotes all share a common theme: marriage, at its most fundamental level, represents the lifelong commitment of two people, at least
in principle. Even Jill, a 24-year-old divorced mother of two young
children, continued to equate marriage with commitment. She noted
during her interview that, "It's [marriage] just like a commitment.
You have to know someone for a really long time before you do it. For
me personally, I would have to know somebody for a really long time
before I'd ever do it again. Like it's being really committed and loyal to
somebody." Although this is not a new idea, the consistency with which
emerging adults mentioned it points to a strongly held belief that marriage *should* be about commitment. This is important for several reasons.
First, it suggests that modern emerging adults think about marriage and
their current dating relationships in very different ways. Many were in
what they themselves called "committed," sexually active, and exclu-
sive relationships, suggesting a certain degree of similarity to marriage.
Yet they still claimed that marriage was a different type of relationship
than they were currently experiencing. They did this largely by distinguishing between different types of commitment. More specifically, current relationships were just that—current. These relationships, although
they shared much in common with what these emerging adults imag-
ined marital relationships to be like, were never intended to last forever.
Marriage, on the other hand, implies *lifelong* commitment, the stuff of
"till death do us part" love scenes. Consider two additional quotes:

Ryan: It's still supposed to be one person with one other person
and with a lifelong commitment.
Brooke: I mean it [marriage] really means making a lifelong
commitment.

That is, marriage is unique not only for the strength of the commitment
you make (very strong) but also in the length (lifelong). As Marty, a 25-
year-old high school dropout who was currently working landscaping
noted, marriage was "to show the commitment and know that you're
committed to that other person. Because I feel like if a person stays
boyfriend and girlfriend, you know, either person could leave at any
time. Marriage kinda shows that you're committed to that person and

you're not just kinda scared to jump in." For emerging adults, marriage is meant to last forever, whereas their current relationships are meant to last until they are no longer needful or useful.

Given the turbulent and chaotic lives of many emerging adults, it is easy to see the appeal of such lifelong commitments. As previously outlined, emerging adults are consistently faced with change or the threat of change. Every day brings with it the possibility of failed educational or career prospects or the beginning or ending of another romantic partnership. Stability, then, naturally holds great value for emerging adults. For many, the idea of having a partner on which to rely, someone to help you through the ups and downs of life, sounds almost like a fairy tale.

Of course, fairy tales usually involve some dark, sinister evil that challenges the hero. In an ironic twist, lifelong commitment plays the role of both villain and victor in the plot played out in the marital and romantic lives of emerging adults. Such commitment scares some emerging adults and makes them hesitant about the idea of marrying. With the United States continuing to experience comparatively high rates of divorce, it is understandable that some emerging adults see lifelong commitment as a challenge. Some even view the idea of being with the same person for the remainder of their days as boring. As Cassidy simply stated in her interview: "I don't want to be committed to one person forever anyway, like getting married to somebody, because what if they turn out to be a butthole or something?"

That is, not only are many emerging adults socialized to expect transition and change, but they also expect novelty. Don't like your current job? Go find another one. Changed your major five times? Great, that represents important personal exploration. Emerging adults are accustomed to the accessibility of possibility in nearly all areas of life (Arnett, 2000). For some, then, the thought of marriage and the accompanying commitment to one person—for life—represents a stability that some emerging adults find quite distasteful.

Marriage as a "Piece of Paper"

Somewhat paradoxically, worries about marriage requiring a lifelong commitment coexist with what may appear to be a conflicting viewpoint. The second common theme that very often emerged during discussions of the institution of marriage was that marriage was merely a piece of paper, a piece of paper that may hold some symbolic value but was no longer essential for the cultural acceptance of one's relationship. Emerging adults recognize that their current relationships are "marriage-like" in many ways. So the transition to marriage, seen by previous generations as a cause to celebrate, can then become a transition of somewhat muted fanfare. After all, if you're already living together, paying bills as a couple, and having regular sex, the only real difference in the relationship may simply be the legal status. This, in turn, leads emerging adults to view marriage as simply a "piece of paper," a phrase used by many emerging adults we interviewed. Importantly, many emerging adults did not use this phrase to reject marriage; rather, they seemed to want to express the idea that marriage was simply a legal hurdle necessary to gain social and economic benefits.

For example, some saw getting married as something that made navigating societal institutions easier. Angelina, 22 years old and recently single when we interviewed her, shared this mentality:

> Personally I would like to be able to get married because it means
> that I can share health insurance ... and establishing credit
> together; all these things if you want to build a life together, to
> me that makes sense to have a marriage. Just because it's easier
> to—if I'm in the hospital it'll be easier for my husband to get into
> the hospital because he'll be married to me rather than having
> to prove he's my significant other. So to me it just makes sense,
> but I think that a lot of people don't necessarily need that social
> construct, that *piece of paper* that says we're married, and I think
> that's really beautiful actually.

Another emerging adult, Brooklyn, was in her first year of medical school when we spoke to her, and she saw marriage as an avenue to easing some of life's challenges. She explained that to her, marriage was "more a legal benefit than anything else" and that she "could take it or leave it." So even though many emerging adults clearly feel that marriage implies long-term, even lifelong, commitment to a partner, others also see it as a means to legal benefits (although what Brooklyn believed these legal benefits to be was never explicit).

Of course, not all see things this way. Still other emerging adults used the "piece of paper" phrase to suggest that marriage adds value to the relationship, that the piece of paper creates an almost symbolic quality to marriage. As Allison pointed out later in her interview, "it [marriage] just makes it [the relationship] feel stronger; there's something about signing that paper, and even though you know you're honest and open in a relationship, there's something different about putting it in writing." In other words, the act of making a commitment legally binding appears to deepen the symbolic nature of marriage.

However, the piece of paper terminology was also used by a segment of emerging adults in a more dismissive manner. For these emerging adults, the use of this phrase appeared to help them justify their dislike or disinterest. These emerging adults spoke of marriage as a social contract with little practical importance. Greyson, a software engineer recently divorced from an early marriage, explained, "I mean, if you're going to be with someone, you just be with someone, and whether or not you go through the ceremony and have that little sheet of paper from the state—that's not a concern of mine." Greyson, likely influenced by the dissolution of his own marriage, was among a handful of emerging adults we interviewed who felt a commitment to a partner was best (and probably solely!) demonstrated through actions, with no need for marriage licenses. David, another divorced emerging adult, also used this term as a way to suggest that marriage was not that important. He explained, "It's not one size fits all. For sure. My belief is, if you love somebody you can love them with or without a piece of paper, but if you want that piece of paper, go ahead and get it. . . . It's just a façade. You know you don't need a piece of paper to show them that you love somebody." This perhaps represented the ultimate extreme of Cherlin's (2004) deinstitutionalization argument—that the role of marriage may erode to such an extent that it is neither a societal norm nor a needed institution. Instead, marriage becomes a niche relationship form, accepted by some but rejected by most. Although this was certainly not a common sentiment, for those who did reject the idea of marriage as an important social institution, reducing marriage to a mere piece of paper was perhaps the ultimate way to express how little marriage meant to them in their lives.

Further evidence of this dismissiveness of marriage can be seen in several quotes by Brianna, Aubrey, and Devon, each of whom, in their own way, suggested that the legal institution of marriage likely continues partially because we can't think of an alternative.

Brianna, a 21-year-old Latino young woman we spoke to, had recently ended an 8-year committed relationship. When discussing marriage, Brianna explained,

> I think we're socialized to think that it [marriage] is [needed]
> and being married gives you a lot more privileges financially

and socially, but I don't really see that it is any kind of glue that's holding society together. I think just a lot of people are taught to value it, so they do.

Brianna saw the value of marriage being "socialized" and almost forced on her and her peers. For her, marriage is an institution that was assumed to have value but might not really be needed at all. Aubrey, a single 26-year-old working a good job in a large metropolitan area, was willing to give marriage a little more credit. She noted,

> I think it's a loose rope that ties the family structure together in a way. It's just we as humans think it's nice to have labels on things and to know our parameters, and I think marriage still provides that, whether it be through law or religion or social standards or even how to interact with other people and other couples and other singles when you're still married. If you have that mind of marriage you know there are certain lines you can't cross.

That marriage might have slight, vague societal importance was a common sentiment among emerging adults. Many recognized that marriage might help structure society, but these same emerging adults were often quick to dismiss individual benefits, again bringing marriage back to the simple piece of paper that might not matter. Devon, a 23-year-old who was in a dating relationship and currently living with his parents, noted that dichotomy when thinking about marriage generally versus at the couple level. He explained,

> I think that it [marriage] benefits the other people that aren't the two getting married, if that makes sense. I think the government needs that and other people need it, but the two people I don't think that they . . . necessarily need that institution.

Devon recognized the irony in his thinking: that marriage was needed for others but not for the actual couple involved. For Devon, marriage almost became a sacrificial offering that couples make on the altar of societal good.

Putting together these first two themes of marriage as commitment and marriage as simply a piece of paper leads us to yet another paradox. Essentially, it boils down to this: Marriage is simultaneously the most private of all personal relationships and the most public of all institutions. On the one hand, the institution of marriage is unique to each individual because of the commitment each partner feels for the other. This obligation makes the idea of marriage different for each emerging adult. It is the ultimate individual expression of commitment in a stable relationship and will look different for everyone. On the other hand, marriage is a public ritual, a legally binding ceremony performed among family and friends that, some emerging adults argue, is really just a legal step that means little beyond state or federal benefits.

Perhaps this paradox is resolved in the minds of many emerging adults through claims that, although marriage is the ultimate expression of commitment, perhaps it is not a *needed* step to demonstrate lifelong commitment. In other words, marriage is not the only game in town when it comes to demonstrating commitment. In Kierra's (a 22-year-old student) words, "The person you're married to is just someone you're making a commitment to, and I just don't think you need a legal piece of paper to make that commitment." Or as Lauren (another 22-year-old female student) put it, "If you need a piece of paper to commit yourself to someone then you're probably not that committed." Perhaps for most emerging adults, marriage really has simply become a piece of paper that legally binds two people together. Although such a step may be symbolically important to some couples, in the relativistic world of emerging adults, such a step is optional at best and restrictive at worst.

Marriage and the Importance of Romantic Love

This paradox, that marriage encompasses lifelong commitment yet represents a simple and perhaps disposable tradition in a relationship, also emerges in a third theme that sprung from our interviews. Regardless of whether marriage entailed lifelong commitment or constituted an arbitrary piece of paper, another concept appeared in the interviews with all but the most cynical emerging adults: Marriage is about love. Candice, a 23-year-old of Native American heritage, provides a good example of this type of mentality. She explained,

> To me it's [marriage] a romantic thing. I guess in the past it was more about joining families and finances, but that's not how I view it at all really. It's more—to me it's about love and wanting to spend the rest of your life with another person and just committing to that.

Other emerging adults seemed to connect romance with a heightened sense of intimacy in a relationship. Capria, a 25-year-old woman considering going to school to become a nurse, thought that romance was essential for any long-term relationship. She said, "Without romance it'd get boring. That's my opinion. Like romance plays so big. Who would you wanna be with if you can't kiss him or you're not attracted to them, you know? . . . Who wants to be with somebody that they are not attracted to?" Like commitment, this description of love and marriage being intertwined as Candice described was very common among the emerging adults we interviewed. The emerging adults we spoke to connected marriage with love in 66% of our interviews. This connection of love and marriage took different forms. The most common was a direct reference to "romantic love" (35% of the sample), whereas many other emerging adults spoke of "lifelong love" or "sacrificial love" being a key element of the institution of marriage. Regardless of the exact definition emerging adults used for love, it was clear that love and marriage were connected in their minds and that such a connection was different from the way previous generations had thought of marriage.

This focus on love reflects the power of romanticism in marriage. Romanticism, of course, has been tied to marriage since at least the medieval rise of courtly love. Today, emerging adults are bombarded by images and messages promoting the power and allure of romanticism. From Disney to the latest young adult bestseller, or TV shows ranging from *iCarly* to *Game of Thrones*, the idea that love conquers all has, in a twist of fate, conquered our society. As the character of Christian in the 2001 movie *Moulin Rouge* declared, "Love is like oxygen, love is a many splendored thing. Love lifts us up where we belong! All you need is love!"

Romanticism often involves ideals and beliefs that love can conquer all obstacles and that ideal relationships are centered on perfect, romantic partners (Spanier, 1972). Internalizing such romantic messages have been shown to influence emerging adults in a variety of ways, including increasing the risk for impulsive sexual behaviors (Ugoji, 2011) and increasing romantic involvement (Montgomery, 2005). Other scholars have noted the potential for extreme romanticism to interfere with long-term healthy relationship formation by creating unrealistic expectations of romantic partners (Baucom & Epstein, 1990; Glenn, 1991). As evidenced by these previous findings and our own current data, marriage continues to be intermixed with romantic ideals for the majority of emerging adults.

What is the net effect of this connection between romanticism and marriage among emerging adults? The specific outcomes of such a link are beyond the scope of the present discussion, but it does suggest an important caveat to emerging adults' insistence that marriage equates to lifelong commitment. It appears as though part of this commitment is rooted in romantic love. Similar to how lifelong commitment separates marriage from the long-term dating or cohabiting relationships most emerging adults are engaged in, marriage was often talked about as a relationship that will have *more* romance than emerging adults' current relationships. This begins to set the stage for a theme we will come back to several times in later chapters. Emerging adults place marriage in a difficult position. Although the institution itself may or may not be needed, if the transition does occur, the relationship is meant to be more committed and more romantic than the relationships that preceded it. That is a high bar to set and gives us our first insight into why marriage may be delayed and deprioritized among emerging adults who still profess to value the relationship.

▲ Variation in Thinking About Marriage

Before moving on, we need to make a final point: Despite the prevalence of the three themes identified, there is no universal way that emerging adults think about marriage. Although most emerging adults value marriage and expect to marry, the nuances and details of emerging adults' paradigms and beliefs are as diverse as the emerging adults themselves. Emerging adults, after all, are given unprecedented freedom and choices about their approach to adulthood and the world in general. Numerous (and likely infinite) are the ways in which emerging adults think about the institution of marriage; this will remain a theme throughout the remainder of this book. The variety of ways in which emerging adults think about marriage lead to numerous marital paradigms (Willoughby & Hall, 2015), which by extension will influence behaviors and actions. Indeed, having established the general patterns surrounding how emerging adults think about the institution of marriage, we will proceed in the following chapters to examine wrinkles in these general beliefs. That is, we assess how emerging adults translate these general ideas and values about marriage into tangible attitudes and beliefs that inform the opinions, decisions, and behaviors that shape their lives. It is in these details and variations where many of the marital paradoxes lie for emerging adults.

4 ⚡

I Want to Get Married ... Just not Right Now

Now that we have covered some of the ground surrounding marriage in general, we will use Marital Paradigm Theory (Willoughby, Hall, & Luczak, 2015), discussed in chapter 3, to shed light on the marital paradox. Specifically, Marital Paradigm Theory suggests that beliefs about getting married are especially significant to emerging adults after they launch from their parents' home and move toward (or away from) an eventual marriage. These beliefs, which encompass marital timing (when to get married), marital salience (how important marriage is), and marital context (the circumstances in which marriage should occur), form the basis for many decisions during the critical period between the ages of 18 and 30 years. In this chapter, we explore emerging adults' beliefs about marital timing as well as how beliefs and thoughts about the ideal time to marry shape our understanding of how emerging adults orient themselves toward committed relationships and marriage.

⚡ When Do Emerging Adults Get Married?

Despite a general trend to delay marriage, many emerging adults still marry at some point in their early to mid-20s. In 2009, only 27% of women between the ages of 30 and 34 years had never been married, suggesting that the majority of individuals in the United States have married at least once by the age of 30 (Kreider & Ellis, 2011). However, marriage continues to creep later and later into the life course for most Americans. As referenced earlier, the median age at marriage in 2015 for all individuals was 29.2 for men and 27.1 for women (U.S. Census Bureau, 2015b), placing marriage for most at the tail end of emerging adulthood. These aggregate numbers, however, mask some stark differences based on class and race. Although 87% of whites have been

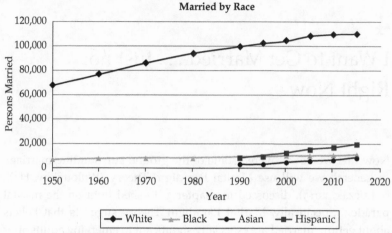

FIGURE 4.1 Number of married persons by race.
Source: Current Population Survey.

married once by their early 30s, only 46% of blacks have been married (Kreider & Ellis, 2011). As seen in Figure 4.1, the number of persons married has increased for all ethnicities since 2000, but the numbers of whites, Hispanics, and Asians who are married increased at a faster rate than the number of blacks.

Income appears to be another important consideration when exploring marriage in the United States. In Figure 4.2, the percentage of married people separated by income is shown. It is interesting that among those reporting a yearly income between $25,000 and $40,000, fewer than 50% were married. Of those with a reported yearly income of $100,000 or more, however, 80% of men and about 65% of women were married.

Despite these important race and socioeconomic caveats, for at least many Americans (especially white, educated Americans), marriage continues to occur at some point in their 20s. However, most would agree that getting married at 21 and 29 are two very different decisions. Indeed, discussing trends and averages that show marriage generally occurs in the late 20s and early 30s sometimes means glossing over emerging adults who marry in their early 20s or failing to consider the variation in marital timing that occurs in the third decade of life. Emerging adults who transition to marriage in their early 20s, for example, are likely very different from those who marry

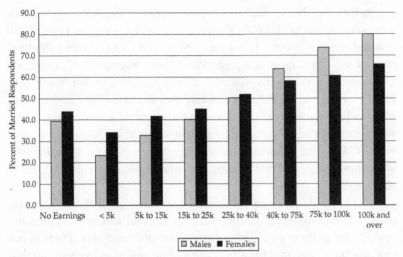

FIGURE 4.2 Percentage married by gender and income level.
Source: Current Population Survey.

in their late 20s. Speaking more generally, we know relatively little about emerging adults who do make transitions to marriage at varying points during their 20s because often they are lumped together with "adults" in the social science research. Because they have chosen to make the transition to the adult roles that marriage entails, they are often separated from the rest of their age cohort and disregarded in many ways by developmental scholars. Although we will discuss those emerging adults who marry early in more detail in chapter 10, at this point it will suffice to simply point out that less than 20% of emerging adults have married by the age of 25 years (Copen, Daniels, Vespa, & Mosher, 2012), suggesting that this group is certainly a minority in today's culture.

This variation in when people get married (i.e., marital timing) is important for reasons beyond simple descriptive purposes. For years, scholars have debated the "ideal" age of marriage by examining the probability of a healthy and stable marriage among people married in their teens, 20s, 30s, and so on. The results, as it turns out, are often complex. On the one hand, many studies suggest that the longer one waits to marry, the lower the probability of divorce (Heaton, 2002; Lehrer, 2008), especially because older ages at marriage often come with more education, maturity, and financial resources. These same studies generally show that teenage marriages are among the most risky when it comes to divorce probability. However, Glenn, Uecker, and Love (2010) pointed out that divorce is not the only factor to look at when thinking about the "ideal" age at marriage. What about happiness? Satisfaction? Commitment? When divorce and marital satisfaction are considered jointly, Glenn and his colleagues found that marrying between the ages of 22 and 26 years was associated with the greatest likelihood of success, with emerging adults who delay marriage into their 30s reporting elevated risk-taking behaviors and even poorer mental health compared with those who married earlier (see Hymowitz, Carroll, Wilcox, & Kaye, 2013).

Here, we do not aim to argue the specific age that all emerging adults should marry. Such an endeavor is often foolhardy, given the complexity of most emerging adults' lives and priorities. There is not just one "best" age that fits all people. Rather, we wish to point out that research does suggest that the timing of marriage matters generally—that marrying at some ages does appear to have a higher likelihood of eventual marital success than others do. And because timing matters, at least in terms of divorce and marital satisfaction, how emerging adults think about marital timing, both for themselves and others, becomes of crucial importance. This is especially true given research demonstrating a link between emerging adults' beliefs about marital timing and when they actually choose to marry (Willoughby, 2012). When emerging adults plan to marry appears to put them on probable trajectories that will influence when an actual marital transition will occur.

▲ When Do Emerging Adults *Want* to Get Married?

Given that marital timing matters, the next logical question is simply this: When do emerging adults want to marry? Why do some of them choose to marry early, whereas others do not marry until their late 20s or even 30s? How many of them *do* wish to marry during this potentially optimal time during their 20s? Despite the extensive talk among scholars on trends in age at marriage, what emerging adults desire, expect, or consider ideal in terms of marital timing has received less attention. Such an exploration of beliefs about marital timing is not quite as simple as merely asking emerging adults when they want to marry. Indeed, one thing became increasingly clear to us over the course of our study of emerging adults: Emerging adults give very different answers based on whether you ask them what they feel is the *ideal* age at marriage or what age they *expect* to marry.

The Ideal Versus the Expected

One of the most consistent marital beliefs emerging adults in our study reported is that the ideal age at marriage is about 25 years. First reported by Carroll and colleagues (2007), the magic number of 25 has appeared in other studies as well (Willoughby & Carroll, 2012). Among the almost 700 emerging adults we surveyed during our initial data collection, the average ideal age of marriage reported was 25.7 years old, with 38% of the sample specifying exactly 25 years old as the ideal age. Why 25, a seemingly arbitrary choice conveniently in the middle of the 20s, is the ideal remains unclear. Perhaps 20 is too young and 30 too old, so 25 feels safe and normal. Many of the emerging adults surveyed in the previously cited studies were in their late teens and early 20s when they were surveyed, so 25 may seem like a far-off goal for many of them.

Leo, a 21-year-old single when we interviewed him, noted when asked about when he wanted to marry, "I'm 21 currently, so by the time I'm 26, 27 maybe, it would be nice to have found somebody by then. But it's not something that will preoccupy me specifically." This does not leave the impression that the mid-20s are some magical age. Rather, 25 sounds more like a rough approximation of what constitutes "the future" date at which marriage seems like a nice idea. Like Leo, many younger emerging adults may believe the mid-20s are far enough away that, when they get there, they will be ready for marriage.

Many studies on the ideal age of marriage have utilized mostly middle-class college students, for whom 25 may also represent a completed college degree and a reasonably established career. Thus, this number may largely be about sequencing, or the ordering of life events. Sydney, a 22-year-old student on the cusp of graduation who recently ended a long-term committed relationship, noted that as she approached her mid-20s she began to realize she was in the age range in which marriage, for her at least, would ideally happen. When asked about her thoughts on marital timing, she immediately thought of her impending graduation, noting that, "I just assumed it would happen at some point when I was an adult. And now that I am suddenly 22 and about to graduate college, it's like, 'Oh, that might actually happen soon.' And it's kind of a real and soon possibility."

Still others view their mid-20s as an internal deadline. Avery, 22 years old, who was recently married and finishing a human development degree when we interviewed her, spoke of 25 as a deadline, of sorts, for singlehood. She explained, "I've always thought I will be married by the time I'm 25. If I'm not married by the time I'm 25, there's no hope. I'll never get married—that's always what I thought." Like Avery, Sydney, and Leo, many emerging adults seem to believe the mid-20s, for a variety of reasons, is the ideal age to marry.

Of course, the ideal is often different from the expected. For some, ideals may seem out of reach and unrealistic. Many college students, for example, expect to make much less money than they would consider ideal! They may have aspirations for Hollywood success or launching a successful independent business, but also realize that expecting such dreams to be fulfilled will result in frustration. Research on beliefs about marital timing is often interested in what emerging adults think is the ideal age of marriage, but we wondered if emerging adults might expect something different from the ideal. We wondered how well their expected age at marriage matched with whatever ideal age they carried with them internally. After all, emerging adulthood is the age of possibilities but also of anxiety, stress, and uncertainty. Tellingly, when emerging adults talk about *expected* rather than *ideal* age at marriage, the answers become more varied. Although the bulk of our respondents agreed that 25 was the ideal age at marriage, there was far less agreement on the expected age at marriage (Figure 4.3). The average expected age at marriage in our sample was only slightly later than the ideal (26.1), but the variation of responses was much greater. The standard deviation, used to assess how much "spread" there is around the mean, indicated much more variation in "expected" versus "ideal" marital timing (standard deviation [SD] = 3.06 for ideal; SD = 4.22 for expected timing). What this means, in practical terms, is that although our respondents, on average, thought the ideal age at marriage was anytime between 22 and 28 (the average being right in the middle at 25), the expected age at marriage tended to range from 21 to 30. Similarly, although less than one fifth (16%) of the emerging adults we surveyed reported an ideal age at marriage as older than 28 years, more than one fourth (26%) reported an expected age older than 28 years, a 10% increase. Figure 4.3 shows the ideal and expected ages at marriage frequencies for the emerging adults in our sample. Although 25 years may be the most common answer for

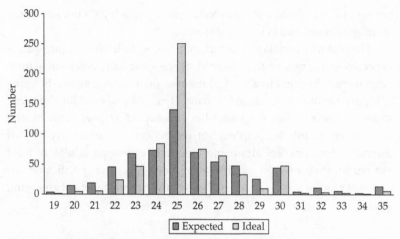

FIGURE 4.3 Ideal and expected age of marriage at time 1.

both questions, this figure visually shows how the expected age distribution suggested more variation than the ideal age question.

Another important element of the data is not clear when simply looking at these aggregate numbers. Generally, most emerging adults appear to place their expected age at marriage later than their ideal. On average, emerging adults in our sample expected to marry about a year later than what they thought was ideal. However, this pattern did not hold for all emerging adults, and, again, variation was apparent. A sizable minority of emerging adults expected to marry sooner than their ideal. In fact, 36% expected to marry sooner than their ideal, whereas 40% expected to marry later than their ideal. Among those who expected to marry later, the average difference was 3.2 years. Interestingly, gender appeared to be an important factor in understanding these differences. Men were much more likely to expect to marry later than their ideal than women. In total, 50% of the men we surveyed expected to marry later than their ideal, compared with only 38% of women. In fact, women only differed by 0.2 years in their expected versus ideal marital timing, a difference that, in practice, is essentially irrelevant.

Overall, these numbers suggest some interesting variations among emerging adults in their beliefs about the timing of marriage. Many emerging adults expected to marry after their ideal age, yet more than half of the emerging adults we sampled expected to marry at their ideal age or sooner. Like many aspects of emerging adulthood, "variation" appears to be the best way to describe emerging adults' views on when marriage should and is expected to occur.

Despite this variation, the fact that almost half of emerging adults expected to marry later than their ideal age, especially when such questions were submitted in a neutral manner on a survey, suggests a specific paradox about marriage for many. If marriage would ideally occur sooner in their minds, why not plan and expect to meet those ideals? The answer to this is complex, but we believe it may simply be that marriage does not feel attainable for many emerging adults, at least not within their desired window of opportunity. The specifics of this paradox require some deeper analysis of the timing beliefs of emerging adults.

There Is No Ideal—The Influence of Relativism and Individualism

There is an interesting caveat to the previous findings—for many emerging adults, there is no ideal age at marriage. That this might be true occurred to us after some feedback from the emerging adults in our study. During the second year of data collection, we decided to ask a question that to our knowledge had never been asked before. Instead of simply asking emerging adults what the ideal age at marriage was, we asked them if they thought there even was such a thing. The results initially surprised us, but with further reflection we see that the responses fall in line with previous themes.

Surprisingly, a solid majority, not just a handful, of emerging adults believed there was no ideal age at marriage. Only 35% of our sample in the second study year even reported that there was an ideal age. One year later, that percentage had dropped to less than one third (29%). Is it possible that scholars have been forcing a question on emerging adults that they consider irrelevant? What is clear in these data is that most emerging adults do not believe there is an ideal age at marriage at all. For these emerging adults, at least, the internal paradox of ideal versus expected age at marriage is more mirage than substance.

This idea (that there is no ideal age at marriage) was a recurring theme in our interviews when we probed emerging adults for more detail on the issue. Nearly every time we prodded, statements about the ascendency of individualism and relativism reigned supreme. To have an ideal age at marriage, they argued, implies that marriage at a given age will be better (or more successful) than others. Emerging adults often reject such thoughts on any topic, including marriage, instead choosing to emphasize how unique circumstances in each individual's life could make a wide variety of ages the "ideal." Ashlyn, a 22-year-old "lifelong single," for example, did not mince words with us when we asked her about the ideal age to get married, stating simply that "the ideal time is when you find the right person to marry." Biological age is inconsequential; it's about context. The ideal age is individualized and specific to each person. Kendall, a 26-year-old who was engaged to be married at the time we interviewed her, summarized this perfectly when she explained, "I think everyone has a specific age for them in their life that is like, you can get married around this age and you know this is good for you. And for some people that's in their 40s, for some people that's in their 20s. It depends on what's good for you and where you are in your life, so I think everyone has an ideal age for them." Taya, in her early 20s and working to complete her General Educational Development (GED) certification, likewise believed in this relativism of marital timing. Taya had a child out of wedlock several years earlier with her current partner. She explained, "I feel like every person is different and every relationship is different. We started out with children and there's different circumstances for everyone. I feel like when you know you know, and if you're ready for it then you're ready for it. It could be 19, it could be 30. So, I think it's different for everyone."

For many, this sentiment seems strongly connected to the experience of emerging adulthood itself. Although children and teens idealize marriage and weddings and have their lives mapped out, emerging adults who have navigated the curves and dips of their early 20s have faced the stark reality of an unstable future and (sometimes wildly) unpredictable circumstances. Consequently, this has made many of them sympathetic to the shifting context of others. Matthew, a 24-year-old law student, explained how his views about ideal timing of marriage have shifted during the past few years. He noted, "I used to [think there was an ideal] when I was younger, but everybody is so different. Life is going to change and you never know where you're going to meet that person, so I don't think there is one now." Lauren, a 22-year-old on the cusp of engagement with a long-term boyfriend, also noted how her views have shifted, "I think it's just different for everybody. If you would have asked me 4 or 5 years ago, I would have wanted to be married by the time I was 22 and [have] kids when I was 25. I think it's different for everybody, and you do it when it's the right time."

Although it may be tempting to believe that this relativism was reserved for only the secular among our sample, such sentiment could easily be translated into a religious context. Claire, a devout Christian who was engaged and about to transition to marriage much sooner than her peers, explained her beliefs in this way, "I am all about [marrying] in God's timing, so whenever he opens the door for an opportunity for marriage, if it's with the right person, then I think you could be 19—as crazy as that sounds—and get married, or you could be 55 and get married." Thus, even among our most religious emerging adults, the concept of "God's timing" allowed many to incorporate within their spiritual beliefs the same relativistic beliefs about marital timing.

▲ Too Young Versus Too Old: Marriage Windows

Beyond whether an ideal age of marriage exists, another theme that emerged in our interviews suggested a conflicting (or paradoxical) belief. As emerging adults discussed when they expected to marry, it became clear that many emerging adults had what might be considered an ideal marriage window rather than a particular age. Over and over again, emerging adults discussed marital timing less in terms of specific ages and more in terms of "too young" and "too old." Their thoughts and examples on both ends of this spectrum suggest some interesting caveats to their belief that marital timing is a relative and individualistic choice.

Marrying Too Young

On one end of the spectrum came a strong message surrounding the potential dangers of marrying too young. Indeed, when emerging adults were searching for extreme examples of appropriate ages at marriage, they often cited examples on the older end (e.g., "You could certainly get married at 40, 50, or 60"). In contrast, almost no emerging adults used extremes on the younger end of the age spectrum to justify the importance of relative ideal timing. Instead, many emerging adults claimed that marrying "young" carried distinct disadvantages, often tied to maturity. Devon, a 23-year-old in that awkward period between graduating college and finding a career, noted that brain development would hinder healthy relationship development if marriage happened too early. He stated, "I think a lot of people get married way too young; your brain is still developing at age 25 or something and people are getting married at 22, 23. Is this really the best thing to do? I think people get married way too young." David, our struggling musician mentioned in earlier chapters, was disturbed when he saw early marriage around him. He said, "So when I see these 18-, 19-year-olds getting married it just makes me sick, 'cause they're children. They haven't figured anything out. They're just barely out of high school. Do you really have the life experience to deal with everything that entails to giving yourself to another person? Usually more times than not, it's not."

Andrew, a 25-year-old part-time graduate student, explained his thoughts on early marriage this way:

> I would say 18- to 20-year-olds, that age group who gets married, I think they're going to have more issues because they're still pretty immature. They're still kids, to be honest. And then they have kids and they're kind of stuck in a marriage because they have the traditional ideal that we're married, we have kids, we should just tough it out. I feel like they're unhappy and it's just drama, drama, drama. I feel they are unhappy.

This belief, that people getting married young are "stuck" in a marriage, was a common theme among those we interviewed.

It is ironic, then, that the pervasive sense that others should not be judged based on the peculiar circumstances in every person's life does not seem to apply to those who choose to marry at younger ages. Many assumed those getting married in their late teens or early 20s were settling or succumbing to external pressures. Brianna, a 21-year-old college student, connected early marriage to "small town" values, saying, "I think it's more of a small town thing to get married early. I think a lot of it is just that if you're from a small town, you kind of see everything that's ahead of you, you have a kind of limited world. When you get to college you see that you could go anywhere and do anything, and if you marry someone, you have someone that you're accountable for."

It is important, again, to note that this belief cannot be disentangled from the general belief emerging adults have that individual choice and individualism matter. Many emerging adults failed to recognize the potential contradiction in their beliefs. When asked about marital timing, Alexis, 22 when we interviewed her, was at first quick to point out that there is no ideal, that it is up to the couple to decide what works for them. She suggested, "I think it's totally a personal choice and it's up to the couple. It's definitely a big decision to make, you know. Marriage is this giant thing." Although this statement seems to shout the importance of personal choice and the supremacy of relativism, Alexis immediately followed this statement by saying,

> The funny thing is that everybody nowadays is getting married or having babies. You scroll down through Facebook [and] that's all you see is somebody else is getting engaged or married or having a kid. It's like, really? We're so young, so I think it's funny that a lot of people have this idea that—the older generation especially— our grandparents were getting married right away, like out of high school, and that's so weird. But I'm like, dudes, we're doing the same thing. You're just graduating college and you're jumping into a marriage. You don't even know yourself yet. I think that people nowadays are getting married earlier than they maybe should.

This contradiction, that when to marry is up to the couple and their individual circumstances but that her peers who are marrying early are marrying "earlier than they maybe should," was apparent throughout several of our interviews. As if to further drive home the point of contradiction, Alexis ended her thoughts on ideal marital timing with this: "But again, like I said, to each their own." Again, individual choice reigns supreme in the age of variation, despite perhaps underlying beliefs that there is indeed an ideal time.

Marrying Too Late

If marriage, in many emerging adults' eyes, can happen too early, many also feel it can happen too late, but for very different reasons. Instead of worrying about being stuck in a marriage, marrying too late appears to be a fertility issue. Among the middle-class emerging adults we spoke to, marriage and parenthood are still strongly connected. Kierra, a single 22-year-old heading to graduate school, placed marriage ideally in the late 20s. For her, a window rather than an exact age best captured this belief when she explained that marrying before or after this late-20s period may be problematic: "Any sooner, I think you're still finding who you are, your career. Later I guess is okay, but if you did want to have kids, saving it for any later you wouldn't have much time to be married without having kids."

If the early 20s are too young and 25 is the "ideal" age, 30 was where many emerging adults felt marriage might be "too late." Like Kierra, for many this had to do with parenting and fertility. Hayley, another emerging-adult woman, explained, "I expect to get married around 30ish, but it doesn't have to be at a certain time. I just feel like it's a good time [to] be married, by 30, because I want to get married before I have children and I want to be young enough that by the time my children have children I will still be alive." Madison, a 22-year-old in a long-term committed relationship, talked about an "ideal age range," a range she placed at 25 to 30 years old. When asked to elaborate on her thinking, she explained, "I think I say that because you have enough time [to] grow up. Obviously you're not going to be grown up by the time you're 25, but you have time to figure what you want to do out [there] and you have time to be by yourself and experience life. But then you still have enough time to have kids before your biological clock says, 'No more.'"

Piecing this together, an interesting picture of marital timing appears. While believing there is no "ideal" timing for marriage and couples should have the luxury of deciding for themselves, emerging adults often also carry specific, perhaps more personal, beliefs about the best or proper way of choosing when to marry. For most, marriage in the late teens or even early 20s is "too soon" because such marriages may, at least in the eyes of the emerging adults we spoke to, limit opportunities for personal growth and be hampered by issues of immaturity that could potentially make it harder to form stable and healthy committed relationships. They also believe that marriage after 30 may be too late, at least if biological children are part of the emerging adult's intended life course. Despite medical and fertility advances that mitigate at least some of these concerns for women, many emerging adults still adhere to traditional ideals of the young married couple raising their own biological children. These beliefs seem to yield an ideal marriage window that opens up between the mid-20s and early 30s; and this likely has something to with why the average age of first marriage is in this period. Wherever the specific marriage window may fall for a particular emerging adult, such windows may be important in understanding the marital and individual trajectories of each person.

Variation in Marital Timing Beliefs

Despite seeming agreement that the mid-20s to early 30s may be the time for marriage, as noted earlier, there is a great deal of variety around the expected timing of marriage. In fact, the respondents we spoke with varied widely in when they placed marriage both in terms of the ideal and what they expected. Why such variation? For one, emerging adults believe strongly that the "right" time to marry can and should be different for everyone (as long as it is not too early or too late). However, what factors do emerging adults believe matter most when determining why the timing of marriage should vary? If context matters so much, how do we know when someone is truly ready for marriage? In the past, such beliefs have been conceptualized as marriage readiness (Carroll et al., 2009). Within a sample of almost 800 university students, Carroll and colleagues (2009) found that interpersonal competencies, or the ability to communicate and interact well with others, were among the most important factors listed by emerging adults as criteria for marriage. Also, many pragmatic factors such as financial self-sufficiency (91% felt it was necessary) and living apart from parents (80% felt it was necessary) were commonly reported by emerging adults. Interestingly, these criteria differ significantly from the sentiments of emerging adults' parents (Willoughby, Olson, Carroll, Nelson, & Miller, 2012), who place greater emphasis on external benchmarks like avoiding risk-taking rather than internal criteria such as settling on personal values. Among our own interview data, three factors seemed to surface when emerging adults attempted to explain their varying beliefs about the ideal and expected age at marriage. The first of these was maturity.

Maturity

Despite no use of the term on our end, *maturity* was directly mentioned more than 100 times over the course of our interviews. Almost half (45%) of the emerging adults we spoke to brought up the term *maturity* explicitly, and these emerging adults mentioned it on average 2.8 times per interview. This focus on maturity was not unique to us. Research shows that many emerging adults see maturity as a requirement for adulthood generally (Arnett, 2016; Cote, 2000; Monahan, Steinberg, Cauffman, & Mulvey, 2013; Staff, 2013) Almost forty percent (39%) of our participants mentioned that maturity is developed primarily by age and experience. When we asked Robert, a single young man at the time of our interview, why, according to him, marriage should take place before age 30 but not before the early 20s, he explained,

> There is a new level of maturity because hopefully by then you're living out on your own, away from family. Not in your parents' house, I should say—You're living as a single person, going to work or doing [your] job or career and you['re] coming home and taking care of things yourself. So it's all about, mainly, experience. That's the best way, I feel, to explain it. It's the best age because of all the experience you've had growing up between past relationships and whatnot.

But what exactly maturity means to emerging adults seems less clear. Maturity seemed to be more of a buzzword than anything else, one that was easy to reference but difficult to quantify. For some, maturity was about emotional control. Blake noted, "The best time to get married for me is about, I'd say, 30ish. I think that it's not necessarily about your age but about a lot of variables such as your financial stability, your emotional maturity, the dependence you have on your partner and how committed you are to them, and a lot of the other important relationship factors." For others, maturity has to do with establishing and adhering to life goals. Isabelle, a 22-year-old student who had recently become single, expressed frustration with some of her dating and marital prospects and tied these frustrations back to maturity, explaining,

> You know, sometimes people don't even know how to ask people out on a date. It's more just hanging out or talking. Everything is kind of twisted into something a lot more casual. That is okay for some situations and sometimes it's just not. [Dating] just needs to be taken more on a level of maturity. Guys who just like to party and all of that kind of stuff—that's a major turnoff for me. That just shows no work ethic or goals in life, I guess. There's nothing wrong with having a good time, definitely. But it just comes across as lazy and just immature.

For some emerging adults, maturity was simple to explain. Maturity merely means achieving adulthood status and making responsible decisions, something other scholars have noted (Arnett, 2016). After you have satisfactorily settled into an adult role in society and made rational decisions, you are considered mature. Kendall, recently graduated from college, explained why marriage and maturity are linked:

> It [marrying later] gives me 4 years to screw around still and I don't mean that literally; I mean just relax still. I mean, I just graduated so I don't want to get married right out of college. Where you're mid-20s, that's more of an adult; plus, I know I'm going to have a little bit more of a mature mind. I don't think that I'm mature enough, really, at this point to consider something as serious as marriage right now. I think a lot of people go into marriage so unseriously, so that's why a lot of people still get divorced. They don't really take it seriously enough, so 26 sounds solid.

Sage, a 25-year-old who had ambitions to travel the world in the next few years, was even more blunt when asked directly what maturity meant to her. She explained that maturity was

> being responsible; you can pay your bills, you can make your money. Or, if you're not in that stage in life and you're in college, you can get good grades while maintaining a healthy life and not getting a DUI or anything—you know, not being stupid, partying out like that. But, I don't know, just being able to take care of yourself and make good decisions without having to go home to your mama.

Still others tied maturity to financial stability and seemed to equate it directly with having financial resources and a steady job. Sareena noted when asked about the most important factors to consider when marrying that "both people need to at least live out on their own to experience having to pay bills and budget and what it's like in the real world. If you're still living at home and you're not having to pay electricity, and you're not having to worry about, okay, I've got a budget in groceries this week—it's a shock to people. One of the biggest things that couples have issues with is finances."

After hearing such a wide range of opinions on what constituted maturity, we began to wonder if the varied ways that emerging adults use the term *maturity* might give us some insight into the marital paradox. Sure, most emerging adults believe that maturity precedes marriage. However, what actually constitutes maturity appears vague and undefined for many of them. They appear to have internalized societal messaging about the need to grow up and establish themselves, but emerging adults struggle to articulate clear markers for when this maturity is achieved. Perhaps this is the natural result of an age period full of societally approved exploration and experimentation. Without a clear normative road map, emerging adults are left without well-defined indicators that they have, in fact, matured. And because maturity is one of the most critical markers for marriage, at least in their minds, these emerging adults may value marriage but not necessarily wish to embrace it—yet.

Sequencing: Spacing Education, Careers, Marriage, and Childbearing

Another factor determining when emerging adults expect to marry deals with perceptions of how marriage coordinates with other adult roles. As mentioned in previous chapters, societal norms surrounding when and how to transition to parenthood, marriage, and career are less clear than in generations past. Emerging adults feel, in fact, that there is no prescribed order at all and that they can sequence these transitions in virtually any order they choose. On the one hand, this freedom is likely exciting to some emerging adults. On the other hand, with this freedom comes a great deal of ambiguity about how and when these transitions are supposed to take place. After all, careers are dictated by supervisors and bosses, whereas marriage and parenthood involve spouses and partners who have their own input on how life transitions should take place. These two worlds, with their many options, create uncertainty among emerging adults trying to sequence these events in their minds and then plan accordingly.

Consequently, their beliefs about marital timing go hand-in-hand with their expected timing of other life events such as education, career, and parenthood. Jacob, a 22-year-old senior majoring in psychology at the time of our interview, offers a perfect illustration of this sequencing idea. Although Jacob had not been in many romantic relationships at that point, he labeled marriage an important priority for him. Yet he was also very quick to note that marriage should come after other transitions, in no small part because of the importance he placed on marriage. Early in his interview he noted that, "I think it's [marriage] something that comes after other things. Not because it's a lower priority but because I feel like it deserves the utmost attention." He further explained how important it was to complete his education and establish his career before he thought about marriage. He noted, "I feel like that's something once you've got launched out in a career then you can let that [marriage] fall into place. You can really focus your time into that." Later, Jacob expanded on these thoughts, explaining that he thought this sequencing from education to the transition to parenting was key to a successful marriage.

> I think that [marriage] can be successful as long as people are, like I said, staggering things out. I'm going to have a career or I'm going to get involved in my career—start working on that. Then that's comfortable, I can take on an extra [thing in] my life to manage. And then after the marriage is settled in a bit, then you can start thinking about children—you know, I'm ready to take this step and have another life depending on me.

This sequencing of education, career, and then marriage was a common one among the emerging adults we interviewed. Emilee put it perhaps the most directly to us when she quickly informed us, "I hope to get married someday. Once I graduate first and find jobs, but yeah."

This does not mean that other sequences did not emerge. Carli, about to transition to marriage herself, did not believe marriage needed to wait until after all college had been completed. For her, the transition to parenthood was what needed to wait until after establishing a career. This was influenced by the example of her parents. She explained that, "I think they've [her parents] definitely influenced my decision to wait to have kids until I am done with grad school and I'm working because right now I don't really have the time to leave. But I think that when I'm in a more established career I will." Claire, our highly religious and engaged emerging adult mentioned earlier, suggested another sequence. Claire wanted to wait until after graduation to marry, explaining, "[I] definitely wanted to be finished with that [school], just because I felt like it would have been too much for me to handle being a wife and being a student at the same time. So that was our main waiting period—after I graduate." Unlike many of her peers, though, the transition to sexual experience was important to Claire, given her religious upbringing and beliefs, one of which was a desire to abstain from sex until after marriage. When asked why she planned to marry so quickly after graduation (within a few months), Claire said, "Why wait for it when we can be married now and avoid temptations and stuff like that." For Claire, the clear sequence was college, marriage, and then sex.

Other variations were found among the emerging adults who came from more impoverished backgrounds, those who did not have the typical college trajectory. Kamar, a 24-year-old young man, had his GED certification and was working in a low-paying, blue-collar job when we spoke to him. He viewed the ideal age of marriage as 18, much younger than virtually anyone we spoke to. Yet to Kamar, he actually viewed this age as a "delayed" transition and still felt that education should come before a marriage. As he put it, "I would probably say 18 [for an ideal age]. A person at 15, 16, their main focus should be on dating. My mama was 16 and my daddy was 15 when I was born. See that just messed up a lot of stuff. Nobody finished school because of my momma being pregnant." Note that Kamar felt that marriage could interfere with educational trajectories like many emerging adults, he simply was substituting high school graduation for the college plans of most middle-class emerging adults. From Kamar's frame of reference, marriage (and childbearing) could interfere with secondary education as he saw happen with his parents.

This handful of examples illustrates a larger point: Much of the variation in how emerging adults view marriage fitting into their life plans is directly connected to their desired and ideal sequencing of other major events and transitions. For most middle-class emerging adults, this sequence appeared to center around finishing their college education, establishing themselves in a career, and then transitioning to marriage. Such a normative sequence, however, seemingly contradicts the very idea of a marital paradox. After all, if most emerging adults have a clear sequence in mind, why would there be a paradox between their beliefs and actions? Clear social norms, particularly around marriage historically, tend to lead to remarkable conformity to those norms.

Part of the answer may lie in the final theme that emerged that helps us understand the variation in marital timing beliefs. Although career establishment may come before marriage in emerging adults' minds, the instability of employment and career trajectories in the modern era was an important wrinkle in the best-laid plans of many emerging adults.

Uncertainty About Career

Of all the transitions that emerging adults confront, educational and career trajectories are perhaps responsible for the most anxiety that emerging adults feel, as was mentioned in chapter 1. The goal for many in the middle and upper-middle classes, of course, is to finish college and then use that education to launch into a stable career that can support an eventual family. But this plan has increasingly become disrupted by an unstable job market and employment opportunities that may change at a moment's notice. Instability and uncertainty in today's fast-paced economy are the norm. Gone are the days when college graduates could expect to find stable, long-term employment right out of college. More and more middle-class emerging adults today find themselves in entry-level positions in business and service-oriented fields, with dim prospects of long-term stability. Many of these entry-level jobs also come with limited or no benefits and lower salaries compared with their parents' first jobs. Subsequently, despite a hope for marital readiness on starting a career, many emerging adults fear that career instability will make future relationships more difficult. Sydney, 22 and in a steady relationship of 3 years, talked about how her future job prospects may influence her relationship. She explained,

> I am in a place now because I'm in school and because I'[ve] got another year, I am totally just thinking about a job. I realize that if I were to try to get married in the next year I think that might mess up job prospects. And that might make it hard if I have to move somewhere. In my brain it's like, okay, job first and then we think about getting married and then we think about having kids. I think it's important to get comfortable in one before you add another one on. You know, you want to have a solid foundation before you add the next step.

In Sydney's eyes, her future career likely requires flexibility—that is, flexibility she may not have if tied down in a marriage.

For many, though, merely getting a job wasn't the only prerequisite for marriage; rather, it was having a *secure* job. For the emerging adults we spoke to, a typical career trajectory can be divided into two phases. Phase one follows education and usually involves several moves and several different positions (often with different companies). Phase two involves "settling" into a more permanent and stable profession. Parker, a recently graduated 24-year-old with a year's worth of work experience under his belt, noted that although he considered his current relationship very stable and healthy, he still saw marriage as several years away. His explanation? "Because I'm hoping by that time I will feel that I can propose, and then after proposal we'll have time to figure out everything and get married then. And hopefully by maybe 26 I have enough time to have more of a secure job that I'll feel like I'll stay with and that I like doing and that will pay me, and I'll have benefits maybe." Parker's case is not uncommon. Many of his peers also struggle to believe that their current entry-level positions will lead to permanent careers. Because of the importance of having a "secure" job before marrying, it may take two, three, or even four more jobs before finding one that offers the desired level of stability. This, too, contributes to some of the paradoxical beliefs about marriage that emerging adults hold.

▲ Putting It All Together

Clearly, emerging adults' complex beliefs about marital timing intersect with other decisions. Despite clear variations in almost all aspects of how emerging adults think about marital timing, some clear patterns exist. A previous study conducted by Willoughby and Hall (2015) categorized emerging adults, based on this set of complex marital timing beliefs, into three common categories: marriage delayers, marriage hesitants, and marriage enthusiasts. Although other groups likely exist, these three groups help paint a picture of what many emerging adults think concerning their marital timing beliefs. Thus, we have used these three groups for heuristic purposes here to illustrate how emerging adults may differ in how they approach the timing of marriage holistically using what we have learned about emerging adults' view of marital beliefs throughout this chapter.

Delayers

On one end of the spectrum, we have emerging adults who view marriage as a hindrance and as an outdated institution, thus often placing marriage later in the life course than others, if they desire to marry at all. These emerging adults typically put marriage after 30, an age you will remember often considered "too old" by many emerging adults. For these individuals, marriage seems to be a barrier that impedes progress toward their other ambitions. In the Willoughby and Hall

(2015) study, this group represented 10% of the emerging adults in the sample, by far the smallest proportion of the sample. Although small, this group represents an important and perhaps growing segment of the emerging adulthood population. For this group, marriage as an institution seems to have lost its luster. In fact, they view marriage negatively.

Robert, 21, a Native American with divorced parents, is a perfect example of a delayer. He pointed out early in the interview that, "I am in no rush to get married." He elaborated,

> I'm in no rush because right now if I were to get married I would not be able to do very well because that means I have to make that commitment to the other person. Being married is another responsibility because you have that responsibility to take care of the other person and take care of a lot of other things that you both will be accomplishing or paying for. So I'm in no rush because it's not a priority and I know that it's not something that I need to do at this stage; it's just not right for me at this stage. I'm too young right now.

Robert placed the ideal age at marriage after 30 and "very strongly disagreed" that marriage should come before education or career, which we found in all 3 years of our survey. For Robert, the obligation of being partially responsible for another person's emotional and financial well-being is too much of a commitment.

Still, it is not just the finances that make marriage seem unappealing to delayers. Take Jadyn, for example, a 20-year-old woman who enjoyed the sexual experimentation that emerging adulthood was providing her. Marriage was a relationship she wished to delay because of the perceived restrictions such a monogamous relationship would place on her and her concern that she had not yet fully discovered her own sexual appetites. As she explained, "I've never been a big fan of [marriage] just because, for one, if your parts don't fit, but you love each other, why would you condemn each other to a lifetime of bad sex? That just doesn't make sense. That doesn't seem very loving to me. Sex is supposed to be awesome not painful." Jadyn, who expected to marry at 30, wished to delay marriage to more fully experience the sexual freedom and opportunities that emerging adulthood would give her.

Enthusiasts

Not all emerging adults held negative views of marriage, however. Enthusiasts are those emerging adults who generally value marriage and are excited for its arrival in their lives. Carli, for example, was 21 and engaged to be married when she was interviewed and was a good example of what a modern marriage enthusiast looks like. It was clear that marriage was a positive and exciting thing for Carli. She had been engaged for nearly 3 years when we spoke with her and noted that the only reason she and her fiancé waited to get married was to avoid planning a wedding while in school. As she was quick to point out, "It's not that we wanted to necessarily wait for marriage, it's just that a wedding is a lot of work." Interestingly, Carli felt she was taking the slow course toward marriage. In fact, when we first surveyed Carli, she reported an expected age at marriage (23) that was 3 years earlier than her ideal (26). She also disagreed that marriage was among the top priorities in her life or that it should come before an education. When asked about her trajectory toward marriage with her fiancé, she noted, "I know for a fact that I want our marriage to last so I don't feel a lot of pressure to rush into it. I realize that sometimes people who rush into it do it for the wrong reasons. So, that might be one reason why I don't feel bad about having a long engagement, even though a lot of people think it's weird."

Despite reservations about marriage, Carli was moving comparatively quickly toward marriage and was quite positive when she spoke about her own pending marriage. Carli exemplified a group of emerging adults who idealize marriage and therefore integrate it into almost everything they do. They eagerly plan and prepare for marriage, viewing it as a positive and welcome transition in their lives. Willoughby and Hall (2015) called these types of emerging adults *enthusiasts*. Although they are a minority, some emerging adults remain steadfast in the notion of marriage as an institution that not only benefits couples but also society. Claire, our religiously minded emerging adult, described how for her, "marriage definitely is the key for holding a family together and having children and being able to multiply. I believe that marriage is a great example for relationships and how they are supposed to be." Such enthusiasts seem to value marriage not only for its perceived personal benefits but also for the benefits it gives others. Seeing marriage as a union that is assumed to generate so many positive things, such emerging adults hold timing beliefs that place marriage comparatively early in the life course and often are willing to prioritize the sequencing of marriage before other major transitions.

Hesitants

The final group of emerging adults, the *hesitants*, was the largest, representing more than half of the Willoughby and Hall (2015) sample. It was a group that certainly seemed to value marriage and expected to marry only slightly later than the enthusiasts. Yet they also expressed some strong fears and apprehensions about marriage. When asked about whether marriage should be a permanent arrangement, the hesitants resembled those in the delayer group. It was this group that commonly appeared in our interviews, the group that appears to best capture the current emerging adult approach to marriage. It was among this group that we saw the most grappling with issues like maturity and sequencing mentioned earlier. These emerging adults often expected to marry later than what they considered "ideal."

Chelsea, for example, described marriage as "kind of a scary thing." When asked to elaborate, she explained, "Just to imagine being with the same person in the same place for a long time or forever." The use of the word *scary*, which we heard numerous times, exemplifies the fear so many of these emerging adults have when it comes to marriage. As with just about everything in emerging adulthood, this fear took a variety of forms. Sometimes it was fear of rejection, sometimes it was fear of never finding true love. For many emerging adults, that fear was tied to the ubiquitous anxiety and uncertainty that pervades this period, dramatically influencing how they thought about marriage. Brooke explained that she feared marriage because of its permanence, unlike so many other things in her life. She explained, "It's one of those things where we're not really used to thinking of anything in permanence. Things change really quickly, and going through all of those changes all of the time but saying this person is going to be there forever and for always, no matter what—that's scary. It's a scary thing ... it's a scary, scary thing."

Fear of divorce was another common source of angst. Melissa, who ideally placed marriage at 26 but expected to marry at 28, put it this way, "I'm religious, so I think it's [marriage is] meant to be a good thing. I just think it's kind of scary, our society, I mean the divorce rate is so terrible. I don't know, I have a lot of mixed feelings about it." When asked whether marriage should precede education or career, among other things, Melissa was right in the middle, often selecting neutral responses—that is, with one exception. When we asked if she felt ready for marriage, she selected the lowest possible response, "very strongly disagree." Together, Chelsea, Brooke, and Melissa represent a very typical pattern for emerging adults and their views of marital timing. Marriage should happen, it should probably happen in the late 20s, but the prospect of actually getting married is tied to the general fear and anxiety of an uncertain future.

Although there are likely many other types of marital paradigms that emerging adults hold, these three types illustrate the common themes we currently see among emerging adults and how the timing of marriage has become a complicated and paradoxical notion in the minds of emerging adults. No longer simply about a person's relationship, when to get married is clearly connected to a complex web of personal, relational, and career development, creating ambiguity that may provide the foundation of many of the paradoxes regarding marriage currently seen among emerging adults.

What, then, is the collective sum of the beliefs about marital timing explored in this chapter? Emerging adults appear to embrace individualism with their timing beliefs. Although the age of 25 continues to be a magic number of sorts when emerging adults think of marriage, most do not believe there is a truly ideal age to marry. Instead, they believe each couple should be free to blaze their own path. This pathway is often based on personal decisions rooted in educational and career trajectories, the sequencing of which seem to be important factors in determining each emerging adult's personal expectations about marital timing. However, paradoxes abound: Emerging adults also believe that one can marry both too early and too late, providing pressure to marry within a window of time in the late 20s for most. As mentioned previously, this makes most emerging adults marriage hesitants, hoping for a future marriage within the next decade yet hesitant about when and if it should occur in their own life.

5 ▲

Marriage Is Important . . . Just Not *That* Important

Having discussed the beliefs emerging adults hold about marital timing, we now turn to a second important area of beliefs about marriage: beliefs about the *importance* of marriage. Both Marital Horizon Theory and Marital Paradigm Theory recognize marital importance, or salience, as a key dimension explaining an individual's marital beliefs and attitudes. Generally, marital importance can be divided into three broad categories of beliefs: an individual's beliefs about the importance of marriage for society, beliefs about the specific importance of marriage in the individual's own life, and the relative importance of marriage compared with other life goals. In this chapter, we will explore how emerging adults think about marriage across each of these three broad categories to better understand how they weigh the importance of marriage and marital transitions.

▲ Does Marriage Still Matter?

Even after discussing how emerging adults view marriage and seeing that emerging adults believe marriage is largely defined by commitment and lifelong love (see chapter 3), a fundamental question about marriage remains: Do we need it? Is marriage generally important for people? Is it an important institution and pillar of our modern society? Many emerging adults believe, as noted in chapter 3, that marriage is simply an unnecessary "piece of paper." The assumption, of course, is that if something is unnecessary, it must therefore be unimportant. Although there is certainly a link between the two, it is essential to understand that, among the emerging adults we spoke with, *unnecessary* and *unimportant* are not necessarily synonyms. Indeed, the very essence of the marital paradox is that emerging adults act and talk like they value marriage yet seem to devalue it for themselves and for others.

In an attempt to further understand this specific paradox, we asked emerging adults directly whether marriage was in fact *needed* in our modern society. What we got was plenty of confusion and conflicting internal evaluations of what marriage meant in our larger society, and a lot of uncertainty.

Is Marriage Still an Institution?

The question of whether marriage still constitutes a societal institution is not unique, of course, to our specific study and discussion. Indeed, many scholars have monitored the belief across cohorts regarding whether marriage is needed or important in society. According to the Monitoring the Future Study, in 1976 having a good marriage was very important to 72% of the high school seniors surveyed. This number stayed steady with a small increase of 2% by 2014 (74%). Between 1976 and 2004, the highest percentage was in 1990 at 78%.

Our own data suggested that emerging adults continue to think marriage is needed, although only by a slim majority. Generally speaking, the emerging adults we interviewed agreed at some level that marriage was an important institution. Of our emerging adults sampled, 56% believed marriage was still a needed institution, whereas another 9% were somewhat mixed. Yet this agreement was often tempered by hesitation and a struggle to articulate *why* marriage was still important. Many emerging adults felt that life would certainly go on if marriage went the way of stagecoaches and horse buggies, items that served their purpose but whose usefulness has long since eroded. For these emerging adults, believing marriage was integral to society's well-being was something of a misnomer. Brianna, for example, noted that, "I think we're socialized to think that it is [needed]—being married gives you a lot more privileges financially and socially, I guess. But I don't really see that it is any kind of glue that's holding society together." For her, marriage was almost an archaic idea foisted on her by society. Twenty-three-year-old David held a similar belief, acknowledging that marriage was now more of a choice rather than a requirement, stating, "I don't feel like anybody has to get married. Marriage is definitely a choice. It's more of a thing you gotta want for yourself I guess. Everybody wants to grow up, get married, and have kids. It's all part of the status quo. But, I don't think it's necessary, no."

Lindsay, a 22-year-old who was engaged and already had a young child with her fiancé, held an even more negative view of the role marriage should play in society: "People can still be committed to each other without this imaginary marriage concept around them." Blunt, perhaps, especially for one about to actually transition to marriage, but quite representative of many of the views we heard expressed.

Although there were certainly emerging adults we spoke to who believed in the power of marriage as a societal institution, it seems abundantly clear that some emerging adults are beginning to question whether marriage is still needed. Some emerging adults have likely always disregarded marriage, but the number of emerging adults who are questioning its validity appears to be growing. However, like many marital beliefs, several nuances warrant further discussion.

What Would We Do Without It?

We asked many of the emerging adults who felt marriage was not needed what life would be like without marriage. Many of our emerging adults seemed genuinely confused about our question regarding what society would be like or do without marriage. Although they had a clear sense that marriage may not be that important or needed, they struggled to articulate what an alternative arrangement would look like. Despite their seeming apathy toward marriage, most did not wish to rid society of institutionalized relationship norms, thus leaving marriage as the only option left standing. Rather than filling some essential societal role, marriage was seen as important merely because, in the eyes of emerging adults, we need something to help people commit to each other. Other relational options, such as committed and long-term cohabitation, were almost never mentioned as viable alternatives by these emerging adults. Perhaps, some suggested, marriage should be available moving forward, but only as something that remained for those who wished to utilize it. Hayley, for example, noted that marriage should be an option for those who continued to want it, saying, "I don't think people should be forced to get married, but I think if people want to be able to get married they should be able to. So, I think that the institution of marriage should continue but not everybody should have to get married if they decide they don't want to."

The more we spoke with emerging adults, the clearer it became that, for many of them, marriage has an unspoken heft to it, as though it's historical significance warranted at least some reverence. To a certain extent, of course, they're quite right. Many scholars have noted the key economic, social, and familial role marriage has played across time and culture (Sweeney, 2002; Thornton, Axinn, & Xie, 2008) because of its gatekeeper function in many societies. For example, marriage traditionally served as the primary pathway through which mate selection and eventual parenthood occurred (Thornton et al., 2008). This notion continues to influence us today as many continue to believe marriage is the proper avenue though which to bear children (Cherlin, 2010). However, marriage and its place in society have shifted away from this gatekeeping function (Cherlin, 2004, 2010). In lieu of its organizational benefits, many feel marriage now primarily has to do with romance and relationships. You might recall from chapter 3 that commitment and lifelong love were key themes in how emerging adults described what marriage meant to them.

Although marriage clearly had a historical place in society, that place has shifted, and many are unsure what the new normal is. When asked whether marriage was needed, Tori, a 26-year-old engaged female, noted that, "I feel like there's too much history embedded, though, for it not to be [important]. To just abolish marriage—people would be like, what? I think it's not necessary. To me, I want it and I know a lot of people do, but in our society I think it's shifting away from that." Lindsay expressed a similar sentiment when she said, "I don't know if it ever was a needed institution. I mean, I don't know when marriages started. But since it is one [an institution], we kind of have to just accept that it is."

Some emerging adults shared Lindsay's resignation that marriage is here to stay, even if it is not a needed part of society. Marriage, thus, appears to have taken on itself a very uncertain role in their lives. Marriage should perhaps have a purpose, but many emerging adults struggle to grasp or articulate it. As marriage has become less about economic stability, less a part of the bedrock of society's structure, and more about a long-term and romantic committed relationship, emerging adults struggle to articulate why we have marriage for structural reasons or what society would be like without it.

Two Married Parents Are Still Important

However, although marriage itself may have lost much of its luster for emerging adults as an institution, many still felt marriage did have one important gatekeeping function: to provide a mechanism to create stable two-parent families. As mentioned in chapter 4, many middle-class emerging adults still believe that parenthood should come after a marital transition. In fact, a new paradox surfaced as emerging adults laid out their thoughts on the importance of marriage generally. Many emerging adults believe that marriage should ideally occur toward the natural limits of female fertility (i.e., later rather than sooner in the life course). Yet they also seem to believe that marriage is an essential part of creating the ideal environment in which to raise children. This argument is not new in the relationship and family literature because marriage often provides many resources for children's development (Hanson, McLanahan, & Thomson, 1994; Sun & Li, 2011), and its relative stability affords positive emotional and physical health benefits for children (Carr & Springer, 2010; Ryan & Claessens, 2013).

Beyond research and scholarship, the ideal of the two-parent married family is a pillar of Western norms about childbearing and childrearing, particularly in the United States. Modern television, often seen as both a reflection and harbinger of cultural change, suggests that families with children are still often depicted as being led by two married parents. The popular show *Modern Family* perhaps illustrates this concept best. The show centers on three very different families with children (one traditional couple, one same-sex couple, and one remarried couple with a large age gap), yet all three couples hold one important factor in common: they are all married.

This fact is not lost on emerging adults. One of the bluntest about this connection was Melissa. When discussing the importance of marriage and whether it was needed, she noted that, "I would say definitely. I think in order for a child to really grow and develop properly and everything, you need a strong mother role and a strong father role. You can't just have one or the other. And obviously you need a marriage to procreate. I don't think it's a good idea just to live together, there's no commitment there. So I think it's important." Notably, she believed that marriage was not just desirable but needed to have children.

Many emerging adults we spoke to quickly shifted the focus from marriage to family when we discussed whether marriage was needed. Tom, a 21-year-old embarking on a career as an accountant, explained it this way:

I would think it's [marriage] absolutely needed. It's all centered on the family; it's the basis of the family, right? And the family, obviously it's the basis of society. I don't think you need a science teacher to tell you that much. A marriage seems to solidify, at least in my experience and what I've seen in recent study stuff, that marriage itself kind of solidifies the whole communion aspect and the community aspects. And human beings, we have a natural need, I suppose, to live in that community, and families really provide that. So I suppose families in some ways conform out of the community as a whole, but I think marriage is still the foundation, or at least it is the first place to start.

Ellen, a 27-year-old physical therapist, made the connection even more explicit, referencing what she considered an impact on her niece who was living with unmarried parents. She explained,

I think it's [marriage] still needed. The traditional way is, I think, good for children just to say that their mom and dad are married, and because I think it's a little weird for my niece; her friend's parents are married and my brother is not married to her mom. Socially it's become more accepted to be married and [then] have kids.

Although marriage may be less important to society, it remains important in many of their minds as the gateway to parenting. Even among those who did not explicitly connect marriage to parenting, it was rare among the middle-class emerging adults we interviewed to anticipate marrying after becoming a parent. This is, of course, in sharp contrast to the trends seen among the lower socioeconomic class in the United States. In 2012, 45.5% of all never-married parents in the United States lived below the poverty line (Solomon-Fears, 2014). This phenomenon has been actively discussed by scholars and policy makers. McLanahan (2004) referred to the "diverging destinies" of children from upper- and lower-class families. Although we will refrain here from getting into a long discussion of child outcome and family formation research, it is sufficient to simply point out that this strong connection between sequencing marriage before childbearing continues to be more often a middle- to upper-middle class belief.

Taken together, emerging adults' beliefs about whether marriage is indeed still important seem full of many paradoxes. A comment from David exemplifies many of these themes while also illustrating these paradoxes. When discussing if marriage is needed, David said, "I don't feel like anybody has to get married. Marriage is definitely a choice. It's more of a thing you gotta want for yourself I guess. Everybody wants to grow up, get married, and have kids. It's all part of the status quo. But, I don't think it's necessary, no." Notice some important elements of this comment. First, David clearly does not believe everyone needs to be married. It is a personal choice and, by extension, not important at a societal level. Yet he also notes that marriage is part of the "status quo" and that his peers desire a parental transition that follows a marriage, suggesting a normative sequence. Like many emerging adults, David seems caught between wanting marriage to be the ultimate expression of personal choice (and likely commitment) in a relationship yet also acknowledging that marriage continues to dominate the cultural narrative around relationship progression and fertility.

▲ Relative Importance: How Marriage Stacks Up to Other Life Priorities

Unlike marital timing beliefs, which tend to be much more varied, scholars have long noted remarkable consistency in beliefs about marital importance. In fact, one of the hallmarks of American youth and emerging adults is their long-standing and persistent belief in the overall importance of marriage as a personal life goal. When we first began collecting data, for example, 79% of the emerging adults we surveyed agreed that marriage was "a very important goal" for them.

Perhaps, then, understanding emerging adults and their beliefs about marital importance is more about *relative* importance and less about *general* importance. The idea is simple: Although most emerging adults value marriage and believe it is important, their behavior and other specific beliefs about marriage are more varied. This suggests that the general importance placed on marriage may have less utility in determining daily behavior and life trajectories. Instead, the beliefs emerging adults hold about how marriage is prioritized against other life priorities provides something more focused and individual. Emerging adults, then, not only must decide how generally important marriage is to them but also must work out how marriage stacks up against their many other goals and priorities. In reality, even though marriage is important to most emerging adults, having a good career, getting an education, traveling, and even having fun are also very important (sometimes more important) to them (see Ravert, 2009). Each emerging adult must then rank and prioritize these wants and goals. Although global and general beliefs about the importance of marriage provide us some insights, it is this *relative* ranking where the rubber hits the road, where emerging adults must decide what marriage really means in their life. It is these beliefs that determine whether emerging adults will act in ways that move them toward or away from marriage. This ranking, the relative importance placed on marriage compared with other life goals, provides in some ways a more instructive understanding of the real importance emerging adults place on marriage in their own lives and provides further understanding of the marital paradox.

Balancing Adult Roles (Career, Marriage, and Family)

So what are the other things in emerging adults' lives jockeying for position in the zero-sum game of life? Scholarship on emerging adulthood has identified three key life goals, each of which is particularly salient during emerging adults' 20s: career (often intertwined with educational goals), marriage, and parenting. These three factors appear to serve as milestones that orient and structure the life course for many emerging adults. Indeed, in chapter 4 we already recognized that the sequencing of parenting, education, and marriage provides one of the more useful tools for understanding emerging adults' beliefs about the timing of marriage. Here, we focus not on sequence but on importance, although the two are clearly connected. Individuals tend to consider all three areas of their lives together. Focusing in on marriage, emerging adults are actively considering both parenting and educational goals as they plan for their own marriages. Education and career goals appear to be particularly key for many emerging adults, as noted in several previous chapters.

Willoughby, Hall, and Goff (2015) recently explored such priorities among a sample of almost 600 emerging adults currently attending college. Emerging adults were asked to indicate how much importance they expected to place on different adult roles (being a parent, being a spouse, having a career, and leisure) as they looked into the future. To make things interesting, they were forced to divide "100%" importance across these areas. In other words, greater importance placed in one area meant there was less importance to divide between the remaining areas. Strikingly, emerging adults expected to place almost the exact same importance on marriage (29.9%), parenting (27.6%), and career (26.7%), with less importance being placed on leisure (15.8%), the final category. This suggests a desire for balance in the lives of emerging adults.

Although this desire for balance seems practical on the surface, given the economic realities mentioned in previous chapter, is it possible? Anxiety ruled the day when we asked emerging adults in our own sample how they planned to achieve balance in these roles. As we spoke with them about future plans for marriage, careers, and parenthood, a sense of impending difficulties and frustrations arose. Two clear themes emerged for us: the perceived difficulty of balancing these roles with the inherent sacrifice required to get there and the belief that having success in all areas of life may be simply impossible.

It Will Be Hard

The phrase *"It's hard"* captures the dominant message we received whenever we asked emerging adults about balancing work, parenting, and marriage, partly because of cultural values centered on individualism. The American dream tells us that if we work hard enough, success is just around the corner, leading many to internalize messages about the importance of personal hard work. The downside of such messages, of course, is that they leave no room for failure. If someone is not successful, it must be because he or she did not work hard enough. Consequently, emerging adults want to be perfect parents, perfect marital partners, and perfect employees but are also confronted by the harsh reality of limited resources. In fact, these resources play a central role in the minds of many emerging adults we talked to. Ryan, a 23-year-old working an entry-level job, explained that understanding resources was a key to success in all three areas.

> So if you choose to have a child, what has to give might be work. But then there's things like childcare and, I don't know, it's complicated. I'm 23 and I'm not even married, so what does my opinion count for? But I think that they [parenting, career, and

marriage] can be equally successful as long as you are realistic about the resources you have and the relative cost of how you divide those [resources], especially time.

To deal with this reality, many emerging adults engaged in deliberate sequencing, meaning the prioritization of one area over the others, in hopes of being equally successful with enough effort. This, again, weds the concepts of timing and importance. As Marty put it, "You can have all those things [success in multiple areas of your life], just not at the same time ... unless you're Superman." Many emerging adults believed that it was necessary to sequence roles in order to maximize your probability of success over time. Alexis, an emerging adult mentioned in previous chapters who was working in Texas, had recently broke things off with her boyfriend to focus on a career. She noted that although becoming a parent was her highest priority, she hoped for success in all three areas. She said, "I really want to have kids. I want to have a good working career, but to make sure that both of those things can be well established I have to have a good marriage. So I think that they all are pretty much equal. But kids are definitely my top priority in looking into the future and figuring out what that means." Alexis believed that success in all three areas was interconnected, that a truly balanced life necessitated balance of effort and resources and focusing on one area at a time. Others found comfort in the belief that they did not need to be successful in all three areas all at once. For example, Rosie, a 22-year-old engaged to her boyfriend, explained, "I think there will be ups and downs to each one of them [career, parenting, and marriage] at each stage in your life, they don't all have to be perfect at once. They're easily manageable, but you have to decide which one is important to you." Rosie was one of the few emerging adults we interviewed that used the word *easy* when describing this balance.

Shaina represents the far more common mentality. She noted, "It's a very delicate, difficult balance that parents and people have to consciously make an effort to be successful in all of them. And I don't think it's quite ideal to think that they're all going to be successful at the same time. You can try real hard and really aim for that and I think that's an admirable goal, I just think it's very difficult." In other words, some emerging adults almost revere those who accomplish equal success in all three areas. They seem to believe that balance could occur even if it's unlikely to happen in their own lives. Take the following quotes from two of the women we interviewed as examples:

> Candice: I think if you try to make them all equal then they're all going to suffer a little bit. I would say that there has to be emphasis on at least one of those things because I think I would lose my mind if I tried to equally put my time between children, my marriage, and my career. I just feel like I would lose it somewhere in there.
>
> Hayley: I think it's possible for them to be equal but it's not necessarily likely. It's not probable, it's possible but not probable. If I choose to have children then I better be taking care of them or my husband better be taking care of them.

Thus, Shaina, Candice, and Hayley each claim that, though theoretically possible, success in marriage, career, and parenting is almost never practical. Or as Candice suggested, those who try will "suffer" in the long-term. According to many, doing so may even be unhealthy or at least unwise, notwithstanding their expressed desire to have all three.

Picking and Choosing

Despite beliefs in some quarters that balancing marriage, parenting, and career may be possible (if unlikely), the majority of emerging adults we interviewed believed differently: success in all areas of life is unrealistic; consequently, each person must prioritize and select certain life roles to engage in, focusing on some aspects while letting others slide. In fact, a significant minority (25%) felt it was simply impossible to be successful in a marriage, in a career, and as a parent simultaneously. As Jill, a single mom working as a customer service agent explained, "I don't think you can do all of them [be a good parent, be a good spouse, and have a successful career] at once. I don't think that. I think you could if you tried really, really hard. But it would be a lot of work, and you'd be pretty stressed." For Jill, while such overall success may be theoretically possible, it was, in practical terms, unattainable.

Emerging adults' worry about their ability to successfully navigate adult roles leads us to a critical insight into marital importance: many emerging adults believe painful choices between adult roles are inevitable. Note that this does not mean emerging adults are choosing whether to engage in a particular role. Rather, they feel obligated to choose the roles that matter most to them while either rejecting or neglecting at least one area. This reality is both stark and depressing. Having just arrived into adulthood, many of these emerging adults were already planning to be a less-than-stellar employee, parent, or spouse, resigned to mediocrity in one of the three most critical roles of modern American society.

A few illustrations from the tail end of emerging adulthood may flesh out the view expressed by so many emerging adults. These were individuals in their late 20s who were markedly less optimistic about their ability to balance adult roles than those we interviewed in their early 20s. When we interviewed Steven, 27, he was working at a Best Buy almost 70 hours per week to save money for graduate school. With a degree in music history, he had not found many career prospects after graduation. On the relationship front, Steven had been in a relationship for more than a year but had no plans to marry. In many ways, Steven represents many emerging adults in their late 20s as they try to navigate the complex and often disheartening worlds of career and family. When asked if he felt he could be equally successful in marriage, parenting, and his career, he shared an analogy that helped him balance the importance of each aspect:

> I'm gonna say no, that not all three of them [can be successful], and that reminds me of an analogy. It has to do with cars. You're gonna have a reliable car, a cheap car, or a fast car, but you can only pick two of them and if you pick all three you just can't do it. You got a fast, cheap car but it's not gonna be reliable, you can have a reliable, cheap car but it's not gonna be fast, or you can have a fast, reliable car but it's not gonna be cheap. So I think it's kind of a similar sort of thing; you're gonna spread yourself too thin and you're just not gonna do that good of a job at any of them. I think you can probably favor two of the three. Probably not all three though.

Thus, in Steven's mind at least, one can balance two but not three of these areas of life. For Steven, our survey suggested it was parenting (35% importance) and marital (25%) importance that he valued the most over career.

At 32, Jack, returning to school to pursue an engineering degree, was "very single and not looking" and had moved past the age that most would consider emerging adulthood. After combining personal experience with observations of those around him, he concluded that emerging adults must decide what is most important to them if they are going to get what they want out of life. When asked about success in all three areas, Jack said, "I feel like my answer would be yes and no because you hope that an individual can balance all three. But the reality that I've seen is that unfortunately one or the other is usually what has to be emphasized over time to have success. Especially because I've read recently: To be successful in business, women usually have to give up marriage and children. You know?"

Together, these examples indicate a common belief pattern, one that evolves during the 20s for many emerging adults. Although many begin with hope and optimism that success in parenting, marriage, and career is within their reach, the economic and relational realities of the modern 20s leave many feeling forced to reconsider their priorities; some feeling forced to abandon one role or perhaps two. When combined with the fact that many emerging adults no longer view marriage as a needed transition, it is easier to understand why it has become a transition and adult role that more and more emerging adults are willing to drop.

Career Oriented Versus Family Oriented

As they spoke of the need to prioritize areas for success, emerging adults largely fell into two camps: those valuing career over family transitions (marriage and parenting) and those valuing marriage and parenting over career. In the first year of our study, most emerging adults overwhelmingly placed themselves in the family camp, with 76% of the sample placing more importance on their eventual role as a spouse or parent compared with the importance their careers.

In this finding, however, another paradox arises: Many emerging adults appeared across our interviews to have an orientation that emphasizes careers over marriage and parenting transitions. In chapter 4, we highlighted education and career goals as one of the major reasons emerging adults gave for a desire to delay marriage. However, these previous data on the importance of marriage raise an interesting issue. Rather than rejecting marriage, emerging adults may be valuing education and career goals in their 20s precisely because they believe such goals will enable them to *eventually* focus on marriage. Take Jamie, 22 years old and recently graduated from college, as an example. When we spoke with her, she was working in a service-oriented job and was in a long-distance relationship with her boyfriend. When asked about ideal marital timing, she was clear that, like many emerging adults, "I think there's an ideal age for everyone individually." Jamie expected to marry at the age of 26, although she noted that the ideal would probably be closer to 24. So, like many of her peers, Jamie expected to marry in her mid to late 20s. However, she felt many emerging adults were moving too quickly. She noted that, "I think that, to me it feels like everyone is rushing it [marriage]. The majority of my friends are getting married right now and for me it's like I still feel like I'm a kid. I mean I'm 22 but I still feel like a kid." When asked directly if marriage was a priority for her, she said, "I wouldn't consider marriage my number one right now. I would consider my relationship like top, but marriage is not right there right now." On the surface, Jamie might not appear to value marriage much, a label often given to emerging adults who express similar views. However, in another part of the interview, Jamie labeled herself as "pro-marriage," and her survey results indicated that she expected to place much more importance on marriage and parenting (38% each) than on career (14%) in her adult life. Additionally, Jamie believed that success across all three simply was not possible, stating,

> I feel like I've seen people try really hard to make all three of those number one, but I've never personally seen it successfully done. That sounds awful, but it's just so hard because for me, whenever I've seen it, one always comes up over the other. I've never seen where all three are fully satisfied all of the time. One always gets a little more than the other and one gets a little bit less, so I wouldn't say that one or all three are always fully satisfied.

Such an example gives us insight into the minds and paradoxes of emerging adults like Jamie. She values marriage and parenting—in some ways over her future career. However, she questions her ability to be successful at all three. To make sense of this paradox, she has done what seems very rational—her relative importance shifts across her life course. Right now, in her early 20s and several years away from when she expects to marry, she is putting her time, energy, and other resources into educational and career goals. As Jamie reaches her mid to late 20s, we may expect her focus to shift toward family transitions. Importantly, economic considerations beyond emerging adults' control may factor heavily into this as well because evidence from our older emerging adults such as Jack and Steven suggests that in a struggling economy, many emerging adults may never reach the point at which they are able to "ramp-down" their career goals and refocus on marriage and family goals.

Although Jamie represented perhaps the average emerging adult, some emerging adults take more extreme views on the topic. These emerging adults likely fall in the "enthusiast" category described in the chapter 4 (see also Willoughby & Hall, 2015) because they place an overwhelmingly strong importance on marriage relative to other life goals, even earlier in the life course. Clayton, for instance, was 22, already married, and on his way to dental school when we interviewed him. For Clayton, putting marriage first was the clear and obvious choice. Perhaps unsurprisingly, he came from a very religious background. But even with a solid marital example from parents and his fellow religious congregants, he still did not believe marriage, parenting, and career goals could all be equally successful in any practical way. When asked directly, he explained,

> I think you can be equally successful at being a spouse and parent and an employee but I don't know if that's a good thing. I think that you should try to be like, the effort you put in to being a good spouse should come first and then being a good parent and then being a good employee. In terms of the importance, at least to me, that's the hierarchy; your marriage is important, your kids are less important, and then your job and your career are less important than that.

Unlike many emerging adults who have decided to prioritize career and education during their early 20s, Clayton had likewise decided to prioritize the importance of adult roles but had already prioritized marriage and parenting over career.

Despite acknowledging the importance of marriage, many middle-class emerging adults are increasingly choosing career over family. Although some emerging adults planned to shift increasingly toward marriage and away from career goals as time went on, many of the emerging adults in our sample instead reported placing increased importance on career goals as they got older. By the third year of data collection, career roles were listed as the highest priority in emerging adults over marriage and parenting (29.7% vs. 26.1% and 25%, respectively). Between the first and third years of the study, the proportion of emerging adults who expected to place more importance on marriage or parenting dropped by 14%. This seems to leave open the possibility that emerging adults in the coming generation will continue placing career goals above marriage and parenting.

▲ Is Marriage Too Important?—Idealizing Marriage

To this point, we have emphasized how marriage for emerging adults is largely future focused rather than a persistent part of their daily existence, in large part because they struggle to balance the importance of marriage with other life goals. But we have not yet focused on an aspect that may be among the most important in understanding the marital paradox of emerging adulthood. Similar to how emerging adults insist that people can and should be free to marry whenever they choose and yet still believe in an ideal marriage window, emerging adults also paradoxically seem to *overwhelmingly* romanticize marriage without according it *overwhelming* importance. As mentioned previously, such a belief permeated almost all our interviews except among the most jaded and negative about marriage. Marriage, it seems, has achieved a nearly mystical status among many emerging adults as it continues to be romanticized in our modern culture. Despite eroding norms that everyone must be married, middle-class emerging adults we spoke to now appear to believe that marriage is largely reserved for the elite among them. The fact that marriage is romanticized *and* delayed connects the topics of the last two chapters. One of the key reasons that so many emerging adults expected to marry after their ideal age or why they delayed marriage at all was that they believed marriage was so important. Although previous work (Edin & Kefalas, 2005) has found this mentality among the poor and has used it to partially explain the plummeting marital rates among low-income parents, this same problem appears to be resurfacing among the middle class as well.

Blake, a 22-year-old student about to finish his college degree, spoke passionately about the ills of modern marriage as he saw it, discussing the pressures to marry that many feel and the problems inherent with marriage being what he called just a "stepping stone" in relationships. His expected and ideal age of marriage were both 30, comparatively late among his peers. However, he also considered marriage a "wonderful institution" that he believes is "great, it's really good for people. It helps them. Most of the things I've said so far have been kind of negative because I feel that that's important to express. But I think that marriage is a wonderful institution, especially the legal version." Blake wasn't delaying marriage because he didn't care. Quite the opposite. He was delaying marriage because of how important he felt it was, how much importance he placed on that relational transition, and how strongly he felt that such relationships should be permanent, calling divorce "the absolute 100% last thing I would like to do in my life."

Chloe, a 22-year-old aspiring pharmacist, expressed a similar mentality. She expected to marry at 28 and described marriage as a "very strong commitment between two people." Expressive and thoughtful, she articulated how holding marriage in high esteem can subversively lead to delayed marriage: "I think it's [marriage] something that kind of comes after other things. Not because it's a lower priority but because I feel like it deserves the utmost attention." Both Chloe and Blake employed complex internal conceptualization to fit the square peg of marriage timing in the round hole of marital importance. Because marriage, the ultimate expression of commitment between two people, is so important, it needs to happen after one is established, mature, and financially secure. But because it is no longer needed, failure to fulfill these prerequisites may result in marriage ending up on the back burner.

Another manifestation of the idealization of marriage appeared when emerging adults spoke of divorce. If marriage does not matter much and is just "another" relationship for emerging adults, divorce should not carry that much stigma. Yet the fear of divorce was palpable in the interviews, moving beyond the legal and financial consequences that often accompany marital dissolution. Amelia, a 20-year-old public relations student, spoke of the fear of divorce among her and her friends. She related, "I know, especially among my friends, a lot of them don't like it [divorce] or don't like the idea of it because they see all their parents getting divorced, and you see more divorce than you do marriage." Faced with the reality of a high divorce rate, many emerging adults spoke of their worries and anxieties about an eventual divorce. They actively spoke about trying to avoid becoming another divorce statistic. Nate, a single 22-year-old, explained how his own marital plans were connected to his thinking about divorce. He said, "The divorce rate is really high. I'm in the military and the divorce rate is extra-alarmingly high in the military so I would actually like to finish in the military before I get married to give me a better chance of staying with my spouse." One of the young women we interviewed, Tenli, spoke the most passionately about divorce. Twenty-one and struggling with a job she hated, Tenli had seen her own parents divorce and had seen firsthand the effect it had on both her and her parents. She articulated it in this way: "I think that they're [emerging adults] delaying it [marriage] because I mean, it is scary. And a lot of us, we've seen our parents get divorced. We are the children of every divorced person ever. So we're just looking at it like, wow. You know, I'm a little scared because divorce sucks."

These types of quotes, very common across our interviews, betray some of these emerging adults' true feelings. If marriage does not matter, if marriage truly is an individual choice that you can take or leave, then divorce should not necessarily be feared. Yet the data overwhelmingly suggest that marriage, and divorce with it, does continue to matter to emerging adults. But *how* it matters and *why* it is important is perhaps what is shifting. Marriage is romanticized, a relationship of permanent, lifelong love that should uplift and enrich one's life. It should be a relationship that distracts from the anxieties and stresses of career and educational pursuits. After you commit to marriage, you should do everything you can to make that relationship last. To perhaps put it more bluntly, marriage now serves the individuals and has lost much of its inherent societal good in the eyes of many emerging adults. Much of the marriage paradox hinges on these sometimes contradictory beliefs and on the ways in which emerging adults attempt to balance their own individualized goals and ambitions.

6 ▲
Finding the Right Person to Marry

We turn now to beliefs about marital context, or the beliefs about the circumstances and conditions in which marital decisions are considered, debated, and ultimately made. Although such beliefs come from many places, from personal preferences to social norms and conditions, in this chapter we focus on the beliefs emerging adults hold regarding the ideal and necessary characteristics of potential spouses. In other words, we are interested in the beliefs emerging adults hold regarding the type of partner they are searching for. Such beliefs are very different from those explored in previous chapters, where we have mostly focused on marital beliefs that are decidedly self-focused. These include beliefs about the timing and the importance of marriage in an individual's own varying life trajectory and involve a single person in the decision-making process. When do *I* want to get married? How important is marriage to *me*? Do *I* believe that marriage still matters?

In contrast, this chapter explores beliefs about mate selection, or the process people go through to select romantic partners. Although still individual beliefs, these beliefs are more focused on others because they require us to evaluate the characteristics of potential partners. While remaining very personalized, the themes and commonalities within such beliefs will give us more pieces to the puzzle of understanding emerging adults' paradoxical beliefs and behaviors regarding marriage.

Before delving into the specific beliefs emerging adults hold about potential partners, we first consider some of the theoretical concepts that govern the mate-selection process. Like other areas of this book, this is not meant to be an exhaustive review of the hundreds of articles, books, and other discussions on the mate-selection process; rather, we merely note some of the ideas that guide scholarship in this area.

No discussion of mate-selection preferences can ignore how evolutionary theories have influenced the research on how and why individuals favor and select potential dating and marriage partners (Buss, 1989, 2006). This scholarship focuses on the basic psychological and physical human needs to bond and reproduce. In this framework, mate selection is structured around the objective assessment of the potential fertility and potential resources a partner brings to the relationship. One of the key elements of mate selection from this perspective is physical attraction. Physical attraction often provides a gauge of a future partner's fertility (Buss, Shackelford, Kirkpatrick, & Larsen, 2001) and has been shown to be a key aspect in the mate-selection process, with men tending to value it more than women do (Buss & Schmitt, 1993; Janz, Pepping, & Halford, 2015). Physical attraction also appears to be key in the initial dating phase, serving as an important evaluative tool of potential partners (Lee, Loewenstein, Ariely, Hong, & Young, 2008; Li et al., 2013). Because emerging adults often lack financial stability or other indicators of social standing or future success, there is some indication that they may value physical attraction particularly highly (Miller & Maner, 2011).

What evolutionary theories gain in terms of universal understanding of the mate-selection process and the role genetics and innate drive play therein, they lack in cultural sensitivity. After all, from an evolutionary perspective, marriage becomes merely a convenient cultural label to direct the fertility process. But marriage and relationships, as we've seen, are no longer as closely linked to fertility decisions among modern emerging adults as they once were. Although mate selection still occurs in an environment largely structured by evolutionary desires, emerging adults utilize broader criteria than ever before when considering dating and eventual marital partners.

Some scholars, for example, argue that mate selection is a three-phase social process that involves strategic self-presentation (seeking the best way to present one's best self to the potential partner), evaluation of the potential partner (considering the pros and cons of a committed relationship), and self-protection from rejection (shielding oneself from the pain and anguish that accompany rejection (Beck & Clark, 2010). This process, much like emerging adulthood itself, need not happen in any particular order. Rather, individuals can be in any of the phases and can even revisit them throughout the early stages of a romantic relationship.

For our discussion, we are mostly interested in the second step, the evaluation of the potential partner. This process was argued to begin at the initiation of a relationship, but as Clark and Beck (2010) noted, "the felt need to evaluate the potential partner should grow across time as one finds that the other is interested in a relationship and becomes more serious about the relationship" (p. 203). That is to say, as emerging adults move into a committed relationship, they begin to consider the ramifications of both the relationship and their partner. These evaluations likely crescendo as marriage becomes more realistic. Because marriage remains a strong cultural norm symbolizing lifelong commitment (at least in theory), emerging adults must come to terms with what characteristics they are willing (or not willing) to live with in a spouse during this key time.

So what does this process look like? What exactly are emerging adults looking for in a partner? We posed these and similar questions to our emerging adults. The remainder of the chapter summarizes our findings regarding what exactly emerging adults look for in a dating partner and an eventual spouse and how such findings dovetail with their other beliefs about marriage.

▲ The Ideal Dating Partner and the Ideal Marriage Partner

Beliefs about potential romantic partners represent a very intimate and specific type of belief about preferences, people, and relationships. All are interconnected, yet they emerge out of larger beliefs about the meaning, sequencing, and importance of marriage. As we explored how emerging adults think about dating and marital partners, several important trends emerged. The first answers the most basic of questions— what do emerging adults look for in their dating and marriage partners?

In assessing the traits emerging adults seek in potential romantic partners, we asked them two key questions. First, we asked what traits they look for in a potential marital partner. Then we asked specifically about which traits they consider when committing to date someone without any long-term implications. Sometimes responses to these questions were identical; other times we got quite different answers.

Several interesting patterns emerged. First, it was clear that the umbrella term *good personality* was key for many emerging adults (20% mentioned this as important for marriage partners and 28% for dating partners). Why personality was more frequently mentioned for dating (short-term relationships) than for marriage (long-term relationships) is puzzling. This trend may be related to emerging adults' desire for personality traits such as "fun" and "outgoing" because these traits may lend themselves to the more stress-relieving dating relationships many emerging adults long for. Another common trait identified was *similar beliefs and values* (23% of lists for marriage partners, 11% of lists for dating partners). Together, these two criteria point to the importance of similarity—and, quite obviously, emerging adults often seek partners that are like them in terms of traits and backgrounds (Byrne, 1997; Garcia & Markey, 2007). In other words, emerging adults appear to be seeking someone who thinks about the world in a way they can relate to.

Of course, such findings should be fairly self-evident. Having a "good personality" and finding someone with shared values are universally understood to be benchmarks for partner evaluation in our modern society. However, before moving further into this analysis, we need to address another very basic question. Although these two previous criteria showed some strong overlap as emerging adults considered short-term and long-term partners, how much overlap is there in how emerging adults perceive their ideal dating and marital partners? As noted previously, we asked emerging adults for their ideal traits in *both* a dating and marriage partner. On the one hand, most emerging adults do not plan to marry for several years, if not almost a decade, so they must find more proximate evaluation criteria for their current relationships. The question is whether those evaluative criteria match the criteria they'll eventually use to select a marriage partner.

Previous research suggests that dating and marital partner criteria may be different. For example, several studies have documented that sexual history preference varies based on whether individuals are seeking a dating or marital partner, with individuals generally preferring those with little sexual history for marriage partners but those with high sexual experience as dating partners (O'Sullivan, 1995; Williams & Jacoby, 1989). Another study (Sylwester & Pawlowski, 2010) found that both men and women find risk-takers more attractive as short-term dating partners; risk-avoiders were more attractive as long-term dating partners.

When looking for differences in our own study, we first noted that emerging adults cited far more criteria when considering a marriage partner. In all, we identified seventeen different criteria that were mentioned by at least 5% of our sample when considering a potential long-term relationship. In contrast, only twelve traits made the cut when considering a dating partner. Perhaps it is unsurprising and understandable that emerging adults hold higher standards for committing to a partner long-term. But beyond the sheer quantity of criteria, the content of the criteria was also different. The most mentioned criterion for a dating partner was *physical appearance and attraction* (mentioned by a whopping 35% of the sample). The most mentioned trait for a long-term and marital partner was *commitment*, mentioned by more than one fourth (28%) of the sample. This simple difference suggests a fundamental shift in partner evaluation when emerging adults consider marriage. Although attraction was key in early dating situations, when switching to the long-term view involving marriage, these emerging adults immediately began to talk about commitment, a buzzword noted back in chapter 3 that many emerging adults employ when they consider marriage.

The second most common trait suggested a similar disconnect. For dating partners, it was *humor* or *being a fun person* (34% of the sample), whereas for marriage it was the previously mentioned *similarity in beliefs and values* (23% of the sample). Just for comparison's sake, *humor and fun* did show up on the marriage criteria list, but it was only noted by 5% of the sample. *Attractiveness* was on the marriage list, too, mentioned by only 8% of the sample. Although emerging adults appear to be looking for the same traits in both dating and potential marriage partners, their emphasis on specific traits appears to shift based on which type of partner they are considering.

The storyline here appears clear. Emerging adults seek fun and sexy partners for dating, whereas for marriage they want a committed partner who shares their outlook, values, and life goals. What is less clear is whether emerging adults make such a drastic internal shift in their head as they move through their 20s. Do emerging adults flip the marriage switch in their head and decide, "Today I think I will radically change who I date because I'm ready for marriage!"? Or perhaps do emerging adults expect their fun and sexy partners to eventually mature into the long-term spouses they hope for? Although the answer to that question moves beyond the scope of the current discussion and would require a comprehensive longitudinal study to address, it does raise the interesting possibility of another key marital paradox for emerging adults.

The Potential Rejection of Casual Dating

Interestingly, as we discussed their beliefs about dating and marriage partners, most emerging adults told us that they were tired of the casual relationship scene. As mentioned back in chapter 2, casual relationships and hookups are now staples of the emerging adult dating experience. The emerging adults in our sample had experienced this firsthand, with about 40% of our sample reporting at least one casual hookup that included sexual intercourse. In fact, the average emerging adults we surveyed in the first year of the study engaged in 2.5 sexual hookups in their lifetime, a full partner higher in our study than the average of 1.5 sexual partners within a committed relationship these same emerging adults reported. However, by the time we interviewed them, often as they were approaching their mid-20s, many saw few, if any, benefits to such casual encounters. Their goals had turned to focus more on the long-term, and many spoke of their relationships with this in mind. Here are some examples of such sentiments that we heard:

> Rosalie, 22 and single: I enjoy being in a relationship, and I want to date people that I could potentially end up with.
> Ashlyn, 22 and single: I don't like the idea of dating someone who, like what my mom says, "Is he boyfriend material?" I tend to think, "Is he marriage material?
> Ember, 22 and single: [Long- and short-term partners are] the same thing because I'm not looking for short-term relationships anymore. For me, when I first get in a relationship I'm pursuing someone hopefully in the long run I'd like to marry. I'm tired of crying over boys.

As evidenced by these quotes, it was clear that by the early to mid-20s, many emerging adults desired to evaluate dating partners on a scale that at least considered the possibility of marriage. If popular culture is to be believed, we may think that women would be more likely to do this. However, men were among the most passionate of the voices. Blake, 22, finishing up a college degree, and in a committed relation- ship when we spoke to him, was adamant that he is looking for a long-term partner in relationships. He noted, "I myself am incredibly uncomfortable with casual relationships. I've never had one. I don't like the ideas behind them. I don't like the methods through which you find casual relationships. I have only had long-term serious rela- tionships in the past." Interestingly, despite such strong sentiment against casual relationships, he did report one sexual partner outside of a committed relationship. It seems that even for the most long-term focused among our sample, casual hookups were still around. Despite this, however, evaluating potential partners was clearly a long-term game for Blake.

Tom, a 21-year-old just recently launched into the job market, expressed similar sentiments. During his interview he noted, "I see [relationships] almost as a waste of time unless you're discerning marriage. If you're in this relationship just for fun, it is kind of a waste of time, and my personality doesn't like wasting time as it is." It is important to remember that most of these emerging adults have no desire to marry for several years down the line. Perhaps more important, however, marriage appears to always hover in the background as they evaluate partners and relationships.

For many of these middle-class emerging adults, this shift toward the long-term was linked to college. They often viewed college relationships as inherently short-term and less committed than the relationship mecca they believe awaits them after receiving their diploma. For example, Chelsea, 24 and traveling the world after graduation, said she viewed marriage negatively because it forced her into a lifestyle she wanted to avoid. Marriage for Chelsea meant "not being able to do what I want to do all the time anymore." Chelsea was currently dating someone, and when asked about her current relationship she immediately contrasted it with those from her past. She noted, "you know in high school and college you don't really find the greatest guys all of the time, so no serious relationships came out of that [time], I think because I never found someone that was willing to be that equal partner." Chelsea was quick to dismiss most of her relationship experience during schooling, alluding to the possible immaturity of the men in her dating pool. Similarly, Isabelle, a 22-year-old student, equated this idea with her ideal age of marriage. When asked why she expected to marry at 25, she connected it directly with the type of relationships people have after college, explaining, " 'Because people are more mature. They know they're [men] out of college. Definitely done partying, done kind of having fun. I've been through a lot. I've dated people, and I know what I want. I know what I don't want." Isabelle wanted a mature relationship with someone who had moved beyond the college party scene. Notice how both of the previous illustrations allude to *maturity*, an important term we mentioned in chapter 4. Although maturity is certainly a buzzword among emerging adults, it appears not only to be key to their own personal marriage evaluations but also to be an important criterion they place on others.

It is also important to note that not all emerging adults made a clear distinction between short-term and long-term dating partners. Some emerging adults took the cultural messaging about individualism and relativism so common in emerging adulthood and translated it to dating, rejecting traditional notions of long- or short-term daters. One emerging adult we spoke with had been in a relationship for the past 4 years but rejected the notion of differences between short-term and long-term partners. She passionately repudiated the idea that people can be categorized into "long-term dateable, short-term dateable" but rather asked herself a broader question: "Is the relationship working for us?"

Career Blending With Potential Partners

Given the centrality of career and educational trajectories on how emerging adults currently consider marriage for themselves, it was natural for us to inquire about how career considerations may likewise influence the mate-selection process. Nearly all these ideas, as well as many from previous chapters, culminate in a cacophony of marital ambivalence when emerging adults are asked about how career and educational trajectories mesh with selecting potential marriage partners. In particular, they often expressed a great deal of concern about blending two career trajectories. Success in this arena was seen as key components of finding a successful partner. Middle-class emerging adults were well aware of the fact that much of their personal identities and priorities had been latched to the wagon of career success. They recognized that their dating partners will also likely have this mentality. Indeed, many of them seemed to revere and respect the career trajectories of others as a vital component in the matching process. Ryan, 21, enrolled in school and in a relatively long relationship (about 2 years), wanted to wait at least 4 to 5 years before marrying. In his mind, he needed that time to accomplish his educational and career goals. He also noted, however, that this had caused tension in his current relationship. He wondered if being in a long-term relationship right now was ethical, given the incongruity between his and his girlfriend's ambitions. He reflected, "I feel like sometimes I push too far in my dreams to make her match my dreams, and I don't particularly like that in myself. And it's those moments where I feel like, if I'm more forcing something on her then I don't want to push her that direction." Ryan was life-planning with his girlfriend in mind but felt caught between a desire to have her in his life and wanting her to make her own independent plans and goals. Another student, Max, also 21, noted an eerily similar thought process, one that ultimately led him to end his previous relationship. He recalled,

> While I was in that relationship, I was having to think more about "Okay, if this becomes a marriage, then how does that fit in with my career?" and it was starting to impact what type of career choices I was looking into. So it got to the point where we decided to have a mutual breakup. We had become different people, and I realized in this process that while I would be happy in a relationship, I wanted a relationship that wouldn't pull me away from my desired career in the same way that that relationship had.

Although such individualistic sentiments may fly in the face of those who argue for the importance of a more collectivist approach to blending lives, these examples illustrate the power of career trajectories on emerging adults' evaluations of their partners and the relationships they do or do not choose to pursue. For many emerging adults, partner evaluation today is no longer about only attraction levels or even similar values; it's about the compatibility of life and career trajectories.

Of course, not all emerging adults interject careers into their evaluation process in such an individualistic way. Indeed, some emerging adults we spoke with endorsed a more traditional approach that suggested compromise and sacrifice in the blending process. Chelsea, the 24-year-old world traveler mentioned previously, suggested a more traditional approach with us when discussing her current arrangement with her boyfriend. Chelsea has been working a series of seasonal jobs while her boyfriend had a steady job to go along with two children from a previous relationship. Chelsea expressed a willingness to bend her future career trajectory to cope with his inflexibility. When discussing how this relationship has influenced her, she noted, "It's definitely influenced where I've been looking for jobs and what kind of jobs I've been looking for, to stay closer to him. Before my family was in Ohio, and now my sister and brother-in-law live in Florida, but I just would go where I wanted to go and I'd see them again in a few months and that was fine. With him I've focused more on finding jobs that are close to him and the kids." The cynic, of course, might point out that Chelsea's flexibility is due, in part, to her general lack of career goals—this may be true of many emerging adults. Emerging adults who lack firm career goals may be in a better position to adapt to the career goals of their partners as they consider the implications of forming long-term relationships. Others, those with firmer career goals, may find it harder to sacrifice future career success for the sake of a relationship.

Coping With the Increased Likelihood of Long-Distance Relationships

The increased focus on career trajectories among middle-class emerging adults intersects with another element of today's emerging adulthood experience: residential mobility. Modern emerging adults are among the most mobile segments of the population, and residential mobility tends to peak during the early 20s (Arnett, 2014). Much of this mobility is due to shifts in the amount of education required for a successful career. Over the past few decades, higher levels of education and multiple employment transitions have meant greater geographic mobility. In this way, employment and the residency shifts it often requires represent another obstacle for relationship formation. Consequently, emerging adults are confronted with the need to balance employment offers that may hinder their ability to nurture a particular relationship because of distance. In the past, often aided by strict gender roles that favored male employment patterns, couples may have favored one partner's career path over another. However, modern emerging adults want, feel they deserve, and expect to have both successful careers and marriages (or, as we mentioned in chapter 5, they may feel like they need to pick one over the other). With instability now front and center during their 20s, many emerging adults recognize that residential mobility and uncertainty will likely influence their romantic relationships now and into the future. The natural extension of this reality on relationships is straightforward; the likelihood that two emerging adult romantic partners may end up in a long-distance relationship is increasing.

This potential for distance in committed relationships, however, may simply push some emerging adults away from relationships altogether. Two emerging adults we spoke to provide insight into the types of cautionary tales that drive many emerging adults away from committed relationship during the 20s. First, let's return to Alexis, our 22-year-old recent college graduate mentioned in previous chapters.

When she graduated college she had been in a long-term committed relationship for 4 years. Like many in her age cohort, she now faced a decision between her career and relationship. She had received a job offer that would force her to move out of state. Would she move for her job or remain to focus on her relationship? Alexis's boyfriend faced a similar dilemma, also receiving a job offer that required a significant move. They both decided to focus on careers and try to maintain a long-distance relationship. As she put it, "I moved in August. At the time I was dating my boyfriend of 4 years. Well we hit 4 years in January. So we were going really well, he came to visit me in November of last year, right after I moved basically, we had a great time, everything was going really well. When January came around he moved from Indiana to Illinois for an internship." While Alexis reported that they had a great relationship, their jobs had taken them to two very different parts of the country. Such a relationship would be difficult to maintain, even within the committed bounds of a marriage. When the relationship is founded on less commitment, such as dating, the outcome is probably not hard to figure out. She explained, "... his schedule and my schedule were very different so we started to kind of drift a little bit ... there was a lot of stuff going on and I was kind of freaking out because I'm like wow I've been with this person for 4 years but I'm only 22 years old, you know, what am I doing?" Alexis eventually ended the relationship with her boyfriend, a common outcome among middle-class emerging adults facing similar circumstances. When forced to choose between education/career and relationships, emerging adults often choose the former and try to cling to the latter. The outcome is not always (or even usually) the desired one. Yet emerging adults seem more and more willing to let romantic relationships become a sacrifice on the altar of individual career success.

Elizabeth, another emerging adult we interviewed, shows the reverse problem with this dilemma. Elizabeth was 21, recently graduated, and on her way to graduate school when she entered our study. In terms of relationships, she was in a committed and long-term relationship and was already engaged. After graduation, Elizabeth, too, faced the challenge of negotiating her career choices with those of her fiancé. Unlike Alexis, Elizabeth decided to compromise, eventually settling on a graduate program that would also work for her fiancé's plans and keep them close together. However, shortly before entering graduate school, Elizabeth and her fiancé ended their relationship. When asked how relationships had influenced her career and educational decisions,

Elizabeth was rather blunt, saying, "Well, actually I picked my graduate school based upon the guy I was dating, and then that didn't turn out well." Sarcasm and anger echoed through the room as she spoke about her feelings of frustration. In her eyes, she had, at least to some extent, compromised her personal future for the sake of a relational future that never materialized.

These are the cautionary tales that emerging adults hear. Even if few in number, such stories would likely raise serious doubts in the minds of emerging adults thinking about how to rank relational concerns relative to their educational or employment opportunities.

▲ How Will Emerging Adults Know They've Found the Right Person?

At this point, it should be fairly clear that emerging adults have much on their minds as they consider relationships and their long-term implications. For now, let's momentarily narrow our focus. Beyond worries about life trajectories, what about the actual decision of marrying a particular partner? For example, when do emerging adults feel comfortable making a decision about a particular person in a particular context? At the heart of Marital Paradigm Theory is a desire to understand the circumstances in which emerging adults make the transition to marriage. Although how marriage will affect one's career and educational opportunities is important generally, we must not disregard the emotional part of relational decision making and the way romantic relationships are idealized in our culture. Romanticism, after all, still holds a strong place in the hearts of modern emerging adults. Of course, such decisions, as discussed previously, are heavily influenced by emerging adults' beliefs that the mid to late 20s are the correct time to marry in their specific life course. But even when such milestones as achieving interpersonal maturity and college graduation have been reached, how do emerging adults decide to take the plunge with a particular person? In other words, how do emerging adults identify the right person to marry? With this question in mind, we discuss two more aspects vital to understanding the mate-selection process. First, we will discuss the concept of a soul mate, an idea that persists among many emerging adults. Second, we will examine the critical place that cohabitation currently occupies in the mate-selection process.

Despite their penchant for pragmatism, many emerging adults still very much believe in the concept of a soul mate. Interestingly, many of our emerging adults seemed to believe that the decision to get married would ultimately hinge on whether they had found their soul mate. This is despite their often meticulous plans regarding the sequencing and relative timing of educational and relational transitions. In this, emerging adults are not alone. In a national sample, 64% of the participants said that finding their soul mate would be a good reason to get married. Just more than 3% of the sample said that it was a somewhat bad reason or a very bad reason to get married. Figure 6.1 shows the full results of the sample.

Scholars have noted that a belief in soul mates is one of the major ways many individuals believe long-term relationships are formed (Franiuk, Cohen, & Pomerantz, 2002). Interestingly, most adults in committed relationships also believe they have in fact found their soul mate (Arnett & Schwab, 2014). Among those emerging adults who do believe strongly in soul mates, current partners are evaluated differently than those who reject such a notion, often with a harsher light. This is because these emerging adults view their relationships not just as trial relationships but also as trials for the *perfect* relationship. Similarly, their

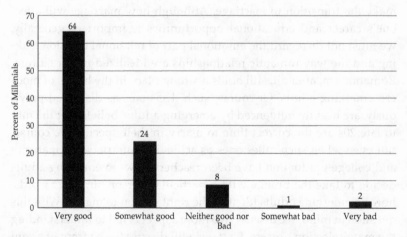

FIGURE 6.1 Do you believe that finding your soul mate is a good reason to marry?

Source: Millennials and Marriage Message Assessment.

partners are not seen as merely *a* potential partner but as the *only* possible partner. Research has shown that these harsh evaluations and high standards for partners have implications for relationship satisfaction, forgiveness of partners, and the general evaluation of the relationship (Burnette & Franiuk, 2010; Franiuk, Cohen, & Pomerantz, 2002; Franiuk, Shain, Bieritz, & Murray, 2012).

The emerging adults we spoke to mirror many of these research findings. Despite the disconnected way that so many emerging adults spoke about marriage, most still clung to the belief that the "one and only" was right around the corner (or at least down the road) when they thought about marriage. Among the emerging adults included in our initial survey, 77% of women and 74% of men agreed that they have a soul mate out there somewhere (Figure 6.2).

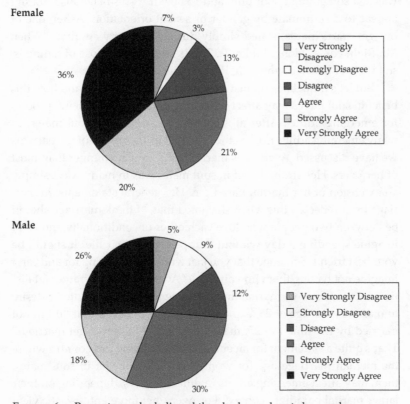

FIGURE 6.2 Percentage who believed they had a soul mate by gender.

Take Kaden, a bachelor at 21 and nearly finished with college. Kaden seemed to firmly believe that when he did find the right person for him, he would just know, despite his lack of practical experience in romantic relationships. He stated, "I think it has to be one of those things that you just know that it's right. Like you just know that, this is the person. I mean obviously I haven't been in this situation, but I think it's one of those moments that you just look over at somebody and think 'Oh, this is right.' You just realize." It doesn't get much more romantic than that! For Kaden, love at first sight is not just a nice thought—it's an expectation! And Kaden was far from alone in this idealized view of "knowing." Even those with relationship experience expressed similar viewpoints. Avery, a 22-year-old who was already married when we spoke to her, expressed her clear belief that she and her husband were simply meant for each other. She said, "From the day my boyfriend asked me to be his girlfriend, I knew I was going to marry him. There was just something about him, and I knew it." This belief also doesn't appear to discriminate by gender or sexual orientation. Asher, one of our gay participants, stated simply during his interview that, "When Mr. Right comes along, I'll know. That's what the purpose of dating is, so I will get married when Mr. Right comes around."

But let's think back for just a moment to better understand how this belief in soul mates may affect the dating and decision-making process for emerging adults. After all, having a clear belief in soul mates, as many emerging adults do, has the potential to alter many of the patterns we have discussed. Avery was married at 22, much younger than most of her peers. Her strong belief in soul mates was in many ways simply an extension of her marital paradigm. Her general statements on marriage itself reflected this when she noted that, "I think marriage should be between two people who love each other unconditionally and can't imagine spending a day without that person in their life. It should be your best friend. Someone that you just would do anything for and can't imagine not having them [in your life]." Avery also took a rather fatalistic stance on her own marital timing. Remember, she recounted a desire to marry by the age of 25, explaining that she believed that "if I'm not married by the time I'm 25, there's not hope—I'll never get married." That's quite a statement for an emerging adult living in a country where the median marriage age for women is 27. This belief in soul mates, then, may affect emerging adults in different ways, depending on their larger marital paradigm context. For Avery, her more enthusiastic view of marriage and desire for an early marital timing created a soul mate belief set that allowed her to make an early and quick decision to transition to marriage when she found the "one." For others, like Kaden discussed earlier, who have a more hesitant paradigm about marriage, soul mate beliefs may represent one more barrier to the marital transition process.

With this strong belief in soul mates noted, let us take a moment to take stock of the picture emerging adults have painted in terms of potential partners. Emerging adults are looking for a partner who can fit with their very individualistic life and career plans, one who also shares similar values and beliefs. In addition, for many, this person must be their soul mate, creating the instant internal spark that takes any ambiguity out of the decision-making process. This high bar for potential partners likely becomes a critical reason that so many emerging adults (most of whom fit into the hesitant camp with Kaden) feel the need to delay or avoid marriage despite its proclaimed importance.

Cohabitation and Marriage

As mentioned previously, cohabitation has become the relationship of choice for most emerging adults, particularly those in their mid-20s; however, how cohabitation fits into the marital landscape remains a bit murky. Indeed, as already mentioned in chapter 2 and as suggested by several scholars, cohabitation could be viewed not only as a precursor to marriage but also as an alternative to marriage (Seltzer, 2000; Shafer & James, 2013; Smock, 2000) or even as an alternative to being single (Rindfuss & VandenHeuvel, 1990). Most cohabiting couples also report that their decision to live with each other was made for practical, not relational reasons (Manning & Smock, 2005; Owen, Rhoades, & Stanley, 2013). For example, cohabitation may occur because one partner's lease is up or because both partners realize they are spending the majority of their time together anyway, so why pay two rents? In this way, defining what cohabitation is and what it is not has given some relational and marital scholars fits as they struggle to find structure and norms within the complexities of modern cohabitation. Part of the answer to understanding how cohabitation fits into the marital decision-making process lies in this complexity. As cohabitation itself becomes normative, it is perhaps unsurprising that the reasons that couples cohabit have become as varied as the people who cohabit.

As we spoke with emerging adults about dating, relationships, and marriage, it became clear that cohabitation did play an important role in the marital transition process of selecting a partner. More than half (56%) said, yes, cohabitation was a needed step toward marriage, whereas 40% said it wasn't (another 4% were somewhere in the middle, unwilling to lean one direction or another). The origin of this desire for cohabitation became clear among our early interviewees and stayed relatively consistent throughout the conversations we had. Outside of a small minority of emerging adults, most of whom were highly religious and outright rejected the idea of cohabitation at all, cohabitation's role highlighted another interesting aspect of modern emerging adults' fears and anxieties about marriage. For many, cohabitation was all about trust. Many emerging adults expressed a lack of trust in their romantic partners, current or in the future. Cohabitation, then, became a way to peek behind the relational curtain and see what type of person they were really dating.

This lack of trust was brought up across many interviews. Blair, one of our oldest participants at 29, explained that he generally distrusted his romantic partners. He attributed this to his time in the military when he saw numerous examples of unfaithful spouses. He mentioned, "I'm definitely a little more skeptical. I definitely try to watch what's going on with it. Like if she's trying to spend all my money, I may just have to step back for a minute." Similarly, Brooklyn, a 22-year-old medical student, also expressed a fear that romantic partners might be hiding their true selves while dating. She feared that one day, after marriage, she would "find out later that this person isn't who they expected them to be. And it's kind of too late at that point."

Cohabitation, then, serves as protection from this sort of deceptive behavior. When we interviewed her, Lauren was 21 and had recently broken up with a romantic partner she was living with, though she was still residing with her ex. Lauren put it bluntly, "Until you live with someone you don't know what their true habits are." Ellen, 27 and dating a divorcé for 8 months with no clear plans for relationship progression, referenced her boyfriend's previous relationships, many of which had ended poorly. She explained the benefit of cohabitation in this way: "I think it would be easier to catch people if they're not being truthful; if they're telling somebody one thing, and another thing, and another, like, 'Oh, sorry, I can't come over, I'm really busy over here.'"

This way of thinking seemed to cut across age and gender. Matthew, 24 and planning to move in with his girlfriend shortly after our interview, explained what he felt cohabitation would bring to his relationship. He said,

I think it's going to be a lot harder to hide little things about yourself. I mean, I don't think in a healthy relationship you intentionally hide anything, but especially at a younger age you're probably not going to be living in a three bedroom house with just the two of you. It's probably going to be a smaller apartment, so you're going to have to deal with them when you're not in a good mood, and [learn] how to deal with them when they're not in a good mood, and [show] all those little parts of yourself you just change about yourself when you're around them that you don't even notice you were changing. Eventually you're going to have to be yourself, so I think figuring out the full extent of who that other person is would be probably a big thing that would end relationships.

For at least some emerging adults, then, the discovery of undesirable traits was not necessarily about large or deviant behavior (like infidelity or substance use). Instead, it was the possibly incompatible habits of daily living that intrigued them. Particularly for those seriously considering marrying their current partner, cohabitation was a way to peek at what marriage might be like on a day-to-day basis. The emerging adults we spoke to were very specific about what they were testing. Let the following examples serve as illustration, all taken from emerging adults in committed relationships in which marriage was very much on the table:

Emilee, 22: In high school I would have never thought of living with somebody before getting married, but now looking at it I would want to live with Emmett before getting married, just to see how it would go, just for that last final check. I think it's important so you know what life every day is going to be like.
    Megan, 23: There are some annoying things about Carson. I'm not going to lie. Carson is a really annoying person so if I just got married and I didn't live with him, I would be like "Oh my god, like really?!" Yes, I definitely think living together is an important

thing to do before you get married because you don't know what they're like if you don't live with them.

Samantha, 21: I would like to live with the person that I would be potentially marrying before we get married because it's one thing to date someone, it's another one to live with them. And I think that's just something that, based on living with them, we figure out, "Okay, what's working? What isn't working? I love to cook, you don't know how to cook. I would be happy to do the cooking if you clean the dishes."

It's interesting to note again that the issues raised here are not large in nature. Cohabitation was not about learning a partner's communication or conflict resolution traits. Nor was it about making sure they were fully committed. It was about daily tasks and roles. This parallels the issues raised earlier in this chapter about intertwining career trajectories. More and more, emerging adults appear to be concerned that romantic partners and eventual marital partners will "get in the way" of their daily routine. As one emerging adult explained to us, it is about a fear of being "stuck." Jill, a single mother in her early 20s, noted, "It's nice to know how somebody lives before you marry them, so that when you marry them, you're not stuck. Or, you don't feel stuck." For many modern emerging adults, finding a romantic partner and eventual spouse is about finding someone who will cause the least disruption in their daily lives. Someone who won't impede personal goals and life trajectories. Across virtually all our interviews, it was this criterion above all else, manifest in slightly different ways, that encapsulated how modern emerging adults are thinking about who they want to marry.

To summarize, partner selection among modern emerging adults is perhaps one of the clearest areas of marriage in which individualism shines through. As emerging adults consider the characteristics and traits they are seeking in eventual spouses, they not only hope to find a partner to whom they are physically attracted and who has similar values but also seek a partner who will allow them to maintain their own goals, hobbies, and interests. Modern relational trajectories and the realities of emerging adulthood have also placed additional criteria in the way of forming marital unions. Emerging adults must now navigate complex and uncertain career trajectories as well as find a partner to whom they have an instant connection and attraction. Related to the discussions from previous chapters, not only is the institution of marriage perhaps now placed on too high a pedestal for some emerging adults to reach, but also the list of characteristics that a potential marital partner must have appears to be increasing.

7 ▲
The Influence of Parents and Families

To this point in our discussion of the marriage paradox, we have largely described the specific beliefs and aspirations that emerging adults have about marriage (and many of the paradoxes these beliefs create). Now, we are going to spend some time considering where such beliefs come from. The first few chapters of the book helped us recognize that understanding the context of emerging adulthood is necessary to fully appreciate the specific beliefs and attitudes emerging adults hold toward marriage. Likewise, to fully understand these beliefs we must also understand the contextual factors from which these beliefs have arisen. In the following chapters, we will do just that, relying heavily on those points of influence that emerging adults identified as key factors in the development of their beliefs and aspirations about marriage.

To do this, we rely on a family ecological perspective (Bubolz & Sontag, 1993) and social learning theories (Bandura, 1977), both of which stress the importance of intersecting environmental factors that influence how an individual navigates the social environment and the role one plays within it. In turn, we shape and are shaped by our social environments. That is, marital beliefs do not simply appear out of nowhere. Each person is embedded in overlapping family, social, and cultural environments; how important each one is depends on individual circumstances. Each context had some say in the type and intensity of an individual's beliefs and views on marriage. In other words, many of the themes and patterns we have described in the previous chapters are the result of shared influences that most modern emerging adults have encountered. Our goals now are to identify those collective points of influence and note where interesting and potentially revealing variations might occur.

We turn first to perhaps the most salient of these factors: an emerging adult's family of origin, focusing on parents. Although other familial influences, such as siblings, certainly matter, it is often parents who have the most lasting effect on emerging adults and their marital trajectories, attitudes, and behaviors.

▲ Why Parents Matter: Socialization and Intergenerational Transmission

The first stop on the road to understanding the roots of most emerging adults' beliefs about marriage looks at what is often their primary example of marriage: their parents. Much of the research on parents has focused on two key roles parents play in their children's lives in terms of future behavior and current orientations: socialization and the intergenerational transmission of values.

Socialization refers to children's learning through observing their parents. Most research in this area, taking cues from social learning theories (Bandura, 1977, 1986), has focused on how parents become primary role models in the lives of their children. Children learn from an early age how to behave in social situations by watching how their parents act. In terms of romantic relationships, parents help children learn interpersonal skills such as communication, conflict resolution, and empathy (Dadds et al., 1999; Feng, Giarrusso, Bengtson, & Frye, 1999; Riggio & Weiser, 2008). For most emerging adults, their parents' marriage was the marital relationship they interacted with and observed the most. For this reason, parents become a particularly strong socialization factor when it comes to marriage. Consequently, many emerging adults had a front row seat for both the successes and failures of their parents' marriage, despite many parents' desire to shield their children from any marital strife. These experiences, however subtle and unassuming, help shape the view emerging adults carry into their 20s about marriage.

Related to socialization, *intergenerational transmission* refers to the process through which parents transmit their values and beliefs to the next generation. This happens through a process called *generativity*, which occurs when the older generation desires to transmit knowledge, values, and behavior to the next. Although this process can certainly take place through socialization, much of this transmission occurs through the sharing of advice and stories or the expression of hopes and dreams for children to the children themselves. Scholars have noted that giving such parental advice about relationships, dating, and marriage is common for many parents (Brody, Moore, & Glei, 1994; Goodsell, James, Yorgason, & Call, 2013; Willoughby, Carroll, Vitas, & Hill, 2011). Particularly as children move through adolescence and into emerging adulthood, parents

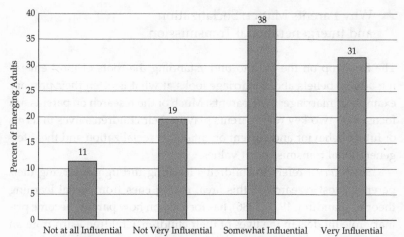

FIGURE 7.1 Extent to which emerging adults reported their parents influenced their beliefs on marriage.

Source: Millennials and Marriage Message Assessment.

usually become increasingly concerned with relaying opinions about dating partners, relationships, and eventual marriage (at times much to the distaste of their children!). Like socialization, this can shape how an emerging adult thinks about both short-term and long-term relationships. According to the Millennials and Marriage Message Assessment, a national sample of emerging adults, 30% of young adults said their parents were very influential on their impressions of marriage. As can also be seen in Figure 7.1 only 11% of the participants said their parents were not at all influential on their impressions of marriage.

To understand how much this parental influence shapes emerging adults, however, we must delve further into the specifics of how emerging adults believe their parents have informed their views on marriage. Emerging adults in our study had much to say about their parents and both the positive and negative influence they felt their parents had on their lives.

▲ Parents as Positive Role Models

Let's begin with the positive: many of the emerging adults in our study spoke about the healthy example their parents had given them. In fact, for emerging adults with happily married parents, many of the marital paradoxes appeared to vanish. Fortunately, just more than half (51%) of emerging adults we interviewed described their parents' marriage as generally positive, and praise for their parents came quickly and often as they looked to their parents' marriage as a source of both inspiration and aspiration. For these emerging adults, their parents' marriage served as the standard against which their own eventual marriages would be judged.

Adam provides an excellent example of this type of healthy influence. Adam, you may recall, was our 22-year-old engaged comparative literature graduate who was struggling to find consistent employment after college. Adam, young and eager to marry (as he put it, marriage was "one of my top goals"), saw a direct connection between his strong desire to marry and his parents' positive example. He explained,

> It's something that I really want to do, to be married. My parents have a really, really healthy marriage, just the way that they are together. I saw something that works really well. I think that really helped me figure out what I wanted in a marriage. Which is something that's very selfless and loving and understanding.

Although Adam did not mention anything in particular that his parents had said to him about marriage, this positive example clearly excited him. He seemed eager to establish a relationship that would mirror his parents' model of marriage.

Often, the word *inspiring* surfaced when emerging adults described these positive examples. Samantha, for example, was 21 and in a 4-year relationship when we spoke to her. Although she was not engaged, it was clear that marriage was on the forefront of her mind. In classic emerging adult terms, she explained that her boyfriend and she had "toyed with the idea" of marriage. When asked about the influence her parents had, she said,

> I think that the way that they're having their relationship is inspiring to me and I think as a result my perception of how marriage should be has been heavily based on the way that they've demonstrated.

Elizabeth, a 21-year-old who had already broken off an engagement in her young life, expressed a similar sentiment, saying, "I mean they're [parents] the closest marriage I've been around for 21 years. It's really been a healthy marriage to be around. I'm so thankful that I've been able to see that and witness it firsthand." These emerging adults appeared genuinely appreciative of their parents' relational role modeling. Perhaps knowing the divorce statistics and seeing broken families play out firsthand among their friends, these emerging adults recognize that their experience of having a stable parental relationship is becoming much less common. In many ways, these positive examples seemed to make these emerging adults value marriage more and fear it less than other emerging adults we spoke to.

Another positive theme among these strong parental marriages was longevity, suggesting that positive parental role models might influence emerging adults' beliefs about not just the importance of marriage but also its permanence. Rosie, a 23-year-old about to be engaged, noted that her parents' long-standing relationship shaped her thinking about divorce. She noted,

> I think my parents definitely influence how I think about
> marriage. They've been married for 30 years and they influence
> what I think about marriage and choosing someone you're going
> to spend your whole life with. To me divorce isn't really an option;
> to me you marry and that's it.

Ember, a 21-year-old single student, provided another example of this mentality, employing almost fairy tale overtones when describing her parents' marriage. She explained,

> Last year was their 25th wedding anniversary so they threw a big
> party together. Then we had a lot of family friends come together
> and they all stood up, each one by one, and talked about how they
> look to my parents as an example. Because, you know, nowadays,
> every other day you hear somebody else is getting divorced or
> you hear things that aren't working out and then all these people
> are saying we look to you guys for hope. To see that they're such
> an example to other people just stands out to me. And all my
> friends are like, "Wow your parents' marriage is so amazing. You
> can see how much your parents love each other." And you can!
> I remember that day just looking at my dad and it's like they're
> 20 years old again. I want to be 50 years old and still be madly in
> love with my husband.

Jessalyn, another emerging adult woman we spoke to, mentioned how her parental example was a reflection of trying to correct for a previous family history of failed marriages. She noted, "Well my grandparents on both sides got divorced. I think it was my parents' firm choice to make sure that never happened with them. I mean of course they would get in disagreements. But they never talked about getting divorced or anything. Which was awesome. So I always knew once you get married, you stay married."

Finally, Eliza, 21 and married when we interviewed her, also had high praise for her parents. She said,

I think definitely seeing their [her parents'] relationship has kind of been a bar I've set for myself regarding marriage. Just the fact that it is so strong for them. It's a source of encouragement for me and it's a source of aspiration.

Such quotes unquestionably paint a rosy picture of parental influence on emerging adults' marital beliefs. Is it possible that emerging adults with strong parental marriages are spared the marital paradox? Not necessarily. Although this may be the case for some, for others it is unlikely to be so simple. Remember, emerging adults value marriage but are also scared by it. And many hold unrealistic standards for marriage. For some, strong parental role models may feed into this anxiety and fear. If marriage itself already feels out of reach, does observing or aspiring to the "perfect" marriage of their parents make it feel farther away? Probably so. But the number of engaged and early-married emerging adults in the previous examples clearly suggests that for some, these positive examples did not push them away from marriage altogether.

Perhaps one answer to why having positive parental role models so fortifies emerging adults' positive conceptions of marriage lies in one specific element in how emerging adults appear to view parental relationships. Even these generally positive emerging adults realized that their parents were in fact not perfect and did not have perfect marriages. They noticed their parents' imperfections and yet still watched their parents maintain strong relationships. Unlike the fairy tale romances depicted in the media, most relationships have serious problems, the natural results of the imperfect people trying to make them work. Although many emerging adults praised their parents' relationships, they also realized that such relationships took years of work and effort to both build and sustain. Amy, recently single at 22, identified her parents as a major factor in her positive view of marriage, noting that her parents' marriage has made her believe that marriage is a "part of having a successful life." At the same time, she was also aware and very open about her parents' struggles. She noted,

> I don't think it's been an easy road for 27 years and they've [my parents] made it. There are times where they were on their last limb and they didn't split up because of us, because of me and my siblings, and I definitely admire them for that. I see how happy they are now, and it goes to show that hard work like that was probably the hardest thing that they've ever been through and hard work can lead to a successful relationship.

Preston, 27 and preparing to ask his long-term girlfriend to marry him, expressed a similar sentiment. As he reflected on his parents' example, he shared that,

> I know they [his parents] argued and fought a lot more when I was younger, so seeing them now is just like night and day. It's made me realize that if both sides truly want it then they can make it happen, and that there will be disagreements that you have to live with and you have to fight for [it].

Blair, 29 and divorced, had every reason to look at marriage in negative terms based on his own past relationship struggles. Yet he still viewed marriage positively, attributing much of his positive marital outlook to his parents. He explained,

> I mean they've been together through thick and thin. I've seen them fight and I've seen them happy together so apparently that's what a marriage is. It's going to have its ups and downs but they're still together. I look up to that and always thought that's how it's supposed to be. That's what I wanted.

When we step back to consider these sentiments, perhaps one of the keys to overcoming the marriage paradox is relatively straightforward: stable families with committed and married parents can give emerging adults a realistic yet hopeful view of marriage. Such emerging adults have seen the strength their parents have derived from marriage yet have also seen the sacrifices it took to get there.

These themes were not confined to those with married parents either. Clark, 22, experienced his parents' divorce when he was young but also saw them work to maintain a positive co-parenting relationship, which had a profound effect on Clark. He explained,

> My family, even though my parents are divorced, I mean it's not the ideal thing, they always stayed ... not together as a relationship but together as a friendship for the kids. So I've never heard my mom say a negative thing about my dad or my dad say a negative thing about my mom.

Although perhaps not getting the same positive message about marriage generally, Clark clearly learned about the effort it takes to maintain a strong relationship, regardless of the legal status of that relationship. Such an example suggests that having married parents is not the only way emerging adults may form positive and perhaps less paradoxical beliefs about marriage.

▲ Unhealthy Parental Examples

Unfortunately, many of our emerging adults painted a drearier picture of their parents' marriages. This was the other main segment of our participants, those who often saw their parents' marriage as an example of what *not* to do. For these emerging adults, the marriages they saw up close were marred by conflict and divorce. A significant amount of our emerging adults (30%) reported that their parents' marriage had a negative influence on how they viewed marriage. Here, words like *inspiration* and *awe* rarely surfaced, yielding instead to descriptors such as *frustration, heartache*, and, in some cases, *betrayal*.

We should note that some of these stories came from people whose parents were stable, if unhappily, married and were not reserved solely for those who had experienced a parental divorce. Parental socialization, after all, is about modeling, about emerging adults seeing up close what relationships are like. For some, what they saw from their married parents pushed them farther away from any desire for marriage. Commonly, emerging adults who witnessed high levels of conflict in their parents' marriages expressed reservations about the institution of marriage. Research suggests that conflict in marriages often teaches children that marriage is an inherently unstable union, even in the absence of divorce. In turn, emerging adults may begin to alter the way they view dating and how they act in relationships (see Lichter & McCloskey, 2004; Long, 1987; Rodrigues & Kitzmann, 2007; Weigel, Bennett, & Ballard-Reisch, 2003).

Unfortunately, these negative examples had the same direct and powerful effect as the powerful positive examples noted earlier. Take Brooklyn, our medical student with unfavorable views of marriage. During our discussion about influences, she noted, "Well, I mean, my parents' marriage is terrible, so it doesn't seem like a super worthwhile institution in that it just tends to make people really miserable." Brooklyn had generalized her parents' marriage to mean one simple thing: marriage = misery. Why would someone want that? Many in situations similar to Brooklyn's appeared to wonder this exact question. Remember Jadyn? She was enjoying the sexual freedom that her 20s afforded and was completely uninterested in a traditional monogamous marriage. She, too, spoke of this misery, saying,

> I think a lot of other things have had more influence, but I think seeing my mother miserable at home, not able to teach.....
> I have learned a lot from my parents about what not to do in relationships.

These illustrations lead us to a question: Why would emerging adults' parents stay in such openly hostile relationships? A full answer to that question would require a lengthy detour into relationship formation and commitment patterns, but for our purposes, suffice it to say that many baby-boomer parents believed in the idea that you "stayed together for the kids." Fearing the negative individual and parental turmoil that divorce may bring, many parents may have decided to tough things out. Still others may have been oblivious to how much conflict their children saw. Either way, such efforts appear to have had unintended consequences, resulting in deeply seated relational scars for their children, making marriage a frightening prospect. Lindsay, a 24-year-old engaged female, seemed to express such thoughts and provides a compelling illustration. Although engaged and in what was, by all appearances, a strong and flourishing relationship, Lindsay struggled with wanting to move forward with her wedding plans. She explained her reservations this way:

I think I've always had so many reservations about getting married [because] I've grown up in a household where my parents should have [broken up] before they got married. I try not to compare myself to them, because if I did, I would never get married and I would never want to be in a relationship because, from watching their relationship, it's just not something that you would want to mirror.

Despite everything going well in her relationship, Lindsay could not shake the fear that she would end up trapped, like she believed her parents were.

Parental Divorce and Emerging Adults' Marital Beliefs

Observing conflict generally appears to diminish many emerging adults' view of marriage regardless of the current marital status of their parents; however, experiencing a parental divorce likely does have a unique effect. Although divorce may shield some children from the highly conflictual marriages of their parents (Ahrons, 1994), most research suggests that divorce has pervasive and negative effects on children (Amato, Kane, & James, 2011; Amato & Sobolewski, 2001; Cartwright, 2006; Christensen & Brooks, 2001; Strohschein, 2012; VanderValk, Spruijt, de Goede, Maas, & Meeus, 2005). Divorce has also been linked to negative relationship consequences, including strong evidence of the intergenerational transmission of divorce from one generation to the next (Amato & Cheadle, 2005; Diekmann & Schmidheiny, 2013; Dronkers & Härkönen, 2008). This link has perhaps been best articulated by the book *Between Two Worlds*, summarizing a study of more than 1,000 emerging adults (Marquardt, 2005), which found that children from divorced homes often change how they act in and think about relationships, even decades after the divorce occurred. Much of this link is thought to be a result of shifts in marital beliefs and paradigms among children who experience a parental divorce. Evidence already exists that suggests that relational attitudes and beliefs shift after parental divorce, with children of divorced parents often reporting lower levels of commitment (Cui, Fincham, & Durtschi, 2011; Whitton, Rhoades, Stanley, & Markman, 2008) and more anxiety and negative attitudes about marriage (Dennison & Koerner, 2008) compared with their counterparts

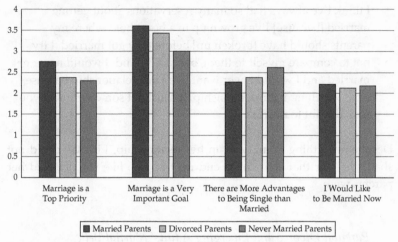

FIGURE 7.2 Marital importance beliefs by parents' marital status. Measured on a scale of 1 (strongly disagree) to 5 (strongly agree).

who had continuously married parents. Renee Dennison and colleagues found that this negative effect is not simply about the actual divorce, either. Continued conflict between parents in post-divorce co-parenting situations has an additional negative influence on how emerging adults view marriage (Dennison & Koerner, 2006, 2008).

Our own data on those with divorced parents illuminated known patterns and uncovered new wrinkles in these previous findings. In many ways, our own data confirm the tendency of emerging adults who experience parental divorce to be more anxious and fearful of marriage. We listened as such emerging adults spoke about marriage with themes of fear, stress, and sadness, largely as a result of their parents' divorce. Twenty-three-year-old Melissa, who had experienced her parents' bitter divorce in high school, put it simply, "I have a lot of mixed feelings about marriage. I'm kind of scared of marriage." She was not alone. Figure 7.2 shows that emerging adults with divorced parents in the first wave of our study were less likely to report marriage as a top priority, less likely to list marriage as an important goal, and more likely to believe that there are more advantages to being single than married compared with those with married parents.

Additionally, parental divorce appears to influence the overall value emerging adults place on marriage. Figure 7.3 tracks how much effort emerging adults expected to place on four roles in their adult life—marriage, parenting, career, and leisure/hobbies. Although not

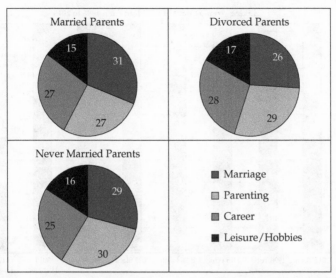

FIGURE 7.3 Percentage of importance placed on four adult roles (marriage, career, parenting, and leisure/hobbies) by parents' marital status.

dramatic, notice how those with divorced parents expected to place slightly less effort into marriage, evenly distributing this freed effort across the remaining three categories.

You may have noticed that we also included information in these previous figures on those emerging adults whose parents never married. Although a small portion of our sample, these emerging adults interestingly tended to report the most negative views and beliefs about marriage, suggesting that parental influence on more pessimistic and negative views on marriage transcends merely experiencing divorce in a person's life. Like research on divorce, such data corroborate with studies that have suggested that single parenthood is linked to negative or pessimistic views of marriage among children (Matamela, Bello, & Idemudia, 2014; Simons, Burt, & Tambling, 2013). This family configuration also appears to be growing among some segments of the US population. According to Figure 7.4 from the Census Bureau: Living Arrangements of Children, although most white and Hispanic children live with two parents, the majority of black children now live with only one parent. Perhaps not surprisingly, these previous figures also reinforce that a solid, stable marriage between parents seems to maximize the chances that their children will expect, seek out, and achieve happy and successful marriages themselves. Children tend to follow in their parents' footsteps, for better or worse.

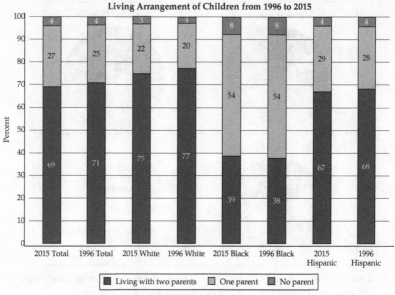

Figure 7.4 Living arrangements by year and race.

Source: Living Arrangements of Children.

Although such findings simply replicated much of what has been discussed in previous studies, there is another effect as well. An often-neglected aspect of emerging adults' marital paradigm centers on their beliefs on how permanent a marriage *should* be. Such beliefs are often labeled as beliefs about marital permanence (Willoughby et al., 2015). Figure 7.5 shows only these results. As can be seen, those with divorced parents also are less likely to believe that marriage is for life and more likely to have favorable attitudes toward divorce compared with those with married parents. These data suggest that the effects of divorce extend beyond devaluing marriage to conceptions about its permanence. Many of the emerging adults we spoke to with divorced parents seemed to struggle with the permanence of marriage. Capria, a young adult working the night shift in a low paying job, spoke of her adopted mother and her never-ending parade of husbands. She related, "I don't know my mother. But, my adopted mom, she got married a lot. Like, I've seen her married probably 16 times. So it's like are you only supposed to be with someone for a couple of months?" Obviously, there was exaggeration in how Capria described her family background, but the half-joking, half-serious

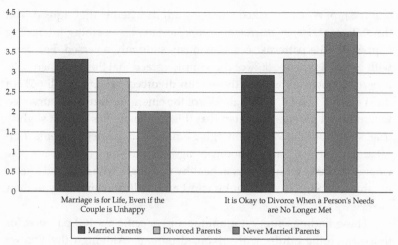

FIGURE 7.5 Belief in marital permanence by parents' marital status.

way she described her mother's churning of marriages made it difficult for Capria to take the permanence of marriage seriously. She went
on to say, "The step-fathers that I did have, they [were always violat-
ing] boundaries. From what I know, there was adultery and stuff like
that. And I don't believe in any of that stuff." Capria saw consistent
instability in her primary parental role models, and it made her seriously question how long marriages typically last.

Collectively, these data echo what we have known for some time—
parental divorce influences how children and emerging adults think
about marriage, often steering them toward a much more negative view
of the institution. For many, this occurs through a loss of trust. Lydia, an
emerging adult with one of the most negative dispositions toward marriage in our sample, noted that,

I'll probably never get over the trust issue of being convinced that
everyone will leave me at some point because when my parents
divorced I didn't see my dad very much for a while. I was also
very angry at both of them.

However, through our exploration of these data, one singular finding stood out to us and made us wonder whether this link was as simple and straightforward as suggested by most data points and previous

scholarship. When we asked emerging adults whether they agreed with the statement, *Happy marriages require hard work*, something interesting happened: The patterns seen previously suddenly reversed. For those with married parents, 56% of the sample agreed that this statement was *very true*. However, among those with divorced parents, a full 66% of them agreed. In total, although 93% of the emerging adults we surveyed with married parents indicated that this statement was at least slightly true, an astounding 97% of emerging adults with divorced parents indicated at least that same amount of agreement. Remember, it was the emerging adults with parents in healthy marriages who reported knowing that marriage would require effort and dedication in many of their interviews.

These findings suggest a unique and specific marital paradox for those emerging adults with divorced parents. Although their views on marriage tended to be negative, it appears as though this was not merely because they view marriage as a relationship that brought misery, frustration, and sadness. For some, it appeared as though their parents' divorce convinced them that if their parents could not make a marriage work, healthy marriages must be too hard—unrealistic for the typical person. Accompanying this is the belief among most emerging adults that divorce in any form should be stringently avoided. Blake, a 22-year-old with unmarried parents, illustrated this belief well, noting, "I hate the idea of divorce. Divorce is the absolute 100% last thing I would like to do in my life. There's just so much emotion, so much baggage. If you have kids it's hard on them." Avery, an emerging adult whose parents separated shortly after she was born, had internalized a strong fear of and desire to avoid divorce. She said,

> My mom's on her third marriage now, and if my dad did marry his current girlfriend that'd be his fourth marriage. So I've never known my parents together. They were married for a year; that was it. Growing up, 21 years now, being the middleman for all that—it's just, I don't ever want to put my kids through that. So I'd definitely say that's probably another really big influence just because I don't want to deal with that in the future.

For many of these emerging adults, marriage was not simply an institution they disregarded; their fear of divorce and fear of heartbreak made marriage seem too risky. As another female emerging adult noted as she explained why she would never marry her current boyfriend, "Divorce is horrible; it's horrible for everybody around. I never want that to happen so we just won't get married."

Certainly, some emerging adults who came from conflictual homes or whose parents divorced did not allow such experiences to destroy their beliefs and hopes for an eventual successful marriage. Indeed, some emerging adults appeared to take their family background as a challenge, something to overcome and improve on so that succeeding generations could avoid the heartaches and challenges that they endured. Shaina, 25 and in a serious long-term relationship, was fully committed to the idea of marriage at some point and of avoiding the mistakes of her parents. She explained that,

> I think marriage, to me, is a lifetime commitment. Divorce really just is not an option for me. My parents were divorced when I was younger and it's not something that I want to put myself through, to put my family through. Of course you never really get to tell what your future holds, but when I get married I want to be sure that divorce isn't an option. It's gonna be something that we're gonna work on—whether you like it or not you're stuck with me type of thing.

Carli, 21 and engaged, offered a similar sentiment. She noted in her interview that,

> My parents got divorced after being married for 20 years and there [were] a lot of reasons behind that, but I still don't necessarily know that I agree with it. So for me to actually take the step and commit to somebody, it was kind of tricky; it was something that I wouldn't have done easily. For me, being able to make that commitment means that I'm willing to work through all of the things that my parents couldn't. To me, marriage just means that even if it sucks I wouldn't want it to suck with anyone else—I'm with you.

Finally, Taya also wanted to avoid the mistakes of her parents. She related the hardships and struggles of her childhood that she felt were due to her parents' divorce and how she never wanted to put her own children through a similar ordeal. She explained,

> Just being with them [her parents] my whole life, it's taught me what I wouldn't want just from being a child of divorce. I want to succeed. I want to come out [with] my marriage [being] just so strong. Being a kid of divorce, it was just really rough. Having to go back and forth. Having two houses and ending up living with my dad and needing my mom there too. I definitely think a kid should have both mom and dad.

Certainly these emerging adults had a more hopeful mentality, but it was clear that for all the positive role models parents had been in the lives of many emerging adults, a significant portion had been struggling with staying positive about marriage as an institution that had brought such suffering into their own lives.

▲ Communication About Relationships and Sex

Regardless of the specific parental marital situations emerging adults have experienced, parents provide an important resource of information about marriage. As noted across several studies, the general intergenerational transmission of relational beliefs from parents to children appears to be an important component of how emerging adults shape their marital beliefs (De Valk & Liefbroer, 2007; Kapinus & Pellerin, 2008; Willoughby et al., 2011). Although much of this intergenerational transmission occurs though socialization and social learning as noted earlier in this chapter, parents may also influence emerging adults through the direct recommendations, advice, and suggestions they give about dating and marriage. This raises an important question. Beyond the lessons about marriage emerging adults learn from watching what their parents do, what exactly are parents telling their children about marriage?

This advice is a little harder to categorize compared with previous topics because such advice is, by nature, highly customized to the specific circumstances of each emerging adult. Nevertheless, some interesting patterns emerged when we spoke to emerging adults about what parents told them about marriage and relationships.

Clearly, one of the messages emerging adults receive from their parents is to wait, to slow down, and to fully experience life before marrying. Sometimes, this message was accompanied by a plea to avoid marriage altogether. Brianna fell into this camp. She had just ended a long-term relationship and was casually dating when we interviewed her. Her generally negative views of marriage (she did not see marriage in her future) appeared to be directly connected to her parents', particularly her mother's, messages about marriage. She related,

> When I was little my mom was actually kind of insane so she would be sitting at the window with a cigarette and she'd be like, "Don't ever marry a man, Brianna." Stuff like that. And when I was a kid I was like, "Okay Mom," and I still wanted to get married and everything so I don't think it affected me at the time.

Despite Brianna's claim that this experience had not influenced her, the link between her mother's suggestion and her own current dismissal of marriage seemed a bit deeper than mere coincidence. Earlier in the same interview her own words seemed to echo her mother's when she said, "I think marriage is for a lot of people, not specifically for me anymore."

Although not all parents discourage marriage, often they suggested delaying marriage in favor of education and other life priorities. These messages seemed particularly strong among the emerging adult females we interviewed. Ember, a 21-year-old college student, shared with us that marriage was among her top goals in life but that she believed that her mother would be disappointed to hear this. She explained her rationale by saying,

> She always tells me, "You're not going to college to get your M-R-S degree. You're going to get an actual career, be a career woman; be something of yourself other than a wife." I'm like, "Ok Mom! Ok! I get it!"

Susan, one of our married emerging adults, appeared to have disregarded similar parental advice that she received from her parents. Susan explained that, "My whole life my parents have worked, and when I decided to get married, I mean, I'm 21, my mom was definitely a little bit upset that I wasn't waiting until after we had graduated." For many middle-class emerging adults we spoke to, parents appeared much more anxious about their children's career prospects than their marital prospects.

Another area where parents were prime socializers for emerging adults regarding marriage was in regard to how gender roles play out in marriage. Although we dedicate an upcoming chapter to gender, it is worth noting here how parental advice and example can influence emerging adults' perceptions of how to "do" gender in marriage. For example, in our quantitative data, gender role beliefs varied significantly by parents' marital status. Although 32% of emerging adults with two married parents agreed that husbands should have the final say in marriage, only 28% of those from single-parent homes and only 16% from divorced homes believed the same thing. That is, although the majority of emerging adults embrace gender egalitarianism in decision making, among those who don't, the experience emerging adults had growing up colors attitudes toward a more traditional shade. Further, although 42% of emerging adults from divorced homes expressed favorable views of the male breadwinner/female homemaker, 56% of those with married parents believed the same thing. Family structure clearly matters in how gender roles are socialized.

Beyond examples based on family structure, however, parents were clearly embracing the direct socialization of their children by talking about gender roles. There was some generational disagreement on the issue, though: Emerging adults often thought differently from their parents, especially expressing disagreement with some of the values openly communicated with them about gender. Time after time, many emerging adults painted their parents as gender-equality dinosaurs, believing in a seemingly ancient system of gender roles that their generation had moved beyond. Take the following quotes from our interviews as common examples of the rhetoric we heard from many emerging adults:

> Tori: She's [my mother] a little more old school and timid and wants to appease him [my father] at times. I think she's just like, "I want to be a good wife," instead of, "I want to get necessarily all my needs and his needs and balance that," if that makes any sense. My definition of *wife* is different clearly because being a good wife to me means communicating.
>
> Carli: My dad just thinks that the husband does the provider and the wife should be super adoring of him for all the work he puts in, but I definitely don't feel that way.

Elizabeth: I love my father but he's still very much in the "men will provide for women, women are not strong enough, they are the weaker sex." So I think even just me going to college has been difficult for him to deal with a little bit because I'm breaking that mold in his mind.

These illustrative quotes suggest that many emerging adults may not be buying the marital messages about gender that their parents are selling, particularly when those messages are connected to what many emerging adults see as an outdated system of power and gender.

▲ Other Family Influences

Before moving on to other influences on emerging adults' marital beliefs, it is important to note that parents, although perhaps the most important and salient familial influence, were not the only family members mentioned by emerging adults. For many of them, other family examples also helped them develop their thoughts on marriage as an institution, often through the same processes of socialization and direct transmission.

For some of our emerging adults, siblings affected their perception and path through relationships, particularly those with older siblings who had already gone through the marital transitions. Perhaps this was because, unlike parents, emerging adults could usually watch their older sibling go through the entire relationship formation process and were also often old enough to recognize and evaluate beneficial and detrimental aspects of their sibling's relationships and partners. Interestingly, this process largely seemed to reinforce their existing beliefs about marriage rather than change them. For example, Rosalie, a 23-year-old college student who valued marriage, spoke about the effect that her siblings and religion had on helping her confirm many of these positive beliefs. She said,

I still sort of identify as Latter-day Saint and my siblings have gotten married, five of them. One got married when I was 4 years old, so getting to see siblings getting married at a really young age and then in turn having nieces and nephews at a very young age, seeing them have kids and get to be homeowners and the things that go along with being married. ... I've always had a really positive outlook on marriage, partially because of the church and partially because of family experiences and things like that.

Like parents, siblings and their marriages also provided opportunities to learn about the realities and difficulties of marriage. Isabelle, a 22-year-old student studying fashion, related the following after watching her sister's marriage: "But I know there [were] also a lot of problems [in her sister's marriage] still as they were trying to work through it and figure it out. It took a while."

Contrary to parental examples, which were mostly positive, exampling of siblings that were shared appeared to be slightly more negative among the emerging adults who brought them up. In total, 19 emerging adults mentioned siblings as an important influence in their views of marriage. Of those 19, 10 spoke of their siblings' marriages in negative tones. Kaden, a 22-year-old college student, provides a good example of this. Kaden watched his sister make an early transition to marriage for what he felt were all the wrong reasons. He related,

My sister actually just got married a few years ago to a guy. She dropped out of college and then went back home and then she was working at a gas station, met some guy, then they you know, dating, and then she got pregnant. Now they're married and it's just very much not a good situation. I feel like threatening to take their child and run away. So it's just one of those things where you don't know this person very well; you've only known this person for—what—two months.

In Kaden's eyes, his sister's marital decisions had resulted in what he deemed as a low-quality marriage. Among other experiences, his sister's (perceived) poor marriage gave him a rather dismal view of marriage, as something that might hinder his own life goals. As he put it later in the interview, "I think my own needs are more pressing in my life right now. Throwing another person into the mix is probably not a good idea."

Next to parents and siblings, grandparents were typically the other family members emerging adults mentioned. Here, however, the tone was typically positive, with many emerging adults admiring and looking up to the stable marriages of their grandparents. Claire, a 22-year-old in the middle of her college graduation, had a glowing review of her grandparents' marriage. She shared,

> I know my grandma got married when she was 16 and they've been together ever since then. That definitely has shown me that okay, no matter what society says about marriage, "Oh it won't work out," it won't fail. It can work out and my parents and grandparents are a proof of that.

Other emerging adults were faced with mixed marital messages among different generations of their family. Carli, our 21-year-old who was engaged to her boyfriend of 4 years, struggled with the mixed messages her parents and grandparents gave through their examples. She noted that, "My grandparents got married at 18 and just celebrated their 51st wedding anniversary. I've also seen my mom and dad have a really successful relationship that just kind of fell to pieces all at once." These conflicting examples provided a unique challenge for Carli, making her question some elements of marriage, despite her grandparents' example of stability. She summarized this internal conflict by saying,

> I think that bearing witness to that and hearing about this really split dichotomy of relationships that last forever and relationships that fall apart in the first 5 years, it has made me think more carefully about the concept of marriage and more carefully about who I would choose for that.

In sum, parents and other family members clearly had a profound effect on the emerging adults in our sample and likely do so for all emerging adults. Regardless of the specific family structure or the specific messages being relayed about marriage, these proximate sources of information about marriage are one of the main factors that contribute to an emerging adult's marital paradigm. In the context of emerging adulthood, it is easy to see the seeds of many marriage paradoxes in these parental role models. Many parents preach a delay of marriage to their children, even if their own marriages were happy and fulfilling. Other emerging adults have developed many of their fears, hesitations, and concerns about marriage by watching their parents' conflictual marriages or experiencing their parents' divorce. Collectively, parents and other family influences appear to be one of the key foundations on which emerging adults have built their internal conceptualization of modern marriage.

8 ▲

Social Influences and Marriage

Think about a typical day in your life. How many times do you interact with someone who is in a romantic relationship each day? How many times do you hear one of your friends mention something about dating or someone on a TV show or movie say something about relationships? Does this happen daily? Hourly? Even more frequently? Although parents and immediate family members may be the biggest influences on emerging adults' views on marriage, they are hardly the only social or cultural context that matter. Emerging adults, like all of us, interact with numerous things in the environment that influence how they think about and value marriage.

Although such potential influences are indeed numerous, perhaps even infinite, in this chapter we focus on three social influences that make a difference in how emerging adults think about marriage and marital transitions: peers, religious institutions, and media, which together have some of the largest effects on the marital paradoxes of emerging adults.

The idea that our behaviors, attitudes, and expectations are influenced by our social surroundings is not a new one, and such ecological views on marriage and human development have been commonplace for decades (see Bronfenbrenner, 1975; Bubolz & Sontag, 1993). The underlying premise of these models is straightforward—individuals and families interact with their surroundings in an interdependent way that creates a living ecosystem of ideas and behaviors.

Emerging adults themselves appear to have some sense that they are being influenced by outside forces beyond their immediate family. They understand that they are engagers in a larger cultural tapestry, experiencing and shaping (while being shaped by) the world around them. Often emerging adults articulate this influence with the general term of "society" or "culture." "Society" is influencing them to do something, or their modern "culture" is pushing them to think a certain way. For example, one emerging adult we interviewed, Jessica, explained how her views of marriage were influenced by this ambiguous society:

> I think that society makes it seem like you're young, you should go explore, travel, do this, do that, and I think it's emphasized a lot with people's bucket list. Well before I do this I want to have this, this, and this accomplished. I think often times society looks at marriage as a checklist and once you've accomplished this many things then you're ready for marriage.

While articulating many of the common marital beliefs of delaying and deprioritizing marriage, Jessica suggested that these views had been influenced by some outside source she calls "society." After some digging and prodding, it became clear that at least three key factors were involved in this vague sense of society and culture.

▲ The Influence of Peer Systems

In most ways, emerging adulthood may seem like the ideal developmental period to explore peer relationships (we will use the terms *peers* and *friends* interchangeably). After all, many emerging adults have already left the parental home. Because most are at least several years away from forming their own long-term committed relationships through marriage or cohabitation, even romantic partners may not be a consistent source of support and interaction. If support does not come from daily, consistent interaction with family or romantic partners, friends are likely to play a particularly large role shaping how emerging adults think about marriages.

Scholarship appears to confirm this point. Friends are often the primary support network for emerging adults as they move through the various transitions that accompany emerging adulthood (Allan, 2008). This is also often a time of expanding friendship networks, something typically not seen later in adulthood (Wrzus, Hänel, Wagner, & Neyer, 2013). As they move from class to class, job to job, and city to city, emerging adults have access to ever-expanding social circles. Perhaps this is the reason, despite the strong and important influence of family members, that emerging adults tend to do more activities, share more personal information, and spend more time with friends than immediate family (Pulakos, 2001). Based on these factors, friends would appear to be poised to exert a large amount of influence on how emerging adults think about relationships and marital formation.

Despite their potential, friends and peers appear to influence the marital paradigms and beliefs of emerging adults less than one might expect, although it is certainly an important touchpoint. In some ways, our data in regard to friendships and emerging adults suggested that the influence of peers appears to be similar to that of siblings. Emerging adults watch their friends and peers make marital decisions and engage in relationships and then glean lessons from them when they encounter similar decisions. Like siblings, when emerging adults spoke of peers and peer influence, they often described specific examples or illustrations. For example, Candice, a 23-year-old about to move in with her boyfriend, had seen both positive and negative examples of marriages through her friends. She stated,

> As I grew older and my friends started getting married, I started knowing more married couples. I've realized that it's kind of a mix between the two [good and bad]. You have your good days and your bad days, and that's shaped how I see marriage and what it's really like as opposed to what media tells us.

Chelsea, a 23-year-old college graduate who had been traveling after graduation, had seen more influences that she perceived as negative among her friends. She explained,

> Seeing all of my friends from high school and my sister's friends getting married so young and kind of being stuck, you know not that they feel stuck, maybe I'm projecting that on to them because I would hate to still be living there [her hometown] in that situation. I think seeing that has taught me more than anything what I don't want. I want the time to go and explore and do what I want to do first and figure out more of who I am before I settle into that lifelong commitment.

Twenty-three-year-old Shaina's examples of marriage, in contrast, had been mostly positive. She explained, "I do have friends who have been married for several years now who got married right out of high school. They've had a successful marriage so far, and I think that's great for them."

As these quotes suggest, friends do exert some pull when it comes to how emerging adults view marriage. However, Shaina also provides an example of perhaps the limited influence peers have. Whereas the connection between parents and emerging adults' views of marriage were rather strong in our own data, the link appeared less reliable for friends. Although Shaina had seen several peers marry early and have, based on her own evaluation, successful marriages, Shaina herself planned to marry at 32, much later than most of her peers. Her views of marriage were generally negative. Why? It appears to have a lot to do with her parents. After experiencing her parents' divorce and being largely raised by a single mother, Shaina summarized this influence in this way:

> My parents divorced, so I grew up with a single mom. I've seen a very strong female role model who didn't need a man. She did not remarry, and there was no other male role model in my life, so I guess that colors my world by saying, "well, you don't need to get married if you don't want to." It's a personal choice, and it's not a need, it's a want.

Shaina's case illustrates an important point: Although friends usually serve as a potential point of reference for emerging adults, they likely will not exceed the more salient experiences of parents.

Fortunately, exploring interactions with friends does provide some unique considerations. One interesting example of this is the influence of not only the emerging adults' own parents but also those of their friends. That is, it is not just an emerging adults' parents but also the example of their friends' parents that influence their marital paradigms. Obviously, this influence is filtered through the perceptions and feelings of their friends, yet still the influence appears to matter, especially when it came to divorce or unhealthy marriages. For example, Adam observed, "I've seen the damage that an unhealthy marriage can do to certain friends of mine who grew up with parents who weren't there. I've seen that sort of effect; a couple of close friends throw off their understanding of family, that sort of stuff." Through observation of his friends, Adam had seen many negative parental influences despite his own happy married parents. In this way, friends and their parents act as a proxy for some emerging adults, enabling emerging adults to observe, for better or worse, the effects of parental marriage from a relatively safe distance. Some emerging adults made assumptions and conclusions about divorce without having experienced divorce in their own families.

Peers and Social Media

In the realm of emerging adulthood, however, peer networks are not confined by geographic proximity. Indeed, the modern emerging adult's social circle may span several states and even countries thanks to numerous social media applications that facilitate interaction and networking with an ever-expanding network of peers. A whopping 90% of emerging adults now use social media on a regular basis (Perrin, 2015), with Facebook remaining among the most popular applications. The interaction these sites provide has both potential positive and negative consequences. For instance, one study suggested that social media access both promoted the growing of a person's social resources (35% of their sample reported finding a new friend via social media) but was also correlated with lower self-esteem if interactions and reactions to profiles and posting were negative (Valkenburg, Peter, & Schouten, 2006).

At the very least, it is clear that modern emerging adults are interconnected at rates never seen before. At the swipe of a finger, emerging adults have instant access to the daily lives of many if not most of their peers. As shown in Figure 8.1, emerging adults are using social media more than any other age group. While the number of emerging adults who use social media has continued to increase, so has the amount of adults in different age groups. According to this research by Pew, when all participants are combined, 75% said they use social media. This study included participants who were categorized into age groups from 18 up to 65+ years.

As noted earlier, in Figure 8.2, it is clear that Facebook is the most common form of social media used by emerging adults.

˙ This pervasive access to the lives of their peers adds another wrinkle to how emerging adults are influenced by their friends. Beyond their immediate social circles, social media allows emerging adults to peek into the lives of not only their close friends but also their general acquaintances, including old schoolmates with whom they had only limited relationships. One natural consequence of this, though, was

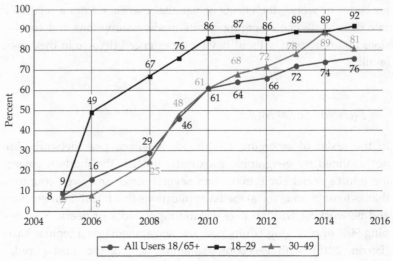

FIGURE 8.1 Social media use by age and year.
Source: Pew Research Center.

access to track major life transitions like marriage. For example, Marty spoke of how Facebook allowed him to get glimpses into the married lives of his peers. He explained, "There's a whole other group of friends, they're all married and from what they say on Facebook everything's going smoothly but you never actually know. They could just be saying that." Although Marty had his doubts about the endless bliss these friends displayed on social media, he identified it as an important point of reference for marriage. Despite values of relativism and individualism strongly embedded through many of our interviews, the emerging adults we spoke to were quick to judge when they weighed in on their peers' lives. Michael, our 25-year-old insurance agent, spoke about what he felt were the poor marital and fertility decisions of his Facebook peers. He said, quite bluntly,

> I see on Facebook people from high school who I know are just—
> not idiots, but are lacking education—and I see them having kids,
> and I'm just like "How are you doing this?" Like financially [for]
> one, they've got to be struggling, I know they have to if they're
> working a factory job and that's it. I just see some of these people,
> and I'm like "Why are you having kids? You should not be
> reproducing." I just see it on Facebook. You do. But that's just the

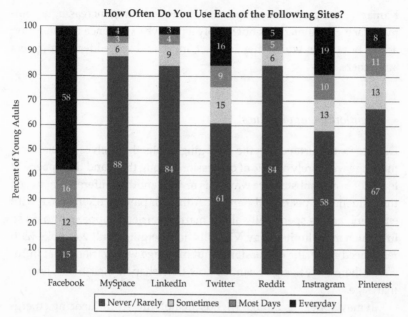

FIGURE 8.2 Social media site use among young adults.
Source: Millennials and Marriage Message Assessment.

truth of it though. People today—kids today should not be having kids. Get stricter birth control or something.

Obviously, Michael had developed some fairly strong opinions about his peers based, at least partially, on what he was seeing on social media.

Beyond access to peers' marital transitions and fertility decisions, social media also serves as a mechanism for expanding emerging adults' dating pool. One of our participants, Kamar, met his current partner through social media. He explained,

I met her on Facebook. She came to my inbox saying, 'Hey, how you doing?' and we just started talking, and then from there we were talking on the phone for about a good week or two. Me and my family, we were having a barbeque at my uncle's house. I invited her to come and meet the family and stuff like that. So she met the family and the family approved. Been together ever since.

Kamar's example is not exceptional and is becoming increasingly commonplace. Social media is not simply a passive experience for emerging adults but one in which they interact, meet, and share ideas with peers and others. .

Reinforcement of Values

Despite its importance, as the emerging adults themselves proclaimed, marriage was rarely a topic of discussion among them and their peers, at least not in any substantive way. This reveals another difference between the influence of peers and parents. Although parents often spoke with emerging adults specifically about marriage, friends appeared to do so in a much more limited way. Virtually no emerging adult we spoke with referenced a specific discussion about marriage with a friend that influenced them or was significant in how they shaped their own views of marriage.

It may appear as though friends are not directly influencing emerging adults' views of marriage through direct conversations, but friends may instead be a source of short-term relationship advice and socialization or, as one emerging adult told us, a "sounding board" for dating advice. Peers are, at least among our sample, a much stronger source of dating advice than marital advice for emerging adults, focused on the immediate and not the long-term. Another emerging adult female said she used her friends to "process all the crap" she went through in dating. To be sure, friends were a vital source of advice about relationships; such advice was just usually about dating rather than about marriage itself.

These conversations likely still influence marital beliefs and values. Take Amberlee as an example. Amberlee, 20 years old, single and in college, related a story in her interview about a friend's relationship. She explained,

> One of my friends right now, she and this guy, they're probably soul mates, but they broke up for one reason or another 2 months ago. I'm really good friends with both of them. They're about to graduate and he's moving to Sacramento and she's staying here, and she just can't wrap her mind around why he doesn't want to date her.

On the surface, this is a common scenario among emerging adults. Two dating partners, about to move on to the next phase in their respective lives and thus deciding to end a college-based romantic relationship, is hardly the stuff of made-for-TV romances. However, Amberlee had clearly had several conversations about this relationship during which she gave input and advice to her friend. Although not directly related to marriage, Amberlee recognized that experiences like this have shaped her own view of relationships. Remember, she called these two partners "soul mates" and seemed frustrated that her friend's boyfriend was not willing to try to make things work, despite the impending distance between them. She went on to explain,

> I think I've been influenced by that—all my friends' relationships that don't make logical sense, and so I think I'm influenced by unhealthy relationships not trying to stick it out together and I just don't get why. I also think that I don't really believe in soul mates. I mean, there's 100 people in this world that I could probably be compatible with for a really long time. It depends on where you are in your life. So I think another influence is that: my friends' stupid relationships.

This experience, and others like it, had partially soured Amberlee's views on long-term relationships and, by extension, marriage. These views, borne of the complex interaction between her own personal experiences and the experiences of her family members, were still malleable, and her friends' experiences helped her shape them. Amberlee believed that her parents were largely unhappy in their marriage, or as she put it at one point in the interview, "It's like they don't even really try." This was a powerful perception for her, leading to a belief that marriage was a relationship that did not bring automatic happiness and that many people in this world simply settled on an eventual marital partner. Amberlee's experience with friends did not create a new view of marriage for her; rather, it fed into her existing perceptions and views.

In this way, peer networks during emerging adulthood may have a reinforcing effect on attitudes and behaviors related to marriage and relationship trajectories. If emerging adults look to peers and few if any of these peers are transitioning to marriage, then emerging adults may feel that marrying might make them out of step with their peers. In our survey data, a sizeable majority (68%) of emerging adults believed that at least half of their friends had a positive view of marriage. In stark contrast, only 5% believed that more than half of their friends thought marriage was an outdated institution. They viewed their friends as generally being positive and energetic about eventual marriage. The word *eventual*, however, is key. Sixty percent of the emerging adults we surveyed reported that 10% or fewer of their friends wanted to get married in the next year. Marriage is important; it is a goal. Just not right now.

In the end, it appears that perhaps the most important influence of friends comes when they reinforce many of the cultural beliefs and behavioral patterns that have created the marriage paradox in the first place. Emerging adults sense that their peers are fearful of marriage and the commitment it entails. Elizabeth, a 21-year-old who had broken off an earlier engagement, noted, "I have friends and that [topic of marriage] freaked them out. They didn't pursue serious relationships because they didn't want to get tied down by anyone or by kids." Susan, another 21-year-old, explained that, "A lot of my peers have the idea that you should fulfill your own happiness before you should fulfill somebody else's." These are all themes (individualism, relative importance, fear) that we have touched on before. Friends and the social environment they create appear to reinforce many of these values and ideas that serve as the core of the marital paradox.

▲ Religious Influences on Marriage

We have largely focused in the previous chapters on the personal interactions emerging adults have with others; however, their interactions with influences that extend beyond personal relationships also affect how emerging adults think and plan for marriage. In fact, these larger cultural systems and societal institutions may influence emerging adults just as much if not more than some specific interactions they have. As emerging adults navigate their 20s, they interact with multiple cultural systems that, like friends and family, have the potential to send direct and indirect messages about marriage. Two of these larger systems appeared to matter to the emerging adults in our study: religion and the media.

In some ways, discussing religion and religious culture among emerging adults seems fruitless. One thing that has been clear in the scholarship and commentary on emerging adulthood is the disillusionment modern emerging adults have regarding traditional religious faiths

(Barry & Abo-Zena, 2014; Smith & Snell, 2009). Several scholars have noted the mass exodus of emerging adults from virtually all religious faiths, observing the drastic declines in religious affiliation and attendance as they launch from their family of origin. One study (Smith & Snell, 2009) suggested that only about one fifth of emerging adults attend church service at least once a week, about a 20% decrease from attendance during adolescence.

This does not mean that religion and spirituality are dead among modern emerging adults. According to another national study (Figure 8.3), there is a large difference between how important emerging adults think religion is in their everyday lives and how often they actually attend church services. Although the highest majority of participants said that religion was either somewhat or very important in their daily lives, the largest number of people said they never attend religious services. That is, whereas for earlier generations religious attendance, affiliation, and importance were one and the same, today these concepts are becoming disentangled, in much the same way that marriage and childrearing are now separate. Consequently, attending

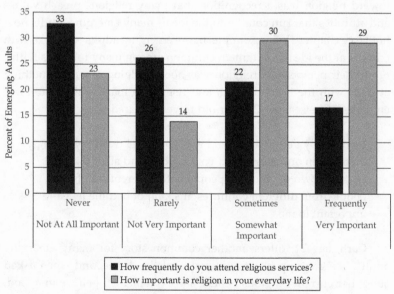

FIGURE 8.3 Religious attendance and importance of religion for emerging adults.

Source: Millennials and Marriage Message Assessment.

services is quickly becoming a smaller part of their religious lives, despite continued belief in the importance of religion.

Such an exodus has implications for marriage because religion and marriage have been interlinked for centuries across most industrialized nations. Although marriage has remained a central goal for most emerging adults, the centrality of religion and spirituality has wavered. In fact, researcher Christian Smith, in his study of emerging adulthood and religion, noted the growing disconnect between marriage and religion. Although 60% of his sample believed that fulfillment in life would be a result of marriage, only 9% believed it would come from religion or God (Smith & Snell, 2009).

Providing further evidence of the decline of religiosity among emerging adults, more than one third of all emerging adults now list themselves as unaffiliated with any religion, a number that has increased by almost 7% in recent years (Smith, 2015). Compared with their parents' generation, modern millennials pray less, believe in God less, and attend church less (Taylor, & Keeter, 2010). Stories of losing faith or at least altering faith were a common theme across the emerging adults we spoke with.

Central to this growing apathy (and in some cases antipathy) toward religion was a recognition that many religions preach values and attitudes that run counter to the ideals many emerging adults now hold (see chapter 1). For example, many emerging adults we spoke with cringed at the idea of judgment common among many religious faiths. From their perspective, religion was about judging others, something at odds with the individualism and relativism many claimed to have embraced. Chelsea, our 24-year-old traveler, shared,

> I would say definitely when I was younger I was very strongly
> involved in our church and youth group and all of that. But
> as I've grown up and met people with different beliefs and
> people from different countries, it's kind of become less and less
> important to me.

Carli, age 21, offers another common story for many emerging adults. She grew up in a traditional Christian home, and when asked about her current religious beliefs, she explained, "I believe in a God, and I used to go to church. But then I guess I got caught up in what denomination am I? I stopped going because it was causing a lot of conflict just within me." Carli, one of our young engaged college students, struggled with her religious identity and eventually concluded that she could be religious without attending or affiliating with one particular religious system.

Many emerging adults feel the same way, using their strong belief in individualism to construct an individualized spirituality that allows for a general moral code that drives actions and decision making but often drops the day-to-day rituals and practices of most religious denominations. Like many things we have discussed, religion and spirituality have also become individualistic and relativistic entities among emerging adults. More than half of all emerging adults now believe that morality is a matter of personal choice (Smith & Snell, 2009).

As noted, this shifting of faith also has implications for marriage. Many, if not most, religious traditions have specific teachings and beliefs about marriage, teachings that many modern emerging adults heard while they attended religious services with their parents. As they shifted their faith during emerging adulthood, many struggled to reconcile these religious messages about marriage with their current values. These religious messages were, in some cases, the only explicit messages about marriage they had received during their formative years. Returning to Carli, as she moved away from organized religion, she sensed that her views on marriage also needed to shift. She explained,

> I think that marriage is a lasting bond, and I grew up in a church
> that really emphasized that when you make that commitment,
> you make that commitment in front of God, and He might not
> necessarily approve if you choose to break it. But, I wouldn't say
> that it made me wait or get married sooner or anything like that.

Despite moving away from the religion she grew up with, Carli was still hearkening back to her religious teachings as she thought about marriage. Lauren offered another example of this shift. Growing up Catholic but currently identifying herself as agnostic, Lauren felt like her shift in religious faith made marriage a much more secular, and perhaps artificial, institution. She explained, "I guess it's [marriage] more of a religious thing, and if you're not really religious, then marriage is just sort of a relationship between two people."

Like many things in emerging adulthood, however, not all emerging adults fit into the common pattern outlined previously. Variation again rules the day, and some emerging adults, although a clear minority, continue to hold strong religious ideals and values. One of the clearest factors that came out of our own study was the stark and widespread differences between the minority of religious emerging adults we spoke with and those emerging adults who were less religious or becoming less religious. These religious differences appeared to cut deep into how these emerging adults thought about and even talked about marriage. For the religious emerging adults we spoke with, marriage was often deeply and strongly interwoven with their faith. Josh, 21, provides a good illustration of this strong connection. Josh grew up in a very religious Christian home, attending private religious schools until he left for college. Josh mentioned religious faith almost immediately in his interview, quickly stating that, "marriage was instituted by God as a covenant between two people, a man and a woman." For many emerging adults like Josh, religion gave marriage a higher and more divine purpose. Josh went on to explain,

> I can be in a relationship with my friend at school and we
> can share our lives together, but it's different than a marriage
> relationship. I think the marriage relationship is a distinct
> relationship set apart for a man and a woman for the purpose of
> knowing each other for their lives but also to have kids obviously.
> [It's] this special relationship that is set apart for them. I think
> it's just a special relationship that imitates what God's idea of a
> perfect relationship is.

Other religious emerging adults saw God's hand not just in how marriage was defined but also in how they moved toward marriage. Jessica, 23 and engaged, spoke of how she felt God had directed her life. She said,

> I believe that there's a path for each of us and He [God] can help
> guide us on the right path, and I think that includes finding
> somebody to be with. I don't think He'd want me to marry
> somebody that wouldn't help me progress to be a better person.
> I think, in my situation, I truly believe that who I marry is who

God intended me to be [with] because he is not who I would ever have picked for myself.

Melissa, while espousing a belief in God's romantic plan similar to Jessica's, had a more depressing story to tell. Twenty-three years old and having grown up in a religious-yet-conflicted home, Melissa noted that her parents divorced when she was young and that she had herself struggled in her dating life. Working at a local technical college, she had recently ended a 3-year relationship just short of a formal engagement. Melissa said this as she described the end of this relationship,

> I'm trying to be okay with God about that [breaking up with her
> boyfriend]; maybe that's [marriage] not His plan for me. But I kind
> of want that. I don't know. I guess I'm kind of bitter and sad,
> and I'm still confused about it all because it ended abruptly. And
> I don't know. I had already given my whole heart to him.

Because Melissa viewed God's hand in her relationships, her relational struggles had made her wonder if marriage was in the cards for her. Emerging adults like Josh, Jessica, and Melissa have strongly intertwined their religious faith with both their trajectory toward marriage and their expectations about what marriage will be like. Ironically, this same tie could also make marriage seem even more out of reach for others.

Although the religious emerging adults we spoke to varied in their religious affiliation (although Christians certainly dominated in our Midwestern sample), the specific influences also varied across the denominations. For example, Susan, an active member of the Church of Jesus Christ of Latter-day Saints (Mormon), referenced her religious faith's belief that marriage and families are eternal. Married at the young age of 21, she related,

> I realize that marriage and families are eternal, you can be together
> forever; [it] definitely puts a lot more meaning and a lot more
> emphasis on getting married because I want to be ready for
> eternity, and the sooner I started that with my husband and was
> able to get married and then continue to get to know each other,
> grow together, go to the temple, different things like that, it has a
> lot more meaning than it would have before.

Mariah, a young Catholic, provided a slightly different take on marriage, referencing the sacramental nature of marriage based on her own faith tradition. She explained,

> Well, with Catholicism I have been taught from a very young age that you need to love the person that you're going to marry, but you also need to love them in Christ and you need to be willing to share your relationship with Christ and put Him in the center of your relationship.

As these quotes illustrate, the exact nature and connection between religion and marriage shifts from faith to faith, but the theme of religion heavily influenced how some emerging adults conceptualized marriage.

These various examples of religious emerging adults contrasted heavily with the majority of emerging adults we spoke with who were either not religious or heading in that direction. Lauren, 22 and studying public relations in college, had a very negative perception of religion, despite having grown up in a somewhat religious home. She had long since stopped attending any religious services and explained that the more of life she experienced the less she felt that religion, as she saw it, was an uplifting experience. She said,

> That [life experience] made me think, "Wow, why, why would anybody join this religion to hate this religion, when they're all basically the same thing?" And I think that definitely is the reason why religion doesn't hit home with me anymore.

Unlike many of our religious emerging adults, Lauren viewed marriage as "outdated" and later explained that,

> The definition of marriage is outdated, and I feel the concept is also a little outdated. Because if there's no real benefit to getting married anymore, besides just being with the person forever, then what's the point of actually going down and getting [married], paying all this money for something?

Lauren's ideal age of marriage was 35, and during the interview it was clear that Lauren would not shed a tear if marriage never came her way.

Clark offers another example of this religious difference in how emerging adults approach marriage. Clark, a 22-year-old finishing school with a financial planning degree, was a youth leader in his church growing up. As he grew older, however, he struggled with what he viewed as the hypocritical behavior of his fellow churchgoers. Eventually, he concluded that religion was simply not for him. As he described it,

> I started thinking about how all those people that just listen to whatever anybody on stage said [at his church], and it just made me think that everything they've taught me was a little bit of a lie. I believe that there is something up there, but I don't know what.

As Clark lost his faith, his views on marriage likewise began to shift. He saw little intrinsic value in marriage, firmly believing that life would go on just fine if marriage went away. He noted,

> No, I don't think it's [marriage] needed. I think it's a choice people can make. People can just be dating and be with each other for the rest of their lives if they want. They don't have to put the name on it.

He was also one of our many emerging adults who felt like marriage should be delayed and that marriage would interfere with the other activities he was hoping to engage in during this period of his life. He went on in the interview to explain his views on when to marry this way:

> When you're younger you're supposed to explore your options. There are so many people out there. I guess some people do pick someone when they're 20 or 21 and they choose them, but there are so many other people out there, and I think if you get married at a younger age you miss out with hanging with all your friends or going out. Nobody wants to hang out with the old couple.

These quotes are obviously quite different from the tone given by many of our more religiously minded participants. This gap in how marriage is perceived seemed to put a wedge between these two segments of the emerging adult population. Take Elizabeth, our emerging adult who had been previously engaged, who noted that such religious differences were one of the reasons that her engagement fell apart. As she put it,

> I met my ex-fiancé through church, actually. His focus was very much religious, and I kind of was like, "I like you, you're fun, I'm going to tag along." So it [the relationship] was much more having to focus on doing things the right way, the biblical way, getting engaged, doing this, waiting until marriage to have sex, and things like that really played into that relationship that I didn't expect to.

Elizabeth quickly realized that her fiancé's perceptions of both marriage and premarital relationships were very different from her own, largely because of the differing religious views they held. After ending her engagement, she quickly retreated from any organized religious faith and has not returned.

Clearly, not all religious emerging adults have positive views of marriage, and not all nonreligious emerging adults revile marriage as an institution. Yet, across all our participants, religious differences were common and pronounced. As religious trends continue to shift among future generations of emerging adults, religion will likely continue to be a major factor influencing the nature of the marital paradoxes that emerging adults encounter.

▲ Media

Our final social and cultural institution is the media, a large topic, to be sure, but one that has clear connections to marriage for many emerging adults. Romance, dating, and marriage are common themes of popular media, and emerging adults often tried to articulate how various media had influenced them.

For some, the media helps create confidence in sexual and dating identity. This was the case for Asher, a gay 21-year old, who said, "I think that's [media] where I got my hope from, honestly." For others, the media offered examples of relationships and marriages that they sought to model in their own relationships. Amy, a 22-year-old pre-med student, shared an example from the popular 1990s television show *Friends* of how she learned about relationships from the media. She said,

> I love the show *Friends,* and Ross and Rachel obviously made it through a whole bunch of different struggles. In the end, as hard as things got, [...] Rachel was supposed to go to Paris at the end of the show, and she didn't because of Ross. I think that at the end of the day, oftentimes as much as you want to do something you have to make big sacrifices for someone that you love.

Ryan, a 21-year-old pharmacy student, drew inspiration from film, particularly romantic comedy. He related,

> I like to think of myself as more the romantic type, I like to be spontaneous, I like that whole side of marriage. I think it should be something that's focused on fun, and so in that case the media, I would say the rom-coms, or romantic comedies, and all those have definitely pushed me towards more of a fun-loving marriage versus a more structured one.

Some emerging adults noted that the media had influenced their desires for the timing of marriage, providing normative guidelines for when transitions should occur. Danica, a 23-year-old recent college graduate, explained that,

> I think media does play a really big part. They always say, "Oh, your time is ticking away," and it's like "Oh my gosh, I'm not even in a relationship." So I want to be engaged for this many years and then not have kids for this many years, and you think about it, and I'll be 40 before any of this happens. I'm not immune to it.

These varying examples all illustrate the influence that the media has on emerging adults by providing education, socialization, and perhaps inspiration centered on romantic relationship formation and eventual marriage.

The influence emerging adults referenced was certainly varied, but a few important themes did emerge. One of the interesting aspects that came out of our interviews was a rather visceral and negative reaction from emerging adults against the messages they were receiving from the media about relationships. Although the scholarship on the effects of media is robust (see Bryant & Oliver, 2009), and decades of research suggest that media use influences everything from behavior (Anderson & Bushman, 2002; Coyne, Padilla-Walker, & Howard, 2013) to beliefs and perceptions (Grabe, Ward, & Hyde, 2008), emerging adults appeared to collectively revile this influence. Despite acknowledgement by some that they had learned from and been influenced by the media, many appeared to, at least on the surface, reject the marital and relational messages they were receiving. Here is just a sample of the types of responses we got from emerging adults as they spoke about the media's influence on their thoughts about marriage and relationships:

> Clark: Media tells me that your spouse will forgive you for doing a lot of things, like cheating on them and stuff on TV shows and movies. I don't really listen to that, it hasn't done anything. Plus it's ridiculous.
>
> Ember: They've [the media] influenced what I don't want it [marriage] to be. The media has shown me where I don't want to get to. I don't want to get to the point where my priorities are above my marriage. Like, I'm not happy so I'm going to leave.
>
> Geoff: I don't pay that much attention to what's going on in the media and what they say about things because they have their own agenda and they have their things they want to push, and I don't care what the media says about it.
>
> Max: There's a lot of times where I won't take the media very seriously on relationships, just because I either know that even if it's not a bad portrayal of relationships, you know, it's been hyper-romanticized or something.
>
> Sierra: Movies and TV shows always give you that unrealistic expectation of things are going to be perfect and there's going to be a fairy tale ending; you might not really have to work on it that hard, just the idea of love that you romanticize.
>
> Taya: I feel like media almost ruins marriage. I don't think that helps at all. I also feel like reality shows these days, they go in the complete opposite of what marriage is. So maybe that's why people don't want to get married.

This final quote from Taya exposes a particular issue we encountered frequently in our study. Perhaps some of the frustration and anger was directed at one of the newer forms of media, namely reality television. In contrast to older generations, emerging adults grew up with numerous television shows depicting seemingly normal people competing with and against each other, with the accompanying celebration of celebrity culture. In fact, one of the strongest themes in our interviews was a continued reference to reality television when emerging adults discussed marriage.

Research suggests that, when centered on dating or relationships (think *The Bachelor*), reality television can have an influence on those who watch it. Because such programming often depicts dating as a game, women as items of conquest, and relationships as highly sexualized, is it any wonder that watching such reality programming is often associated with views that women are sex objects and that physical intimacy is central to relationships (Ferris, Smith, Greenberg, & Smith, 2007; Zurbriggen & Morgan, 2006), or that watching reality television is linked to sexual decision making among college students (Fogel & Kovalenko, 2013)? Although such research is currently limited, it does suggest that emerging adults are likely being affected by the massive amount of reality programming available to them through television channels and various online streaming mechanisms.

One of the more fascinating tidbits that emerged from our interviews was the prominence accorded one particular celebrity couple, despite the fact that we never asked about celebrities or such programming at all. Five of our emerging adults specifically referenced Kim Kardashian's second marriage of 72 days and said it had influenced their views of marriage. The consensus from emerging adults appeared to be rather clear, the Kardashians being only one example. They felt bombarded by celebrity marriages and weddings, marriages that most felt were poor examples of healthy relationships and long-term love. As Claire, a 22-year-old recent college graduate put it, "I think it's [celebrity marriages] shown me, honestly, what not to do in marriage. Honestly, I think media portrays marriage in a sad light, and it's not something I desire." Eliza, a 21-year-old married student, and Madison, a 22-year-old student, both had similar sentiments. Eliza noted, "I think there are some media portrayals of marriage that were, for me, what I do not want to do," while Madison stated, "I don't want that kind of marriage like the Kardashian's, I don't want anything to do with that. I don't want that." Clearly many emerging adults attempt to reject the marriage messages they receive from the ever-increasing celebrity and reality culture of the media.

Yet perhaps the effect is more subtle. After all, is it reasonable to assume that watching numerous failed celebrity marriages or relationships does not influence how emerging adults think about their own relationships? Social learning models of human development would suggest this unlikely at best. David, a 23-year-old living with his parents and searching for a full-time job after college, gave us some insight into this potentially subtle effect. He noted that,

> You have people who are talking about Kim Kardashian and her marriages and Brittney Spears and her marriages and whether those are okay, and it's become such a popular topic that I don't think it's necessarily what it used to be—a commitment between two people. And now [it's] almost like a pop culture thing. Even TV shows for weddings or TLC that's just obsessed with marriage, it becomes just pop culture to talk about as opposed to something that goes on between two people that I'm sure used to be a lot more personal than it is now.

David felt like the immense focus on reality television and our celebrity culture had devalued marriage—it had made marriage something less sacred and more sensational. It also turned him off to the idea of marriage. David went on to explain, "For me with marriage, it's never something that I pictured for me so I didn't even think about what it would be like to be married." David did not feel much urge to engage in an institution that he felt was constantly degraded in the media. This may be the case for other emerging adults as well and may feed into the marital paradox. Emerging adults clearly felt they were exposed to numerous bad examples of marriages in the media, and perhaps that made them more cautious and hesitant about marriage. Perhaps emerging adults wonder, like many of us, if these celebrities with their wealth and fame cannot make a marriage work, how would marriage work for anyone struggling through school or employment?

Ironically, emerging adults rarely admitted being personally influenced by the circus of media marriages, but many of them claimed that the celebrity culture did influence their social circles. Specifically, several emerging adults spoke of how the reality television and celebrity culture may make some of their peers fixate on marriage. Antonio, a 22-year-old graduate student, explained what he felt was the effect of the media among his peers. He said, "Yeah, there's a strong influence from the media here, I think. Especially the celebrity life; you look at divorces happening all the time, marriages, relationships and then people definitely want a piece of that or to be part of that, so we tend to sometimes do what celebrities do." Kimberly, 23 and in college, echoed his remarks, explaining to us that, "Marriage is glorified when we see these celebrities; like, this is what we're supposed to do, this is what we're expected to do." Importantly, the claims regarding possible media influences need to be tempered by noting that we still know relatively little about how this influx of reality programming in the media is shifting relational patterns among emerging adults. But emerging adults themselves certainly appear to acknowledge the influence.

When it came to media influences, one topic that nearly all emerging adults acknowledged as influenced by media depictions was weddings. Weddings are big business in many parts of the world. The average cost of a wedding in the United States is now more than $32,000 (Jacobson, 2016), and weddings today are bigger and more elaborate than ever, with brides and grooms shelling out hundreds if not thousands of dollars for photographers, florists, dresses, and catering. Although it's not altogether clear whether the media is merely reflecting or creating the need for larger and more extravagant weddings, it is certainly one of the avenues through which such grandiosity is portrayed (likely also centered on the celebrity culture mentioned previously).

Emerging adults sensed that such messages were changing how they thought about weddings. Laura, a 22-year-old getting a degree in recreational therapy, was quite animated when expressing her opinion of media-portrayed weddings. She first made a connection to movies and the princess mentality she felt they promoted. She said, "In the princess movies, they have the big wedding and they live happily ever after." She went on to further explain this big wedding messaging, suggesting that the media has made emerging adults much more consumer-minded when it comes to weddings. She explained that she feels that the messaging around weddings given by the media makes her peers desire what they see on television and the Internet. Perhaps influenced by the self-centered nature of social media such as Facebook, Instagram, and Snapchat posts, emerging adults want the spotlight to shine on them, and a wedding is a perfect opportunity. Laura noted, "She [the bride] looks so nice, and everything looks so pretty and everybody's there and doing stuff for them and giving them presents, it's like, 'Aw, I want to feel nice for a couple of hours or something, it looks so nice.'" For Laura, she felt these messages made her lean toward marrying. As she later said, "I think it [the message about weddings] does make me want to get married because I do want to have all of those things."

Such messaging surrounding weddings portrayed by the media may also have the opposite effect as well. Several scholars have noted that the modern wedding, and its cultural expectation of expense, may serve as a barrier to some couples wanting to marry, particularly among low-income couples for whom resources for weddings are scarce (Edin & Kefalas, 2005; Gibson-Davis, Edin, & McLanahan, 2005; Smock, Manning, & Porter, 2005). Regardless of the specific effect on emerging adults, weddings appear to be one more area in which the media and reality television are shaping the marital beliefs of emerging adults.

▲ College as a Socialization Institution

One final stop is in order before we move beyond the social and cultural influences on emerging adults' view of marriage—one that is largely unique to the middle-class and educated emerging adults we spoke with. It was one that was not as strongly referenced as friends, religion, or the media but one that we believe warrants a brief mention. Although many of these emerging adults either had completed or were completing a college education, it appears as though part of their education was also related to marriage, specifically related to the instruction on either relationships, marriage, or general critical thinking they had received in their college classrooms. Several emerging adults told anecdotes about professors or classroom situations that fundamentally altered their view on marriage. Jamie, 22 and a recently graduated nanny, was one of those students. Jamie called herself "pro-marriage" and viewed marriage as a "milestone" in her life, one she hoped would come in her late 20s. As Jamie surveyed her thoughts on marriage, she referenced a very specific experience she had in college. She related,

> One specific professor, who I loved, she gave me so much insight about marriage. Different things she talked about got me really excited about relationships in general [. . .]. It changed my opinion about what I thought about them rather than what I had always been taught by my parents. Rather than seeing relationships as a more of a manipulative situation, it's now more [a] two-way street situation, you know? It took a complete 180 when it came to marriage. Getting into college, my opinion of marriage just completely changed.

Jamie came from a family in which her parents had separated and reconciled many times, yet a few specific encounters in college seemed to have helped solidify her now more positive views of the institution.

Another emerging adult, Sierra, 21 and studying family science, had a similar experience that shifted her views of gender roles in marriage. She explained that,

> Taking a marriage course has changed the way I view
> relationships and that there's more than just the typical gender
> roles of "women do this and men do that." It can be more equal.
> When they do studies about this stuff when it's split up more
> equally, [it] ends up working out better for couples who perceive
> things to be more equal.

Not all emerging adults spoke of such transformative experiences, but such examples may be illustrative. As was mentioned earlier in the book, a growing divide in marriage is occurring between educated and noneducated emerging adults: Educated emerging adults are more likely to marry, value marriage, and put marriage before childbearing than are emerging adults with less education. Perhaps a small part of this difference is actually occurring in our institutions of higher learning, where emerging adults can learn the value of relationships, basic interpersonal skills, and even some of the structural implications of marriage in a variety of social science classrooms.

All told, there are many other contextual and cultural influences that shape how emerging adults view marriage. However, even the main issues addressed in this and the previous chapter make one thing clear—much of the confusion emerging adults experience regarding their views on marriage are rooted in the conflictual messages they receive from the social world around them. Whether it's the direct messages from parents or friends encouraging both the importance of marriage and marital delay, struggles with reconciling shifting religious faith and corresponding messages about marriage, or making sense of the varying marital examples displayed in the media, emerging adults are left to make sense of a mountain of information about dating and marriage that is no longer as consistent or as steady as in generations past and that comes at them at unprecedented speeds. The uniform cultural message about marriage has given way to a complex web of opinion and speculation and has left most emerging adults gleaning what they can from the examples around them.

9 ▲
Gender and Gender Role Expectations

In previous chapters, we have heard from both men and women concerning their views of marriage and have made relatively few distinctions between them. However, you may have noticed some differences in the ways that our respondents talked about marriage based on their gender. These differences, though they appear subtle, have enormous consequences for how these individuals think about marriage. Understanding them, in turn, brings us one step closer to grasping the mechanisms generating the marital paradox.

Of course, gender differences in marriage are hardly new, and hundreds of scholars have written on the topic. Perhaps the most well-known articulation of gender differences in marriage came in 1972, when Jessie Bernard, a noted feminist and eminent scholar, published a book in which she famously claimed there are two marriages: his and hers. This core idea shaped a generation of gender scholars and influenced society for decades to come. Drawing largely from the gender roles and expectations of the 1950s and 1960s, *The Future of Marriage* suggests that marriage is inherently patriarchal, unjust, and rooted in *hegemonic masculinity*, a term that simply means that male domination was at the center of most marriages. Similarly, Thorstein Veblen (1899), a prominent social theorist at the turn of the twentieth century, wrote that women were among the first things to be owned.

Much of the recent theory and scholarship on gender differences has been focused on marriages themselves. Although there is much to be learned by studying the gendered behavior and values of those currently navigating marriage, our focus here is with the emerging adults looking forward to marriage. We wondered: Are there two marriages still today in how emerging adults think about marriage? What do contemporary emerging adults think of this? Particularly, who do they think benefits more from marriage—men or women?

In this chapter, we explore what the emerging adults we spoke with think about gender in marriage. Specifically, we'll talk about who, if anyone, will benefit more from marriage, how emerging adults view feminism, and how emerging adults plan to navigate decisions around gender roles and expectations.

▲ Who Benefits More? Men, Women, or Anyone?

One of the key issues we were interested in at the outset of this project was gender differences in the perceptions of marriage. We, like many others, suspected that men's and women's different perceptions of marriage, on both an individual and a societal level, color the prism through which the marital paradox emerges. For starters, marriage has long served multiple purposes in society. As noted in previous chapters, marriage, in most societies, served as the primary mechanism for bearing and rearing children, organizing sexuality, systematizing commerce and economic production, and establishing rules of proper conduct within communities (Coontz, 2005; Mintz & Kellogg, 1989). But the past several decades have borne witness to dramatic shifts in cohabitation, nonmarital fertility, relationship dissolution, women entering the labor force, and single parenthood, among many others. In turn, these changes have contributed to a sense among many that marriage's roles, purposes, and benefits have changed, resulting in a different mental calculus when people are considering whether and whom to marry. Yet some gendered notions of marriage appear to remain intact.

For some, the perceived benefits of marriage seem tied to ideals about traditional gender roles in marriage, namely the husband breadwinner–wife homemaker model dominant among middle-class white families in the 1950s and made popular by television shows such as *Leave It to Beaver*. Although there was no overall consensus about who benefited more, emerging adults took all sides of the issue. Some felt women benefited more, some felt it was men. Others felt that both benefited equally, and a few even said that no one benefits. Indeed, among all the topics we explored, views of gender and marriage had the most variety and were the hardest to pin down. Little consensus seemed to exist regarding how emerging adults viewed the connection between gender and marriage; perhaps this is a reflection of our current culture, which continues to move toward gender neutrality and the dismissal of gender differences. To give readers a taste, we briefly discuss each of these.

Women Benefit

In contrast to common perception and Jessie Bernard's writing, many of our emerging adults felt that women benefited more from marriage. To be fair, however, many of their reasons for believing women benefit more from marriage had to do with things that they themselves were seeking in marriage. For example, Pierce, 22, working as a part-time editor and looking forward to having children, claimed that, "I think the wife would benefit more because she gets to mess around with the kids all day," whereas Madison, a 22-year-old working on her graduate degree in communication disorders, suggested that "women get deeper emotional satisfaction [from marriage] than men do." For 23-year-old Janessa, marriage was about feeling secure. "Women need security. Being legally married provides a sense of security for women. On a physical level, men [provide this] because there's someone there for them. It benefits women more." Other people, like Parker, a 24-year-old probation officer, felt that "the reason why [women] benefit from [marriage] is that they enjoy more of the social aspect of having someone there all the time, depending on the person."

Sometimes the responses were somewhat more puzzling. Occasionally the interviewees would provide their opinion about who benefits more but without fully explaining why that is. For instance, Melissa, 23 and working for a technology college, curiously said that "if anything, women [benefit more]. The guy usually makes more money. That's a bunch of crap." Melissa claimed women benefited more, then immediately pointed out a way (the gender pay gap) in which women are disadvantaged relative to men. Similarly, Megan, a bank teller in her early 20s, claimed that, "Obviously men and women get the same thing in marriage, but as a woman I think I benefit more." Megan gave no immediate reason for this belief. Even after prodding, it was clear that Megan simply thought women benefited more but could not articulate why.

Men Benefit

More often, however, the emerging adults we spoke with felt that men received the better deal out of marriage. Their reasons for believing this were often rooted in perceptions of unfairness in the way society dictates social norms. Danielle, a 26-year-old occupational therapist, proclaimed that "Men try to brainwash everyone into thinking women are the only ones benefiting and wanting to get married," whereas Cassidy, 21 and finishing up a degree in sociology, said, "I don't think it's fair that women do so much more work in maintaining relationships." Similarly, Alexis, a 22-year-old adoption agent, worried that "somebody might take advantage of my motherly instincts." Together, these three women represent a much larger group of emerging adults who have identified how marriage is seemingly tilted in favor of men and wonder if it's worth it.

These worries were perhaps best articulated by 21-year-old biology major Madilyn who said that men benefit more because "the women today will be working and have to take care of the kids, family, household, laundry. If it was more traditional, it would be more equal." In other words, Madilyn felt that women who are entering the workplace and defying traditional gender roles are being disadvantaged because men are not taking on the traditional female roles in return, leaving women to simply do more with the same time and resources. This adds an interesting wrinkle. Lynette bemoans gender inequality not because women do more housework or childrearing; rather, she says marriage would be more equal if things were more traditional.

These emerging adult women may be tapping into a phenomenon that several scholars have noted in terms of time and role assignments within a marriage. As women have increasingly entered into the workforce, most marriages and families have failed to adjust how they assign household tasks to compensate. Baxter, Hewitt, and Haynes (2008) found in a sample of more than 1,000 men and women that even though men's household labor hours were rarely affected by transitions such as marriage and parenthood, women's hours changed dramatically. It would seem that many men continue to expect their wife to take the brunt of the household duties when it comes to an eventual transition to parenthood, regardless of her employment status. Emerging adult women sense this expectation and have begun to view marriage as an uneven and impractical arrangement. Remember, these emerging adult women are already worried about their career prospects and long-term well-being.

Some concerns were more practical. Twenty-three-year-old Lynette, a social worker, sarcastically lamented, "It's so hard and I hate saying it, but men have better lives because they have nagging wives that make them go to the doctor." This, of course, is true, at least for Lynette's future husband. Danielle, our occupational therapist, stated: "The guys get all the benefits and live longer. The woman's life span gets cut in half. They get healthier because we take care of them, our risk for heart disease goes up." Of course, as a matter of correction, married women's life spans are not cut in half. Rather, married women in the United States (and just about everywhere else) live the longest of any group and have the lowest rate of death at just about any age (National Center for Health Statistics, 2016). But the point stands that the caretaking often expected of married women can take a toll on women's health, and the theme of women believing that marriage was an institution set up to help and protect men was one echoed by many in our sample.

Both Benefit Equally or No One Benefits

As with any argument, there are bound to be peacemakers, and in the artificially induced debate we created in this section of our interviews, we met a few. Jamie, a 22-year-old nanny, was one of these. She felt that both genders benefited equally (or at least differently). "For some women, they would benefit emotionally, and for men it's more financial. I don't know if it's more, but just different ways that they're benefited." Twenty-one-year-old animation major, Kaden, expressed a similar sentiment: "In the past, women would get married to husbands who gave them money and gifts. I think today men and women are benefiting equally." On a somewhat more sardonic note, Amelia, a public relations major, put it rather bluntly, "Women get protection. Both parties get to feel not alone. Men get somebody who takes care of them. It's horrible, but needed." Many of their peers felt similarly, in large part for reasons expressed by Ryan, a 23-year-old landscape technician, because men and women "should benefit equally otherwise there's going to be a lot of resentment" in marriage. This likely has a lot to do with the expectation of equality, voiced by Avery, a 22-year-old human development major looking for work: "There's two completely different perspectives when you bring man and woman together. The woman helps take care of the guy, the guy helps take care of the woman."

Of course, the bells of equality did not sound in everyone's ears when they decided that the contest between who marriage benefited more did not have a winner. Although some people, like those mentioned previously, declared both genders the winner, others said marriage didn't benefit anyone. This group of marriage skeptics can be represented by 22-year-old Kessa, an advertising major, who declared, "I don't know how anybody benefits from [marriage]. What does a woman get out of marriage? A husband, she can invite all her little friends to her wedding." She continued, "If you look at [old examples], women stay at home and make cupcakes all day. The dude gets free cupcakes and a clean house. That's not the way things are. I don't know who benefits or if anybody benefits." Despite continued focus among scholars and others regarding gender roles and gendered behavior in marriage, it seems as though emerging adults themselves have made gender a very personalized and individualized aspect of marriage. There was little sense of cultural norms or strong themes in one direction or another. Instead, each emerging adult had pieced together a view of gender in marriage that fit for them and made the most sense in terms of its connection to other values and attitudes in their lives.

▲ Feminism

When it comes to discussing gender issues with emerging adults, perhaps no topic is quite as divisive as feminism. Like the rest of society, emerging adults' opinions fall on a continuum ranging from strongly in favor to strongly against. It was, however, a common point of conversation among the emerging adults we spoke to when the issue of gender came up. As with most social issues, these emerging adults tend to be more liberal than their parents, although emerging adults' views on feminism were also informed by their peers and the media. In this section, we briefly explore emerging adults' views on feminism and how it works in their personal relationships.

For the most part, when we asked our interviewees about feminism, their views were positive, and they spoke to their beliefs that they truly could "have it all" through feminism, a theme we've already discussed and will continually return to throughout the remainder of the book. Part of the marital paradox, of course, is how emerging adults try to square gendered expectations about work and career with fertility decisions. Although we laid out the generalized beliefs emerging adults have about this balance in chapter 5, there were some uniquely gendered ways in which these beliefs were expressed. Twenty-two-year-old Claire, our graphic designer, best expressed the hopes of many in her generation when she stated, simply, "A woman can work while being a great wife and mother." Of course, this was said more as a hope than a statement of fact. Some emerging adults had seen this attempted firsthand, mostly by their mothers, with mixed results. Twenty-one-year-old Elizabeth's mother appears to have shown her how to "have it all." She said, "She [my mom] always tells me 'be something of yourself other than a wife' and I'm like 'I get it.'" This "getting it," however, came at a personal cost to Elizabeth, whose father clung to more traditional views about gender. "Even me going to college has been difficult for [my father]. I'm breaking the mold. He looks at me like I need a guy to take care of me." Samantha, a 21-year-old studying literature and dance, said she was "raised with a mom who did everything she wanted, that's what I expect. I don't expect to be restricted."

Indeed, emerging adult women often spoke of the difficulty in navigating gender norms. Twenty-two-year old photographer Ashlyn was rather candid in her assessment of how she navigates: "It's more difficult existing as a woman." Similarly, Brooklyn, a 22-year-old medical student, spoke of a faculty member she had in class and said, "He treats women differently; I'd rather be treated like everyone else."

Emerging adult men hear about and view these difficulties and outright mistreatments firsthand, and some, though not all, try to be sensitive to this. Pierce, our part-time editor, believes "everyone has to be a feminist, not just females," and 22 year-old Charles, by no means a feminist, went so far as to proclaim, "I'm not an old fashioned dude who says 'she's going to stay in the kitchen.'" A 32-year-old man, Jack, spoke of the way he was raised, a world in which masculinity, power, and control were rolled up into a single idea of the "macho man." For Jack, rejecting this notion was an essential part of his nascent feminist identity, joining with Pierce in proclaiming that everyone needs to be sensitive and sensitized to feminist issues. Josh, 20 years old, likewise spoke of the importance of gender equality when he said, "It's phenomenal to have successful business women in the world. Society might think different. Women can do basically whatever. They're not limited by stereotypes, like women should be at home with the kids."

Lauren, a 22-year-old college student majoring in communications, rejected any notion that she would be limited by gender norms and cited feminism as a primary reason for that. At one point in our discussion she said, "My personality is driven and motivated to be more than just a housewife. That's what led to my beliefs on marriage." For Shaina, at 25 working as an actuary, it was not her personality that drove her to embrace less traditional views about gendered norms and expectations. Rather, it was her college education. When we asked her about how she had developed her views on marriage and gender roles, she told us, "Some classes empowered women to think they can do it without [a] guy." For many emerging adults, men and women, feminist ideals seemed to drive them to shift their expectations about what marriage would be and how they would approach it.

Not every emerging adult female we spoke with expressed pro-feminist views, however. Janessa, our child development major, tried to blend traditional and modern views about gender roles in marriage when she said, "Women look at [staying home to raise children] as inferior, but not always acknowledging the fact that the role they have is as equal as men's, it's just different." Some of the other women we spoke to implied that they wondered whether "different" can really be "equal." And if this is the case, then equal pay outside the home should result in equal power within the relationship. As with their beliefs about who benefits from marriage, emerging adults also appeared to be sorting through the personal meaning and implications of feminist thought in their lives.

▲ Gender Roles and Expectations

Another key aspect of gender in marital relationships is known as "doing gender," or the way that gender roles are negotiated, enacted, and navigated in marriages. This refers to emerging adults' beliefs about what roles men and women should take in marriage and how they plan to organize gender roles in their own future marriages. This concept has been the subject of a large body of research, and so we were very interested to see how our emerging adults viewed and practiced "doing gender."

In general, most emerging adults sought to have more gender-egalitarian relationships than they had viewed in the past. Many of them reluctantly followed traditional gender roles, impugning various personal strengths and weaknesses as the primary barrier to achieving more equitable relationships. Other emerging adults sought to create a *tabula rasa* of sorts by communicating and negotiating gender roles. We explore each of these, traditional versus blank slate, in the following sections.

Traditional Views of Gender

Although the desire for gender-egalitarian relationships was nearly universal, some emerging adults spoke of the difficulty in turning these societal ideals into relationship realities. One interesting way of dealing with this, at least for many of the emerging adults we spoke with, was to embrace traditional gender roles but to recast them as the natural consequence of differences in individual aptitudes, capabilities, or preferences rather than social norms about what men and women should do. For example, Timothy, an aspiring writer in his early 20s, spoke of how he and his wife divided household and other chores in terms of personal rather than societal choices: "We have sides that we're strong on. I don't really like the fact that we fit into stereotypical male and female roles, but there's some things we're good at. Maren does a lot of the cooking; I do financial stuff." We heard echoes of Timothy when we spoke with Shaina, an actuary in a serious relationship, when she said, "I like more maternal roles, he's an outside person. Playing to our strengths is good, but we still have to share." Similarly, Matthew, a 24-year-old law student, stated, "Each aspect of marriage doesn't need to be equal, whoever is better at said task should pick up slack there. She takes more in some areas, and I take more in others." Of course, the fact that things seemed to end up falling into fairly neat traditional gender roles, with men and women each doing traditional masculine and feminine tasks, respectively, didn't seem to faze either Matthew or the others. In fact, 20-year-old Josh just spat it out,

> There's some things men are better at and some things women are better at. Those aren't strict, but they're there. I think there's areas I'm going to provide leadership. She might be able to provide kids. [It's important to be] able to provide in different areas.

Clayton, 22 and studying pre-dental, said, "She's good at cooking, and I like to clean." Parker, our 24-year-old probation officer, said, "I'm not really a good cook. She's better at that than me, so I let her do that." And it wasn't just men who expressed such sentiments, which may be described as soft sexism because these sentiments provide an acceptable avenue for justifying traditional gender roles. Allison, 24 and working in a grocery store, said she looked forward to embracing the "child care role because I want to, not because of stereotype." Melissa added, "I wouldn't expect my husband to clean the bathroom, I want it done my way." Finally, Taya, working on her GED certification and navigating life with two children, explained that in her relationship, the man does the "hard work." She explained that,

I feel like the yard work is definitely his area, and the manual labor of fixing things around the house and that type of stuff is all him, the car stuff is all him. I'm definitely the appointment setter and taking care of all the things for the kids, and clothing for them. With finances, we both remember things and make sure things are paid on time. So we're very equal except for the hard work.

Such sentiments suggest this may be another area where emerging adults' views about marriage appear contradictory. On the one hand, most appeared to reject the traditional gender norms of their parents, aspiring to a more egalitarian distribution of labor. However, many in long-term relationships and even marriages reported conforming to these traditional roles. Emerging adults appear to rationalize this shift by claiming that they are choosing them, rather than believing they are being forced on them through societal pressures. On some level, traditional gender roles appear to continue to exist and shape relationships, even among modern emerging adults. Despite emerging adults' seeming embrace of feminist ideals and egalitarian values, perhaps such traditional values continue to lurk under the surface, not manifesting until they are forced to enact gender within their committed relationships.

However, it is also quite possible and reasonable to interpret the previous statements in a more charitable light, one that does not require any references to gender. One could, for example, view these comments as advocating for specialization. And specialization, especially in the labor force, is one of the fundamental drivers of advanced economies. Indeed, most people attend college to gain specialized skills that make them more valuable and sought after in the labor market. Couldn't we simply say that these emerging adults are merely choosing to specialize in the activities in which they are most likely to excel, thereby maximizing the benefit gained from that activity personally and relationally, to use the jargon of economics? Of course! And there is likely a great deal of this going on, although it is interesting that this specialization rarely included gender role reversal (we did not come across a male in our sample who claimed to be a better nurturer than his female partner).

Claiming that gender does not play a part requires believing that decision making in relationships is not influenced by gender norms, an assumption that would require a great deal of faith in the face of contrary evidence. For example, if specialization were the sole motivator behind such decisions, one would expect cooking and cleaning to fall roughly equally between men and women because there would be no reason to believe that women should be better at any particular task, on average, than men, or vice versa. But much evidence from the social sciences suggest that men spend more time at traditionally masculine tasks (e.g., yard work, car repair) and women spend more time at traditionally feminine tasks (e.g., housework, child care; Hochschild, 1989; Jacobs & Gerson, 2004). Although men have increased the amount of time they spend engaged in housework and child care, a substantial gender gap persists in the time women spend engaged in such work (Hochschild, 1989; Jacobs & Gerson, 2004). Besides, other problems exist with specialization, as sociologist Valerie Oppenheimer (1997) has pointed out, because specialization has hidden dangers—if one spouse dies or gets sick, there is no one to perform those important tasks, suggesting that gender-egalitarian couples are likely acting rationally as well.

In light of all this, it should not be surprising that emerging adults seem to have a certain amount of cognitive dissonance when they realize they are enacting the very roles that many of them have been taught not only to dislike but also to discard. In large part, this is because gender roles have (likely justly) been implicated in the widespread sexism that ultimately led to the women's rights and feminist movements of the early and mid twentieth century. Therefore, given that the problem is societal expectations about how men and women should behave in romantic relationships, if emerging adults place responsibility for how they choose to "do gender" on individual differences, the cognitive dissonance is reduced. Of course, taking a socially influenced behavior and ascribing it to personal differences is nothing new. In fact, such tactics have been used to justify nearly every behavior at some point. But understanding this process in terms of how people navigate gender roles in marriage unlocks yet another piece of the puzzle we call the marital paradox.

Gender Roles as a Blank Slate

In contrast to the group embracing traditional gender roles, another group of our emerging adults believed that they could and would redraw the boundaries around gendered expectations of housework, child care, employment, and education. That is, they sensed that the deal struck by older generations, their grandparents and often even their parents, was not binding for them and their relationships. Rather, they felt free to consult with their partners and come up with whatever arrangement best suited them. This sense of freedom hearkens back to the sense of autonomy and individualism emerging adults feel, as we discussed in the earliest chapters of the book.

One of the key benefits to equality is the opportunity to negotiate roles based on personal preferences and changing circumstances. Several of our respondents spoke of this. Ryan, 21 and an aspiring pharmacist, said, "If you're saying 'that's not my job' you put a status on it. It would wreck a marriage. If it's rigid you lose ability to negotiate." Claire, a graphic designer, said she believed that "man and woman can share responsibilities," and Samantha, our 21-year-old literature and dance major, added, "I don't think [household labor] is all the women's responsibility. I would say both spouses should be equally contributing, it's not all one person's responsibility." Rosalie, preparing to graduate at age 23 with a degree in marriage and family counseling, explained why. "In a good marriage traditional gender roles don't matter. Ideally you split up tasks and make life easier because you're in a partnership."

Of course, how this is to be accomplished remains unclear at times, especially to those who may never have been in a stable, committed, romantic relationship. Yet emerging adults, at least in our sample, seem remarkably confident about their ability to navigate these difficult waters. Elizabeth, a humanities major, was certain she and her partner would "balance each other out, saying, "Someone's going to be better at this than the other; it's a learning curve to figure out what each other's strengths are." Kimberly, 23 and a sociology major, phrased it in terms of caregiving and housework. "I don't think jobs are for the man or the woman, in order for a house and a relationship to run while you share in the responsibilities. Caregiving was something women would do, but I think it's important for a man to build relationships." And 22-year-old, Kessa, an advertising major, was particularly frank (and slightly vulgar) when she stated,

> If it's "Oh you're the woman so that means you have to clean the house and cook," well I don't want to. There are plenty of people where they both chip in, it's super important. So is the emotional stuff. It doesn't matter how many pork chops he makes, if he doesn't give you a hug, that's a shitty dad.

We're not sure you can say it much more clearly! Finally, Leo, 21 and a journalism major, summed up many of our emerging adults' attitudes toward gender roles in marriage when he said, "I see the use of traditional gender roles, I [just] don't feel those are necessary."

▲ Sexual Orientation and Gender

Additionally, no chapter on gender would be complete without a brief discussion of differences in sexual orientation, an issue separate from but infused with issues of gender. We were surprised to find that, despite a great deal of cultural debate and focus on the topic of sexual orientation, we found very little evidence that heterosexual and homosexual emerging adults viewed issues surrounding gender or marriage very differently. More broadly, homosexual and heterosexual emerging adults spoke similarly about issues such as the importance of commitment, marital timing, and marital importance. So, although we were interested in exploring this topic, especially given its timeliness, when considering the marriage paradox there simply were not sufficient differences to merit a great deal of attention to the issue. Although several heterosexual and homosexual emerging adults we spoke to had commentary regarding the ongoing debate on marital rights, their views about their own future marriages were very congruent. At least when it comes to gender and marital paradigms, the heterosexual and homosexual (mostly men) individuals we spoke with seemed to view the world similarly.

In saying this, we do not wish to paint with too broad a brush because there were a handful of instances when gender clearly was different in homosexual relationships. For instance, Michael, 25, gay and getting his masters in real estate development, spoke of differences between his and his parents' relationships. "My parents are traditional, [so] sometimes Daniel [his partner] and I butt heads over who is the male." Defining gender norms in gay relationships in particular was the source of some strife in other couples as well, although others framed this as an opportunity. As Pierce, our part-time editor, put it, "I try to imagine that me and the person I marry have no gender so it would be equal. Gay marriages are awesome. They have to build [gender roles] from scratch."

Of course, this is no easy task because the historical newness of the legalization of same-sex marriage means many homosexual couples do not have the benefit of widespread acceptance of their relationships—one consequence of which is that they do not have as many examples of how to do gender in their relationships, as Ryan, at 23 a landscape technician, told us when he said that homosexual couples have "tried to model our relationships off straight white people's relationships because that's what you're inundated with since you're 3 years old."

Overall, gender is one more element to how emerging adults are piecing together their complicated and at times contradictory beliefs about marriage. Although egalitarian roles may be the most commonly sought after ideal, many emerging adults continue to struggle with enacting such roles as they face the realities of their own relationships. As mentioned previously, beliefs and perceptions about gender in marriage were among the least structured and most disorganized of all the topics we spoke to emerging adults about. In a world of shifting notions of gender, including whether gender should be promoted as a distinct social construct at all, emerging adults are still making sense of what the current cultural climate means in their personal relationships. Many appear to have adapted a "wait and see" mentality, confident in their ability to negotiate gender once they find their eventual marital partner. What this means for the marriage paradox and the eventual marriages of modern emerging adults is a question still very much up in the air.

10 ▲

The Counterculture of Married Emerging Adults

For most of our discussion, the theme of delayed marriage has been consistent. In fact, the idea that emerging adults are pushing marriage later into the life course while insisting that it still matters is at the heart of this entire exploration. Yet, as we have referenced a few times in previous chapters, not all emerging adults follow this pattern. Remember, emerging adulthood is partially defined as an age of variability and choice, and some emerging adults still choose to marry at an age similar to generations past—an age now considered early (or even too early by many). We have included some of these voices in the previous chapters as we have discussed various aspects of how emerging adults approach marriage, but now we feel that a closer examination of this unique group is warranted.

This examination is relevant for a few reasons. First, these were the emerging adults in our study whose stories and data stuck out on virtually all measures. Their survey data looked unique, their interviews were different, and their entire mentality and approach to marriage made them stand out. They appeared so different in terms of the now more normative road through emerging adulthood that they offer an interesting and insightful look at a very different path through middle-class emerging adulthood. Second, as discussed in chapter 4, one of the themes of how emerging adults think about marital timing is that there is in fact a "too soon" age to marry, often defined as the early 20s. Many emerging adults feel that marrying so young will impede educational trajectories, derail personal progression, and limit individual freedom. The question then becomes, is this actually happening? If we explore the lives of these uniquely early-married emerging adults, can we find evidence of stunted development, unfulfilled career success, or general dissatisfaction in life? Scholarly debate on the best time to marry continues amid a collection of research studies exploring the issue (see Glenn, Uecker, & Love, 2010; Hymowitz, Carroll, Wilcox, & Kaye, 2013), and perhaps the stories of these emerging adults can shed some light on whether marrying early truly does harm their prospects in life.

To do this, we will take a slightly different approach in this chapter. Rather than weaving information from our interviews with other relevant scholarly sources and national data points, we feel this specific task needs a more in-depth approach. Therefore, we will approach this topic with a more case-study-like presentation. We had five emerging adults in our interview sample that fit into this category of early-married emerging adults. In this chapter, we explore their journeys thus far in life and note, where applicable, how these emerging adults are forging a unique path compared with many of the themes mentioned earlier in this book.

▲ Clayton

We will start with Clayton, a 22-year-old college student finishing his undergraduate degree. Clayton grew up in a home with a fair amount of conflict and crisis. His parents were still married when we spoke to him, yet he seemed unsure if staying married was the best option for them. Clayton, like many emerging adults raised by parents with a conflictual marriage, could not help but be affected by this social modeling. Clayton was an emerging adult who wanted to avoid the mistakes he saw his parents make, and it influenced how he approached marriage himself. As Clayton told us, "I think my parents' marriage, growing up in that house, taught me a lot about what not to do. From a kid's perspective, the things that hurt me in turn and made me angry as a child— I think that has definitely shaped how I view marriage."

He seemed to specifically call out his father as the instigator of many of these problems, stating at one point that this father "made fun of her [his mother] in front of us." As Clayton spoke, you could sense frustration and resentment in his voice, even as he moved into adulthood.

Because he seemed to view his father as the cause of many of his parents' marital problems, he seemed to struggle with his relationship with his father generally. His father would spend time with him and even talk about relationships and marriage, but Clayton's perceptions clouded any paternal advice that was given. He explained that,

> My dad was around for my whole life, but we do not have a very good relationship. Whenever we would talk about marriage,

where we could be in an environment where I could observe what he thought about it, I now doubt that he was telling the truth.

Clayton's other major influence in his home environment was religious in nature. He grew up in a religious home that he identified as Christian, although he did not specify a specific denomination. He was homeschooled for the entirety of his schooling, all the way through high school graduation. Although this is not uncommon for religiously conservative families, this experience likely helped foster a closer relationship with his mother (who served as his teacher) while also giving him ample opportunity at home to observe the struggles of his parents.

Clayton showed a background that might have pushed him in a few different directions. On the one hand, his religious background would suggest someone who would be excited and energetic about marriage and would likely prioritize it. On the other hand, his parental and family background were indicative of someone who might very well have many hesitations and concerns about the institution of marriage. It was clear that his parents' marriage weighed on his mind, and many emerging adults in a similar situation would become disillusioned by the prospect of marriage. Yet here he was, as we interviewed him, married for a little less than a year in his early 20s to a woman he had dated for 2 years before marriage. Clearly, his parental example had not kept him from making an early marital transition. What did make a difference? In this case, it appeared that religion had won out over family background.

Clayton's religious values came through early in the interview, and they clearly were the driving factor in how he viewed relationships and marriage. He mentioned that marriage was "something that God created to make us better people." It appeared as though Clayton had used his religious interpretation of marriage to buffer the negative influence of his parents. But there was also another important element to how Clayton spoke of marriage. Clayton was one of the emerging adults we spoke to who clearly felt that marriage was a needed and important part of society, placing a special importance on marriage that went beyond his religious upbringing. To Clayton, marriage was a unique type of relationship that changed people and made the relationship fundamentally different from any other relationship. He explained his belief in this way: "I believe that the longer that you are married to the same person, both people grow more than you would if you weren't married." To him, marriage is a transformative institution, one that changes you the longer you engage in it. Perhaps this was another reason that

Clayton made an earlier transition to marriage—he wanted to give himself as much time as possible in a situation that granted this relational change. He noted at another point, "I always believed what Martin Luther said, that a man who gets married young is always wiser." Again, this suggests that he felt that early marriage was not just possible, but important—a better and more enlightened path. Although he never said so explicitly, to Clayton, being married younger made him better than others, at least relationally.

Clayton recognized that his own relational decisions and views put him out of step with his peers. He mentioned that he was the first one of his peers to get married. However, this was not a negative for him; he saw this as a strength. He was leading the way into an institution that everyone needed to participate in. He also strongly connected marriage to sacrifice, another difference between himself and many of his peers. In fact, Clayton explicitly mentioned this difference in the interview. He noted the same individualism within his peer group that we have also noted across several chapters. In Clayton's mind, this individualism was simply one thing: selfish. He noted,

> I think my generation in particular has become very selfish in many ways. I think one of the aspects of marriage is that you have to be more selfless than you would be if you were single. So I think it's very important that we still get married because I think we'll become more selfish if we don't.

To Clayton, this represented another transformative element of marriage. He viewed the individualism around him as problematic, a problem that at least might partially be solved by entering into a relationship he described as "selfless." Clayton saw marriage as a relationship of sacrifice and giving.

Although Clayton's approach to marriage was certainly unique, what about his life trajectory in other areas? What of educational or career success? Although Clayton may well be entering into a relationship he certainly believed would benefit him, most emerging adults would see his transition as a hindrance to success. Yet Clayton, at least on the surface, seemed to be on track to have a successful career. He was adamant that marriage would not be allowed to derail his education. As he put it, "I don't think we would have gotten married if it would have stopped me from graduating." Finishing his undergraduate degree with an internship when we spoke, he was heading to dental school the next year and seemed determined to succeed. Of course, it would be important to point out that he did not speak of his wife's educational or career plans. As some scholars have noted (Hymowitz et al., 2013), early-married couples sometimes prioritize only one partner's education and career, settling into a much more traditional gender role pattern that may alleviate many of the concerns emerging adults have about blending lives by focusing couple resources on only one person. Based on Clayton's religious background and his own comments in the interview, it is likely that his wife had either already truncated her own career plans or would in the near future.

Related to this, however, he did phrase his discussion of his educational plans in a very interesting way. Here is how he explained his decision to go to dental school during the interview:

> Actually yesterday, we just decided we were going to graduate school. This will be best for both of us and for our future children that don't exist yet.

Notice something interesting about his language. Again, he never mentioned his wife's education or career plans; if anything there was an implicit assumption in his interview that she would stay home with an eventual family. Yet he did not discuss *himself* going to dental school. He said *we* are going to dental school. Throughout the interview, Clayton talked jointly about what on the surface were individual decisions, exhibiting a uniquely collectivist attitude toward life that ran counter to how so many other emerging adults viewed marriage. He further went on to explain how he viewed marriage as a team endeavor, explaining,

> [How] I've come to think of it now at this point in my life is it's more that the marriage is a team and that's what the Bible is trying to communicate. So whatever has to be done, should be done no matter who has to do it.

As Clayton thought of the future and spoke of his career and subsequent balance with family life, he, like so many emerging adults, felt he had to choose and prioritize. However, unlike many middle-class emerging adults that, by graduation, had begun to value careers over marriage (see chapter 5), Clayton explained his priorities this way, "In terms of importance, at least to me, that's the hierarchy: Your marriage is important, your kids are less important, and then your job and your career are less important than that." He even went on to give an example, embedded in his current school culture, noting that "if my wife needs me to do something and I would rather work on this essay that I'm writing, I'd go do what she needs first." Clayton had clear career goals and seemed on track to meet them. However, he was also clear that if push came to shove, marriage (and children) would come first.

Clayton's experience and story provide an interesting and clear example of the differences between this early-married group and the majority of emerging adults we spoke to and surveyed. Clayton's religious mindset when it came to marriage trumped his conflictual family background and pushed marriage to the forefront. He viewed marriage as value added in his life, not as something that would hinder his success. He viewed marriage in terms of a collective endeavor for future success instead of worrying about how his personal goals were consistent or conflicting with his wife's goals. These themes set the stage for many of the other stories we heard from married emerging adults.

▲ Eliza

Let's move on from Clayton to Eliza. Close to Clayton in age at 21, she was also a student when we interviewed her. In Eliza's case, she was a junior working toward a degree in environmental studies. When we spoke with Eliza, she had been married for about 1 year after dating her now-husband for several years. She explained in the interview that her relationship with her current spouse was her first real relationship of any kind. Eliza's family background was different from Clayton's in many respects. Unlike Clayton, Eliza was one of our emerging adults who had glowing praises for her parents and described her parents' marriage as a wonderful example of a healthy relationship. Her parents had been married for 25 years, and Eliza characterized these years as happy and fulfilling. She described the influence of her parents' marriage on her marital beliefs: "I think definitely seeing their relationship has been a bar I've set for myself regarding marriage, just the fact that it is so strong for them. It's a source of encouragement for me, and it's a source of inspiration." Eliza also came from a rather wealthy, upper-middle class background. Eliza noted that both of her parents had successful careers and reported her family's total yearly income around $200,000. She also came from a large family, being the oldest of seven siblings. One thing

Eliza did have in common with Clayton was religion. Like Clayton, she grew up in a religious home, in her case Lutheran.

All of these factors certainly could contribute to Eliza making a decision to transition to marriage early. She came from a religious home with married parents who seemed happy and fulfilled. Yet Eliza's story took an interesting turn around adolescence, when she reported that her views on marriage shifted dramatically from her parents'. She explained,

> When I was a young teenager I had just started getting super into feminism and was reading all these books and was like, "I'm never going to get married because I'm going to be my own person and no man is ever going to have any say over what I do."

Eliza's foray into feminist thought made the patriarchal notion of marriage, likely an image she was getting from her religious culture, unappealing. Although she eventually did believe in the importance of marriage and again expected to marry, Eliza's experiences started her down a path that led her to conceptualize marriage in a way that one might not expect for someone so young and married. Interestingly, whereas Clayton's view of marriage was rather unique and at odds with many of the themes we have mentioned previously, Eliza's views and thoughts were in many cases quite similar to the majority of her peers.

First, it was clear that, unlike Clayton who believed marrying early was beneficial, Eliza had no set belief about an ideal marital timing. Instead, she put it this way:

> I've had cousins get married in their early 20s, I've had cousins get married in their 30s, so I don't think I really had any preconceived notions about what the right age to get married was. I think it's more if you feel like you're in a good point in your life to be able to do it; if all the other factors in your life are taken care of and in a good place.

Marriage came when you had achieved life goals and you were ready to "settle down," a very common sentiment among emerging adults, as we have discussed. She went on to say that marriage was important

> because marriage is such a significant commitment and something you really need to work on. You need to make sure that other parts

of your life are stable enough so that you can devote that time and attention to a marriage.

Eliza's thoughts are right in line with the views held by many other emerging adults her age. Life needed to be, as she put it, stable before marriage occurred. Of course, as we have noted, many emerging adults do not achieve this stability until much later in life, if ever.

Eliza also believed, like many emerging adults, that marriage was about lifelong commitment. She noted that,

> I definitely believe that it's [marriage] a commitment that should be made for life. I feel like a lot of people have the viewpoint, "Oh, we'll try it out for the benefits, and see if it works out, and if it doesn't, whatever, divorce is easy."

Eliza took issue with the belief that divorce should afford couples an easy way out of a bad relationship. She further explained that,

> I believe that it [marriage] has a place both as a religious covenant, but then also has a place as a secular institution. I basically think the main feature of [marriage] is that it is two people who are committing to each other, to love each other and to support each other for their whole lives.

For Eliza, marriage was a lifelong commitment that was serious and important, so serious that individuals should have the other elements of their lives figured out before considering it. Again, many of these views put Eliza right in line with her peers. Marriage mattered, but only in the right context. Marriage was a symbol of commitment, and divorce should be avoided. There was a time and a season for marriage that had little to do with age and more to do with circumstance and context.

So what made Eliza make such an early marital transition, despite this apparent reservation and more hesitant stance on relationships? It may have been that Eliza essentially won the dating partner lottery and triggered the "right time" mentality that evaded many of her peers in their early 20s. She explained that when she met her current husband, his belief and value system completely converged with her own. As she described her husband, it became clear that he believed in the same version of marriage that she did. For Eliza, much of this hearkened back to her feminist past. Her new husband viewed gender roles in a relationship the same way she did, and Eliza felt they were able to create a compatible and egalitarian relationship. As she put it,

> Both of us do believe that regardless that I'm a woman and he's a man, we're still both humans. I think we both have strong career aspirations and then eventually, once that's established, we might try to have a kid or two. If that does become the case, we would both want to be equally involved in that child's life and upbringing.

That being said, like many emerging adults, Eliza continued to struggle with the idea of balancing career, education, and relationship. She actively worried about how they would navigate their future career decisions. She said,

> especially being in college, we're [her and her husband] both at a stage where a lot of opportunities are coming up. You know, travel and jobs and what life after graduation is going to look like, and sometimes it's a challenge to figure out. And the fact that we are this single entity.

Eliza was still worried about what the future would hold and recognized that challenges faced her young marriage in the near future.

So on the one hand, Eliza had found someone who "got her." Someone who believed in the same version of marriage as she did. Of course, there must have still been some catalyst that pushed her into an early marriage. There are many emerging adults who likely would have simply dated each other for a few more years, maybe even have maintained a longer engagement. This would have given them time to navigate future career decisions without the added burden and commitment of a marriage. So why marry? When we asked Eliza this very question, she said,

> I feel like we were already committed to the idea of marriage long before actually discussing having it officially happen. So I think that prepared us for it in a way, maybe earlier then it would for some other people. Aside from the main fact that we just really wanted to and loved each other and felt we were emotionally, spiritually, [and] mentally ready for it.

Although she never mentioned it explicitly, her use of the word "ready" as she gave this answer makes us wonder if the magical buzzword of *maturity* may have had something to do with Eliza's decision. The quote above seems to imply that for Eliza, she and her husband had achieved this mythical milestone of maturity and so, as she put it, "I feel like it [marriage] just made sense."

One other factor appeared to weigh on Eliza's decision. As noted, she recognized the tedious trajectory many emerging adults have in terms of career. Despite her stated belief in having things be stable before marriage, she appeared to have concluded that waiting for a solid career foundation might be a pointless goal. She explained,

> I know that a lot of people in my age group feel like they need
> to have a really strongly established career before even thinking
> about marriage. Obviously, I'm a 21-year-old college student,
> so I don't have a strongly established career. I have career goals
> definitely. I know that I want to go to grad school. I guess for me
> careers are this tenuous thing, especially with the economy the
> way it is. People might not have these strong established careers;
> that might not happen until people are well into their 30s or
> 40s, and I don't know about postponing something that I feel is
> important as marriage is. I don't know that that postponement is
> worth it.

It is in this last point that Eliza's and Clayton's story dovetail: how they viewed the importance of marriage. When we asked Eliza about ranking her goals in life, she replied,

> I think maintaining my marriage is definitely my top goal. Like
> I said, it's a commitment that I believe is for life, and it's also a
> commitment that I believe takes work. I would say it's my top
> goal because I think if I can maintain that relationship with my
> husband, whatever else happens I can roll with it. And I know that
> that's one thing that I don't want to suffer.

Although perhaps more subtle than Clayton, Eliza suggested a life priority list that clearly puts marriage on the top. Although, as she noted, she had career goals and plans, she appeared willing to put those aside as long as her marriage was there, providing a firm foundation. In this,

Eliza recognized her views meant that she might need to let go of certain opportunities in other areas of her life. She went on to say,

> In general, the fact that relationships are a priority to me over success influences how I go about my daily life. My marriage and my relationship are extremely important, and I want decisions I make to support that, whereas, with other aspects of my life, I'm a little more easygoing and accepting.

For Eliza, marriage was at the forefront of how she conceptualized a successful life, and she had made decisions accordingly.

▲ Susan

Our next story comes from Susan. Susan was a 21-year-old student, like Eliza. In fact, Eliza and Susan had many things in common. Susan also came from a stable family with a fair amount of resources. Susan's parents were still married and provided Susan with a generally positive example of marriage. Although this message was positive and supportive, Susan's parents also gave her another very explicit message about marriage. As Susan put it, "I've always been encouraged to get married, but to put it off until after I've gotten my degree." Her parents were very clear that they wanted her to wait until *after* college to marry. Susan related that this message was a consistent one during her childhood and adolescent years. Marriage was important, marriage was expected, but do *not* get married too soon.

Susan was also one of the most religious emerging adults we spoke to and had a unique religious background that influenced her marital trajectory. Susan grew up in a religious home (Pentecostal) but had recently converted to the Church of Jesus Christ of Latter-day Saints (LDS, Mormon) during college. After this conversion, Susan transferred from a public Midwestern school to a religiously affiliated university in the Mountain West. It was here that Susan married her high school sweetheart (also a member of the LDS church), after they dated for all 4 years of high school. They had been married for just 4 months when we spoke to her. Her marital and religious life also intersected in another important way: her now-husband had been the major reason for her religious conversion. Because her husband was a lifelong member of the LDS church, it was Susan's initial relationship with her future husband in high school that led her to explore the beliefs of her current religion. Susan's decision to marry while in school was, of course, at odds with her parents' wishes, and Susan described a certain amount of tension that existed between herself and her parents when she decided to marry. She noted,

When I decided to get married, I mean I'm 21, my mom was definitely a little bit upset that I wasn't waiting until after I had graduated. And since my husband had just gotten home from his [church] mission when we got married, he hadn't started any school, and so my mom was a little bit upset that we weren't waiting. My husband and I, Justin, we both had this idea of "why wait?"

Susan's parents, especially her mom, held a similar fear as many emerging adults, that marriage would derail Susan's life by interfering with her education. Clearly, however, Susan did not feel the same way. As noted in her own words, Susan felt like there was little reason to wait or delay marriage, despite her parents' consistent encouragement to wait until after college. For Susan, her decision to marry early came as a direct disregard of her parents' advice. She also explained later in the interview that she faced opposition from her friends and peers, suggesting she had very little social support for her decision.

Why did she do it, then? In many ways, Susan's views of marriage were in line with Clayton's and provided some insight into her decision. She viewed marriage as a sacrificial relationship, one aimed at pleasing her spouse and God—not outsiders. Her views were heavily influenced by her religious faith, putting marriage and family life on a higher plane than other endeavors in her life. For Susan, she was guided by her new religion into a belief that marriage was a relationship that was destined to persist long after death, an eternal union between herself and her husband. As she put it, marriage was about "eternal progression together." Later on, she again brought up this eternal perspective when talking about the importance of an eventual family. She felt marriage gave others, especially children, a unique relational example of love not found in other places. She explained,

I want to give my kids that opportunity to grow up in a home where they're loved, where they can get that love and then they can grow eternally from that perspective and they don't have to look for it somewhere else because they're not getting it. Everybody needs that love and they can only really get that from a family.

Even later in the interview she simply put it this way, "I feel like my marriage is a lot more meaningful now that I know that I get to be with my husband not only in this life, but in the next." Emboldened by her religious interpretation of love and marriage, Susan believed she was entering into something sacred and eternal. In her mind, there was very little reason to wait to deny herself this type of special relationship.

It appears that for Susan, much of her decision to marry was tied to a specific religious conversion that shifted her view of marriage and perhaps placed more priority on it than she had previously done. Like the preceding stories, Susan also appeared to place many more sacrificial and collective ideals on marriage. As she described it, "I found happiness in making somebody else happy rather than myself." She directly contrasted this belief in selfless marriage with her peers, who she viewed as more selfish and individualist, much like Clayton. She explained that, "A lot of my peers have the idea that you should fulfill your own happiness before you should fulfill somebody else's." As noted in the previous examples, a theme of almost explicit disgust for the individualist tendencies of many other emerging adults seemed to be common among these early-married young adults.

What of Susan's eventual career and educational success that her parents were so concerned with? Despite being close to finishing her undergraduate degree, Susan seemed to suggest that her long-term plans would be in the home, perhaps legitimizing her mother's concern. Susan appeared to hold very traditional gender role beliefs, at one point noting, "If it ever needs be that I need to work, then I work, but it should be a first priority to have a family." Susan hoped for a very traditional arrangement with her husband, one where she would stay at home with the children and he would be the sole provider. She further went on to talk about how her religious conversion, combined with her marriage, made her re-evaluate her life goals and trajectory that brought her to her current views. She said,

I think before I was married, I really valued getting my degree and making it through college. Now I realize it's important to get my degree, but my marriage is the first priority in my life and if my husband is sick or something, then taking care of him takes priority over getting my homework done on time.

There are two important elements to this statement. First, again there is an element of prioritization that is common among the examples we have already explored. Marriage comes first, even at the sacrifice of school, work, or other roles. Second, Susan had appeared in our interview to relegate her own education to a lower tier compared with her husband's schooling. It was still important for her to get her degree, but more because of an abstract notion that "education is important," rather than any long-term life plan. Her degree was seen by her as a backup plan or perhaps as something to just say she had accomplished and finished in her life. For Susan, her religious faith and shifting ideals of marriage had led her to crave and hope for a version of marriage that was in many ways regarded as outdated by many of her peers.

▲ Timothy

Our next example comes from Timothy, a 23-year-old who shared many of the same characteristics as the previous emerging adults we have described. Timothy had recently graduated with a degree in creative writing and was currently working for a Christian organization stationed at a major Midwestern university. This was a temporary job, and Timothy was beginning to look for other job opportunities for the future. Unlike Clayton from our first example, an emerging adult who had a very clear career trajectory, Timothy seemed to be floating through his 20s. He did not seem to have a firm plan in place for where he would be working or even living in a year from now. He had no long-term ambitions that he shared related to his writing degree. This also did not seem to concern Timothy; he seemed confident that something would come around and that he and his wife would figure things out.

Timothy did have one thing in common with Clayton: a less-than-ideal family background. Whereas Clayton's parents stayed together in a conflictual marriage, Timothy came from a home where his parents had divorced. Like many emerging adults in such situations, his parents' divorce left its mark and greatly influenced how Timothy approached marriage. Rather than devaluing marriage or dismissing it, his parents' divorce made Timothy fearful of not just marriage but relationships in general—fearful that he would make the same mistakes as his parents and that he would simply be a bad relational partner because of what his parents had taught him. He worried about ever being able to maintain a healthy relationship. He explained,

> I was really scared of marriage, just scared of my own personal capacity to just do what my dad did, which was just leave. I mean, my mom went into it kind of selfishly—I think they both agree that's what happened.

He saw this parental example as one that involved settling for a less-than-ideal partner, bad interpersonal skills, and, eventually, abandonment.

Yet here he was, talking to us after recently marrying his wife, whom he had been dating for the past 2 years. This had been his first real relationship, and their courtship had happened quickly, even compared with the group of married emerging adults we spoke to. As seen in the previous example with Susan, a catalyst was still needed to shift his views on marriage away from the fearful version of marriage he described. In Timothy's case, that came in the form of a religious conversion, similar to Susan. Timothy was religious and identified as Christian when we spoke to him. In Timothy's case, his conversion began based on interactions with a friend who introduced him to Christianity during college, something he did not have a strong affiliation with growing up. This friend, Bill, was older and married with children, and became a critical mentor in Timothy's life. Timothy viewed this period not only as a time when he came to God but also as a conversion to a new way of viewing marriage. Timothy saw this new view of marriage as a way to escape from the negative example of his parents. He explained this process:

> So that [his conversion to Christianity] changed my life in general, but it also changed the way that I view marriage because of the way that Bill and Julie loved one another, loved their children, loved me. As a family they loved me, even their kids, so much, and it brought me in and welcomed me. What it did was open my eyes to what marriage *can* be and that I'm not enslaved to follow the pattern of my family.

This shift lifted a huge burden from Timothy's shoulders. He felt capable and ready to engage in a relationship. It was shortly after this experience that he began to date his eventual wife.

This experience also led Timothy to develop a very religious view of marriage. As he said within the first 5 minutes of our interview, he "derives all his thinking about marriage from the Bible." A nondenominational Christian, Timothy relied heavily on holy writings to shape how he viewed marriage as a symbolic relationship that was akin to the relationship Jesus Christ had with His church. As Timothy further explained, "That's the background and the reason why that's [marriage] important, because God has created marriage as a picture of that— where Jesus is the groom and the church, the people that have trusted in Christ is the bride."

Interestingly, and similar to our other examples, Timothy viewed marriage as a relationship that changed people for the better. However, Timothy did not feel that all people should get married. Quite the opposite; he seemed to believe that marriage should be reserved only for those who understood its true purpose. He thought declining marriage rates might actually be good, preserving marriage only for those who deserved it. As he put it, "I guess that's [lower marriage rates] good in a sense that [it's] probably better that people don't get married rather than getting married thinking that it's going to just benefit them and then later get divorced." Timothy believed that too many people entered marriage for the wrong reasons and that marriage, as an institution, was better off without these people. Later he went on to say that marriage was no longer needed for much the same reason:

I don't think that it's [marriage] needed. It's not a necessity, but it's a good thing. I think that everyone in our American culture is just like, "Oh, I want to get married, I want to get married." Everyone desires that, but I think that for some people it's [good] not to get married.

Instead, Timothy believed some people married because they were supposed to, or felt obligated. This diminished the sacred nature of marriage in Timothy's mind.

Clearly, a big part of Timothy's decision to marry was tied to his newfound faith and his "discovery" of the true meaning of marriage in his mind. Religious conversion, however, did not appear to be the only reason for Timothy's early transition. Although his views about marriage in general had changed, that alone did not explain why he decided to marry. Like some of our other examples, the question became: Why did Timothy make the specific decision to marry now, not later? Like Eliza, the key for Timothy appeared to be maturity, the word that seems to be at the heart of so many emerging adults' views of marriage. When asked about an ideal age of marriage, Timothy did not believe there was an ideal age, instead noting,

> I think the ideal age to get married is when you're mature enough to get married. I think that in the past that has looked a lot younger than now. I think in America, in the situations that I've grown up in, I think people just don't mature. I don't think that parents discipline their kids very well nowadays; people grow up selfish, so people mature less.

Here we have some ideas that should be familiar after the previous examples already summarized. Marriage happened when you were mature, and Timothy perceived most emerging adults around him as immature and selfish.

When we asked him specifically why he decided to marry young, he again referenced maturity, saying,

> I feel like I was mature enough to get married. I don't mean that I have all my shit together, I just mean that I'm to a point where I can say, "Hey, I understand that marriage is not about myself and we're going to grow together and learn together, but I want to move forward with you."

Timothy offered one of the most explicit definitions of maturity in our sample. To him, the maturity needed for marriage was about selflessness. It was about sacrifice for his partner. Timothy viewed himself as having achieved this milestone of maturity. To him, this is what opened the door to make what he felt was an appropriate transition to marriage. As Timothy spoke of his future, he echoed many of the thoughts portrayed by our previous examples. Marriage came first, above all else. He explained,

> I've got some goals and that'd be cool if those were attained, but at the expense of my marriage, at the expense of our future family? My view of success in a career is pretty low compared to what I feel like everyone else around me has.

Timothy viewed his life's journey as centered on his wife and their relationship. He went on to give an example of how he was considering a potential job opportunity with his wife. He related,

> We're moving on to another job, and we've been talking about it together and praying together, and the biggest thing as I think about moving on to another job is the welfare of my family—like me and my wife—and how is this going to affect her. She is in the back of my mind as I'm making every decision about what I am going to do and where we're going to move. She is in the back of my mind with every decision I make.

Whereas many emerging adults dread this type of interconnectivity with another, Timothy appeared to relish it.

▲ Avery

Our final example comes from Avery. Avery was 22 and preparing to move to Germany to be stationed with her new husband who was serving in the United States Army. She was doing everything she could to finish her degree before her big move. So strong was this desire, Avery was currently living in the Midwest, thousands of miles away from her husband who was living in the Southern states, so she could finish her degree before she moved overseas. Her career was obviously important to Avery. As she explained,

> I don't even live in the same state as my husband right now, he lives in Virginia and I live in Minnesota because I'm finishing up school, and I think that that shows a lot. I need to get my career on track and finish school before I can move on to the next step.

Avery came from a stable family background in which her parents were married and showed her a healthy marital example. They taught her, "If it's broken, fix it, don't throw it away," and they "always worked to make things better and to get back to where they needed to be." In fact, Avery reported that there was no history of divorce across her entire family, going back generations. Connected to her clear desire to finish school, she desired an egalitarian marriage in which both partners were treated equally. This was another value she had picked up from her parents. She explained,

> I think that's important in my marriage that I'm not going to stay home every day, cook and clean and take care of the kids. I would love to do that if we're financially secure enough, but I think that it's a partnership and my husband better be ready to cook, clean, and take care of kids too because it's not just going to be my job. I saw that through my parents, so that's how I want my marriage to be.

Avery was unique among this group of emerging adults we are highlighting because she was clearly the least religious among them and seemed to be more a victim of circumstance than a true enthusiast when it came to marriage. Although she identified as Christian, she was also clear that she did not belong to any particular denomination and disagreed with many elements of the Bible. Her spiritual journey was similar to that of the normative emerging adult in many ways. She grew up with some religious teachings in the home but was quickly abandoning them with the freedom she had during her 20s. Unlike for many of the previous examples, religion did not appear to be a large contributor to how Avery viewed marriage. Instead, her view was very much centered on her choice of partner.

One thing that was clear with Avery was her strong belief in soul mates and love at first sight. She mentioned during the interview, "I think when you know, you just know it's the person you're supposed to be with. That's how I feel, and you make the decision on your own, if you're ready to be married." This idea was directly applied to how she approached her relationship with her partner. After being notified of her boyfriend's deployment to Europe, they were faced with a difficult decision. Here is how her story unfolded, in her own words:

> Seriously, from the day my boyfriend asked me to be his girlfriend, I knew I was going to marry him. There was just something about him, and I knew it. So I always knew that we would get married, but I had always said, "Why do people get married when they're still in college?" It doesn't make sense to me. Why can't you graduate, finish, and then get married? And then my husband found out that he was getting stationed in Germany, and it was, "We get married now and you come with me, or we don't get

married and you stay in Indiana for the year that I'm in Germany."
So truly, honestly, the reason that we got married December 30th
was the army. We would have gotten married, I am very confident
that we would have gotten married, but we definitely sped things
up probably by six months to a year. In order for me to live there
[in Europe], I have to be on his military order, so I have to be his
spouse to go. I was very upset about Germany.

Avery presents an interesting case that is unique compared with the
previous examples. Avery's decision to marry early was based on
a unique situation, and she freely admitted that she would probably
have waited to marry if not for her husband's deployment. However,
before we write off this example to circumstance, we should remember
that she did have the option of waiting until he returned. She did still
decide to move forward with a marriage rather than wait. When we dug
deeper into Avery's beliefs, we uncovered another series of views about
marriage, some that appeared closer to the previous examples than
was apparent when we began to talk to her. Like her peers discussed
elsewhere in this chapter, Avery appeared to believe that marriage was
unique and different from other types of relationships. She believed that
marriage was a distinctive status and had a deeper symbolic quality to
it than simply dating or engagement. She noted at one point,

> I think that there's something different when you're married to
> someone; I think everything changes. And the way that you think
> about life in general changes. It's not something you can explain to
> someone who isn't married, or has never been married.

Notice that despite her clear desire to finish school and have her own
independent career, she was willing to put all of that on hold for at least
a year while she was traveling overseas with her husband.

When pressed about how marriage was different from other relationships, she sang a familiar tune, talking about the sacrifice and other-
centeredness needed in a marriage that made it special. She said,

> I think when you're single you only really have to worry about
> yourself, and you think for yourself and you make decisions for
> yourself. When I was single, I was much more impulsive, and
> I didn't think about my decisions. But when you're married you
> do have to think about it, and you ask someone else's opinion. You

should ask your spouse's opinion on things. It makes you think
about the decisions you're going to make, and I believe it helps
you make better choices.

Notice that Avery, recognizing that being married forced spouses to consider the needs and wants of another person, also felt that this helped them make "better" choices. Despite being more reluctant to marry than those discussed in the other examples, it seems clear that Avery thought marriage helped people grow and become better people, more than simply staying in a nonmarital relationship.

▲ Why Marry Young?

So what is there to learn from these examples? What does this small minority of emerging adults have to tell us about emerging adults who are still making early transitions to marriage? Are there any lessons here about the larger marriage paradox of emerging adulthood? One thing to be clear about is that we do not know how any of these stories end. We cannot cheat and look at the end of the book to see if these emerging adults have their happily-ever-after lives. Most of these emerging adults were newlyweds, and, likely, it would be several more years down the road before anyone could accurately evaluate whether their early marital decisions were helping them flourish or flounder in life. In all likelihood, some of these marriages will fail. Yet as was mentioned at the beginning of the chapter, the very nature of their decision to marry is interesting and enriches our understanding of emerging adults' views on marriage, regardless of the outcome. Although each story is unique, some themes appeared that suggest some specialized ways of approaching marriage for this small subset of emerging adults.

One obvious theme that is not too surprising is religion. Most of our emerging adults who had already married either came from strong religious backgrounds or had unique religious conversion experiences during their early years of emerging adulthood. Unsurprisingly, these highly religious emerging adults had a unique way of looking at marriage. Many mainstream religious faiths view marriage as a sacred institution of importance within human civilization. For these emerging adults, there was an element of marital sanctification (DeMaris, Mahoney, & Pargament, 2010; Mahoney, Pargament, Murray-Swank, & Murray-Swank, 2003), whereby they were placing divine significance on marital roles and marriage itself. Holding these strong religious views appears to allow some of these emerging adults to disregard larger cultural norms in favor of what they may deem a higher path toward marriage. For emerging adults like Clayton and Susan, religious values have likely placed them at odds with many normative emerging adult behaviors. Whether it be premarital sexual behavior, the use of alcohol, or views on gender, these emerging adults have likely already encountered many decisions in their young life with which they have been forced to go against the grain of their peers. Perhaps then, marriage is simply one more way in which they have separated themselves from the mainstream, one more way in which they have actively decided to disregard what they may perceive as the secular approach to marriage.

Yet it would be shortsighted to chalk these experiences up only to religious differences. Avery provides the clearest case of this exception. There appeared to be something deeper going on with these emerging adults as well—something that spoke more to how they viewed the marital relationship in a fundamental way beyond just sanctifying it within their religious tradition. All of these emerging adults appeared to believe that marriage changed both the nature of the individuals who entered into it and the nature of the relationship itself. In contrast to many emerging adults who viewed marriage as a symbolic transition of lifelong commitment at best and a piece of paper at worst, these emerging adults believed, without exception, that marriage changed people. Marriage was not just a symbol of something about the couple, entering into the marital vow changed the nature of the relationship and, by extension, both partners. These emerging adults appeared to believe that marriage made them, for lack of a less narcissistic term, better than other couples around them who were not married. It made their relationship stronger, and it made them more caring and altruistic individuals. Marriage was not something that simply came when the relationship was ready; for many of these emerging adults, marriage became a transformative process (Fincham, Stanley, & Beach, 2007). Perhaps this gives us insight into why they made this transition in the first place. They craved this transformation. They wanted to take the next step in their relational journey. Marriage was not something that was going to hold them back or hinder their lives; it was something that was going to enrich their lives.

Related to this point, there was also a strong collectivist mentality among these emerging adults. Whereas many emerging adults generally struggle with the dualistic nature of marriage and the "baggage" of dealing with another person's life trajectory, these emerging adults seemed to embrace it. Willing to sacrifice their own life trajectory for the good of the marriage, they stood in sharp contrast to the many emerging adults who have grasped a more individualistic approach to life and love. The emerging adults discussed in this chapter were willing to sacrifice their own happiness and personal success for the sake of their relationships.

These themes make these emerging adults different and offer some insight into a small group (and one that will likely continue to shrink) that seems to have solved the marital paradox by embracing a view of the transformational power of marriage. This certainly does not mean that all emerging adults should hold these views or that we are advocating toward this religious and collective view of marriage. There is a perfectly reasonable argument against this mentality that suggests such emerging adults are developing a degree of dependency early in life through marriage that may result in heartache if such relationships do not last. There are legitimate concerns about career trajectory and financial well-being for these couples. Again, until long-term longitudinal data exist on such emerging adults, it is unclear whether this approach does have any long-term benefits. However, in our exploration of the modern approach to marriage among emerging adults, the early-married emerging adults represent an important and sometimes forgotten voice as their numbers dwindle and their perspectives are drowned out by the growing roar of the masses.

11 ▲

Looking Ahead
The Future of the Marriage Paradox

It's now time to step back and ask the most important question of all: So what? What does this all mean? What are the implications of this discussion for emerging adults? For marriage generally? We have reviewed dozens of stories from emerging adults in the thick of making decisions about love and life. We have explored what national trends suggest about the relational lives of emerging adults and what other scholarly sources have to tell us that might shed light on exactly why the marriage paradox exists and how it has emerged. We have reserved a few final pages to both summarize this information and make a few suggestions and comments addressing the previous questions. Because for us, these themes and patterns *do* matter, not only for those interested in studying the trends related to marriage across the last few generations, but also in some ways for the sake of the emerging adults themselves—emerging adults who seem increasingly perplexed and frustrated with how marriage and relationships are playing out in their lives. Although the stories of the emerging adults we have shared were predominantly from white and middle-class emerging adults living in the heart of the United States, such stories represent a large portion of the emerging adult generation currently navigating their 20s. The national trends in the United States we have documented suggest that many of the marriage paradoxes and other issues discussed in previous chapters, though certainly nuanced based on socioeconomic status, cut across many demographic factors.

▲ So What Is the Marriage Paradox?

We begin this final discussion with a perplexing concept at the heart of the marriage paradox that hearkens back to our Introduction. Emerging adults seem consistent, at least across the past 50 years, in their belief that marriage is an important and expected transition for them in their lives. Yet these same 50 years have also seen dramatic shifts in marital behavior and transitions. Clearly, something about how emerging adults approach marriage is creating this paradox between ambition and behavior, whereby emerging adults appear to still value marriage yet seemingly make decisions that deprioritize it. As we mentioned back at the beginning of this book, the reason for this paradox is, on the surface, straightforward. Emerging adults' values and beliefs about marriage have become much more nuanced and varied compared with previous generations. Across our exploration of these intricacies and the origins of these beliefs, a few conclusions can now be drawn that help explain the marriage paradox in more detail and provide some insight into why it may be occurring.

Marriage as an Important yet Unattainable Goal

Perhaps nothing better helps us understand the marriage paradox than to note that for modern emerging adults, a healthy and stable marriage has become a type of Holy Grail in their minds—something that they all aspire to find and establish yet that somehow remains elusive. On the surface, most emerging adults feel as though marriage is an integral part of modern society. Yet their beliefs and comments about marital timing suggest that marriage is not something most plan for in their *immediate* future. Marriage's importance is a future-oriented concept for emerging adults. Put another way, it may be more accurate to say that marriage *will be* important to emerging adults at some point in the future rather than it *is now* important to for them to marry. The 20s, especially the early 20s, is about other things. Often it is about getting relational experience, finishing education, or establishing a career and employment history. On the surface, it is tempting, then, to say that emerging adults really do not care about marriage, that perhaps their insistence on marrying is tied to the remnants of a culture embedded in the marital institution. Yet our data seem to indicate otherwise. Even though marriage has certainly shifted in the minds of emerging adults, it still holds a strong position of importance and occupies a good portion of their thinking when it comes to life planning.

The idea that marriage *will be* important is connected to another theme related to understanding the marriage paradox. As we mentioned back in chapter 5, marriage may have become too mythical in the minds of many emerging adults. Marriage's status in the minds of many emerging adults has taken the form of a gold medal at the end of their turbulent journey to adulthood, the potential relational prize if they reach the finish line.

Here, also, is another shift in how emerging adults are now conceptualizing marriage. Although many reported that they understand marriage will take work and effort (something many learned from their parents), many seemed to be hoping for the easiest route to marital bliss. These largely middle-class emerging adults understood that a good career requires years of education and effort. They seemed to understand that, like a career, achieving a strong personal identity would also take many years of exploration and soul searching. Yet they seemed to believe that a good marriage would be presented to them when they deemed themselves ready. Perhaps perplexingly, there seemed to be little sense that these emerging adults viewed their current dating lives as building toward something greater. Marital relationships would be more stable, more committed, and more romantic than their current relationships. Indeed, most believed in soul mates, most believed that relationships should destress their lives, and many suggested that an eventual marriage would provide a respite from the anxieties of educational and career pressures. This places a lot of pressure on marriage and potential marital partners.

Taking a step away from marriage specifically, emerging adults appear to be struggling with their long-term prospects in life, and marriage may be becoming an unfortunate casualty. Many scholars have argued and struggled over whether emerging adults are flourishing or floundering in their 20s (Arnett, Kloep, Hendry, & Tanner, 2010; Nelson & Padilla-Walker, 2013). The arguments on both sides are compelling (and often based on which outcome one considers the most salient), but in the realm of relationships, many emerging adults seem burdened by the inconsistency of modern life in their 20s. Emerging adults live in a world where multiple moves in a year are normative, where career prospects are shaky at best, and where society places increasing pressure on emerging adults to explore and experiment on their own. Parents often promote delaying long-term commitments, pleading in some cases for them to enjoy the time they have (while also sending the implicit message that life will only go downhill after emerging adulthood). In this sea of uncertainty, emerging adults seem to be craving stability, something that can be constant in an increasingly variable world. They appear to want relationships and marriage to be this constant. This perhaps helps us understand their strong connection between marriage and lifelong commitment. More than anything else, it may be stability rather than companionate love that many emerging adults seek in their life through marriage—a marriage that provides lifelong commitment yet does not interfere with their personal goals and ambitions. It may also be one of the strongest explanations for the marriage paradox. Emerging adults want a type of marriage that may simply not exist for most, if not all, of them. They may be waiting for a shift in life that may never come. Eventually many will marry as they perhaps settle for the "real thing." Others may hold out hope as they wait for a mythical unicorn of a relationship, one that will give them the ultimate satisfaction they seek.

To perhaps put it another way, although marriage remains important across the generations, how and why it is important has likely changed. Today's emerging adults believe marriage is important, not because it provides some greater good to society, but because it can make them happy and fulfilled if certain criteria are met. They understand such happiness is not common. The messages they have received from parents, siblings, and the media have shown them plenty of bad examples. But in a world where emerging adults have been told that they are each special and unique, this fear about an eventual divorce or being stuck in an unhappy marriage only reinforces their resolve to be careful and calculated when they consider if and when to marry.

Marriage Is a Want, Not a Need

Building off this previous concept, such shifting views on the importance of marriage are likewise connected to the growing idea among emerging adults that marriage is no longer needed for society. There is a key and subtle distinction here. Most emerging adults do believe marriage is needed *for them*; they simply no longer believe it is needed *for everyone*. This idea seems to be the largest byproduct of the relativistic approach that many emerging adults now take through life. Despite the importance emerging adults continue to place on marriage, most no longer think they need to be married to have a happy and fulfilling life.

This relativism is creating many paradoxes during emerging adulthood. These paradoxes, likely not just about marriage and relationships but also about many areas of their life, are centered on a potential contradictory element to how emerging adults attempt to implement this relativism. As appears to be the case when it comes to marriage, emerging adults do not seem to be true relativists. Although they may aspire to a utopian mentality in which judgment and prejudice no longer exist and each individual is free to forge her or his own unique path through life, these sentiments appear to be only superficial. In reality, emerging adults do seem to judge others and have strong opinions about right and wrong when it comes to life choices like marriage. With marriage, we pointed out the hypocrisy of believing that there is no ideal age of marriage yet also believing that one can marry too early or too late. We noted the irony of many middle-class emerging adults insisting that marriage is not needed yet explaining how married parents are still the ideal setting for raising children. These are just two of many examples, but they speak to an important aspect of understanding how emerging adults view the need for marriage and the true nature of their relativistic approach to relationships. Much of the marriage paradox perhaps is centered on emerging adults caught in the internal turmoil created by trying to balance a morally relativistic view of marriage with a more absolute truth perspective where some paths are clearly better than others. Although some emerging adults certainly do believe that marriage is no longer needed at all, and others forgo much of this relativistic thinking, the previous paradox appears to exist for the majority of emerging adults.

Beyond this internal struggle, this disconnect from marriage as a personal but not societal requirement has, in practical terms, shifted marriage away from being a true need. Instead, marriage has become a desired transition, a want rather than a need. This shift also changes the nature of marriage in the lives of emerging adults. Wants are just that: wants—to be obtained if possible but discarded if not. If anything, this shift has changed the urgency in which emerging adults seek potential marital partners and is likely propelling some of our current marital trends. As noted in chapter 2, emerging adults are certainly still engaging in romantic relationships and sexual intimacy at rates that suggest relationships still very much matter. Yet marriage, for most, has moved to the periphery. The mid to late 20s has become the ideal age to marry as reported by emerging adults, yet perhaps this ideal is simply a placeholder to put marriage later. Most emerging adults reported that they did not believe in an ideal age to marry, instead putting all the power in each individual emerging adult. With that power, most emerging adults are choosing to push marriage to the back burner, hoping to retrieve it when they are more established or more mature.

On the one hand, there may be some value to delaying marriage until one is ready. Most emerging adults will, in fact, marry between 25 and 30 years of age. On the other hand, marriage rates continue to decline (Wang & Parker, 2014), and the age of first marriage continues to climb (Hymowitz, Carroll, Wilcox, & Kaye, 2013). It seems logical that a sentiment that delays marriage and makes it a want rather than a need could easily leave a growing proportion of emerging adults with a life trajectory that never includes marriage. As we found in our own data, emerging adults seemed to continue to deprioritize marriage over the 3 years of our study, which is odd considering they were approaching the age at which many expected to marry. Like many dreams and hopes of adolescence and emerging adulthood that fade as the realities and challenges of adult life set in, perhaps getting married is occupying the same space as their dreams to become an astronaut or own a pony—eventually we come to understand that such things are only for a select few, and we would be better off setting our sights on more realistic goals. In some ways, marriage may be becoming a similar type of want. Many more emerging adults are deciding as they move through the third decade of life that the ideal of marriage and the type of marriage they desire are neither obtainable nor realistic. They will continue to date, cohabit, and search for love, but marriage itself may increasingly become a childhood dream that is left by the wayside.

▲ Moving Past the Paradox

The marriage paradox, explained in more detail in the previous section, could be viewed in several ways in terms of its overall effect and importance. On the one hand, breaking down each specific shift in values and beliefs among emerging adults might be construed as positive or negative, depending on context. Some may wish to debate whether emerging adults' shifting views on marital timing or soul mates are important touchpoints for healthy or unhealthy development. Such a specific exercise is beyond the scope of our discussion and, frankly, would be of little interest. Research has suggested that each specific belief about marriage and relationships has significant but relatively small effects on the overall experience of emerging adulthood (Willoughby & Carroll, 2015). When we look at this issue more collectively, however, viewing the entire paradox, we argue that there is greater cause for concern and reflection. The concern lies in the fact that emerging adults appear to be seeking a marital relationship that they are increasingly unprepared for because of the collective nature of their paradoxical beliefs. A series of interconnected attitudes centered on pushing marriage into the distance, creating a relationship that is individually gratifying yet free of effort, and finding a partner who is able to seamlessly connect with their life plans has pushed a hoped-for marriage to the fringes of emerging adulthood. Nevertheless, emerging adults still want to marry, and most still do. They simply do so later in the life course, with more hesitation, and with a critical eye fixed squarely on trying to identify any signs that their marriage or spouse may no longer fit their individual needs. This is despite research that suggests that delayed marriage makes the intertwining of life trajectories only more difficult (Glenn, Uecker, & Love, 2010) and the fact that the individualistic mindset of many emerging adults, in which marriage is viewed as a relationship of personal gratification and satisfaction, runs counter to decades of research that suggests healthy marriages are built on a foundation of compassion, commitment, forgiveness, and additional other-focused virtues (Fincham, Stanley, & Beach, 2007; Stanley, Whitton, & Markman, 2004). The argument here is not about forcing marriage on emerging adults who are rejecting it—most clearly are not. Instead, it is about seeking to help emerging adults break out of their current paradox about marriage by teaching them to bring their expressed life goals more in line with a trajectory that helps them succeed. Part of this process is simply shining a light on these paradoxical beliefs, which we have attempted to do in the preceding chapters. Now, we offer three possible ways in which emerging adults and our society might move toward resolving many aspects of the marriage paradox.

Building Resources for Success in All Areas of Life

As we spoke to emerging adults, explored our survey data, and investigated national trends, nothing was more disheartening to us than the fact that emerging adults felt resigned to (what they thought was) the incontrovertible fact that success in three primary areas of life—marriage/family, education, and career—is impossible. As has been pointed out previously, emerging adults feel burdened with a long list of obstacles to success in achieving their educational, career, and family goals. It feels overwhelming—frankly, for many it felt insurmountable—to achieve this overall success in the modern world. This being the case, they prioritized some areas and de-emphasized others, coping with perceived future failure by simply telling themselves that at least one area of their life will not matter because of a lack of interest or energy. For a small group, it was their career trajectory that was put into the crosshairs. Whether it was Avery, who put her life on hold to follow her husband overseas, or Susan, who went against her parents' wishes and put marriage over her educational goals, some emerging adults were willing to sacrifice career success for relational well-being. For others, it was marriage that they planned to disregard, by either avoiding it or setting up fail-safes in their lives in the event of a failed marriage. This group was large and is probably growing. Faced with uncertainty in so many life roles, many emerging adults appear willing to acknowledge that a happy and successful marriage, no matter how enticing, may never happen. What was missing from their narratives was virtually any discussion of having well-rounded success in life. That a person might have a happy, fulfilling, and successful career while also maintaining a happy family life and enjoyable leisure activities felt like fantasy.

Clearly, the solution to this dilemma is multifaceted. Much of this struggle appeared to be economic in nature. The prevailing job market for college and high school graduates does not inspire much confidence, and there was an underlying sense of anxiety among most we spoke to about their career prospects. We will leave any suggestions for employment policy to those much more qualified than we are on the topic, but we will make one key general suggestion that transcends many of these interrelated areas: it is critical to continue to find ways to provide adequate resources to emerging adults across multiple domains of life. Emerging adults seem overwhelmed by stress in their mid-20s. One of the hallmarks of stress theory is the acquisition and use of resources (McCubbin, & Patterson, 1983). Having resources or access to resources in life helps promote positive perceptions and more resiliency (Hawley & DeHaan, 1996; Masten, Burt, Roisman, Obradovic, Long, & Tellegen, 2004). Emerging adults across the socioeconomic spectrum appear to need more resources in their lives. For example, they need more guidance and education about student loans and career opportunities. If our society values giving emerging adults ultimate free will to choose their life path, we need to give them the resources to make educated decisions in these areas of their life.

Relationally, the path is no different. Beyond access to health and sex education, emerging adults receive virtually no education on healthy marriages and rarely are given information about relational resources. We believe this needs to change. Although marriage educators and clinicians have long acknowledged the struggle of getting premarital couples or individuals into any type of relationship education, part of this issue may be a lack of effort at meeting emerging adults where they are. Emerging adults are not likely to be swayed by weekend relationship retreats or the increasingly archaic educational methods employed by most relational educators. Instead, emerging adults need to be educated about relationships through social media, online resources, and other methods that embrace their individualistic and technology-savvy personalities.

We believe such a step is key for helping emerging adults overcome the marital paradoxes in their minds. They need to be educated about healthy dating and relational development. They need to learn about the research that suggests age of marriage matters or how to have healthy communication and conflict resolution in their lives. If knowledge is power, then perhaps some of the marriage paradox can be addressed by giving emerging adults more knowledge about an institution they seem to continue to value and strive for.

Giving Permission and Support for All Marriages

Another important way in which portions of the marriage paradox may be resolved lies in the lessons learned not just from our larger sample but also from our select and small group of married emerging adults in chapter 10. Most emerging adults we spoke to appeared to have an extremely negative outlook on those who married early. Culturally, the message appeared clear: marry early if you want your life to be derailed and you want to be stuck with little hope of future success. Yet, the married emerging adults we spoke to did not appear to share this mentality, and our objective measures of their success, at least within the first few years of their marriage, did not appear to differ dramatically from their peers. Most were still seeking educational opportunities as a family, and none seemed to be wallowing in despair at their marital decisions. We, of course, recognize that some early-married emerging adults are in fact stuck in unhappy marriages (though this is by no means unique to those who marry early in the life course), perhaps pressured to marry by family or other cultural groups, and our small collection of stories in no way represents what all emerging adults who marry early are experiencing. In fact, it is the negative stories that tend to grab the attention of the psyche and become the stories that are circulated among social circles, informing many of the negative stereotypes that seem to prevail among emerging adults about those who married early. However, lost in this rhetoric is the group of emerging adults who married early and were perfectly content and happy, stories reflected in the examples we highlighted. This certainly does not suggest that all emerging adults should marry in their early 20s. Yet, if as a society we wish to truly give emerging adults the freedom of choice they believe they have and deserve, we need to create societal space for everyone, including those who choose to marry early, later, or not at all. The early-married emerging adults in particular may help provide their peers with positive messages that contrast with the negative media messages from celebrity-driven television or the negative familial examples they have witnessed. Perhaps we need more space for emerging adults to hear these stories, to see that if marriage does fit for someone in the early 20s, there is a pathway to success and happiness.

Part of this success likely goes back to resources, not just tangible but also social. If we truly embrace the ideal that each individual should choose his or her own marital adventure, emerging adults and the culture at large should be careful about stigmatizing the early-married (and late-married, for that matter) emerging adults. Early-married emerging adults likely need social resources to maintain educational and career success. Late-marrying emerging adults likely need resources to help them navigate the blending of independent adult lives. Building a supportive culture around marriage that gives space to these varying trajectories into marriage will likely help ease some of the paradoxes in emerging adults' minds whereby they feel implicit pressure to conform to a changing, yet in many ways still rigid, pathway into marriage.

We acknowledge that part of this argument suggesting more resources for supporting marriage does hinge on the assumption that society is better off embracing the social construction we call marriage rather than simply disregarding it in favor of a deinstitutionalized relationship market. We own this assumption and do believe that society benefits from the structure, stability, and symbolism afforded by organizing committed and stable relationships through the institution of marriage.

With this assumption recognized, part of breaking down the marriage paradox lies not only with emerging adults but also with all of us. Supporting marriages at all points in the life course through social avenues, and perhaps policy that recognizes the importance of healthy relationships and the potential social costs of divorce, may also be important elements of resolving the marriage paradox in the coming years.

Recognizing the Messages We Send

Finally, another important step forward may be related to the messages we are sending emerging adults about marriage. As we pointed out, the paradoxes surrounding marriage were not created in a vacuum by emerging adults themselves. Although it is increasingly common to blame millennials for being lazy and having a self-defeating outlook on life, the marriage paradox has its roots not with emerging adults but with parents, the media, and other cultural and social institutions. Even though some positive messages were apparent, emerging adults reported being inundated by negative messages about marriage; their fear and anxiety about finding marital bliss was entrenched in these ongoing messages. Many had been hurt or even scarred by their parental examples (or lack thereof). They were barraged in the media with messages of failed marriages and divorce while at the same time being bombarded with messages of eternal bliss through finding a soul mate. Friends and religious leaders fed into the conflicting messages about the pros and cons about marriage. *Marriage* has become a culture war buzzword that in recent years has been connected more with the ongoing debate about discrimination and human rights than it has with an institution centered on symbolic commitment between two people. In short, when we look at the conflicting and confusing messages about marriage emerging adults hear and internalize, it should come as no surprise that they struggle to make sense of the marital world around them.

This issue also comes with another acknowledgement—that modern emerging adulthood is a very different experience than it was even a generation ago. Emerging adults no longer live in an isolated world where parents, and perhaps local clergy, were their only real sources of relational advice. Emerging adults now live in an interconnected world where virtually limitless information on marriage and relationships are a click or finger swipe away. Emerging adults openly discussed getting some of their marital examples from Facebook and other social media outlets where relational advice and stories are prevalent. Perhaps it is time to be more intentional about the marriage messages we are sending emerging adults and children. Perhaps it is time to explore in more depth what these messages might be. Parents need to be more aware of the socialization that occurs in the home, and social leaders should be deliberate with the messages they send out about marriage. Scholars should begin to explore the nature of the online education emerging adults and children are receiving about marriage and relationships and continue to investigate their effect. In general, we need to be more fully involved with and aware of our cultural messaging about marriage.

This is not a call to attempt to make all our cultural messages about marriage positive. We believe there is value in making sure emerging adults understand the realities of marriage and relationships. Indeed, many emerging adults reported the positive influence of seeing their parents and others overcome struggles in their marriage, helping them form a more realistic vision of the effort involved in building up a marriage. Instead, we believe it is a call to be more realistic and intentional in the messages we send to emerging adults. That is, messaging about marriage should include not only the difficulties and potential downsides of marriage but also the emotional, social, and personal fulfillment that can come from a healthy, stable marriage. It is also a call to be more consistent. As pointed out by some scholars (Willoughby, Olson, Carroll, Nelson, & Miller, 2012), parents are perhaps one of the major sources of the current marriage paradox because they increasingly send mixed messages about the importance of marital delay and the prioritization of education. Such messages would be fine if they were not also likely accompanied by implicit and explicit messages suggesting that an eventual marriage (and grandchildren) is still expected. The result of this current messaging is not surprising: emerging adults struggling to make sense of these sometimes very paradoxical messages.

▲ Conclusion

So, we now bring this discussion to a close. Marriage will likely remain an important element of the life course for at least the near future. Emerging adults will continue to marry and divorce. They will continue to worry about their marriage prospects and wonder what their relational future might hold. Although it may be impossible to know exactly what the future holds for marriage in the United States or other parts of the world, the modern reality of emerging adults has changed how they approach and engage in marriage. Whether this paradox grows or is resolved likely rests on how the cultural narrative and economic milieu surrounding marriage continue to evolve in the years and decades to come. Current trends suggest that despite the continued value most put on marriage, married couples are on their way to becoming a relic of the past, or at least a much smaller part of the US population than they have been. The current mentality and para-doxes of emerging adulthood appear to be feeding into these trends.

For now, the marriage paradox of emerging adulthood is here to stay. Each individual emerging adult must navigate it. Each emerging adult must decide how important marriage truly is to her or him and attempt to balance a multitude of overlapping, overwhelming life roles. It remains one more piece to an increasingly complex puzzle of figuring out life during the 20s. How and if the marriage paradox is resolved will likely have important ramifications for the relationships, families, and children of the next several generations.

APPENDIX ▲

Here we outline the data sources used throughout the book. First, we summarize the methodology of the main longitudinal study used for both the illustrative quotes and some graphs and other statistics throughout the book. We then provide methodological overviews for the national datasets used throughout the book. Finally, we give specific background information on each figure, labeled by chapter.

▲ Methodology of Marital Paradigm Study

Data for the Marital Paradigm Study came from a 3-year longitudinal study of emerging adults located mainly the Midwestern portion of the United States. All aspects of the study were approved by the institutional review boards of Brigham Young University and Ball State University. An initial sample was taken from a population of college students who were attending a Midwestern university during the 2011–2012 academic year. This initial sample was collected by recruitment through email invitation to students at the university who were registered through a university-wide research pool. In this way, the initial sample was able to collect data from students across majors. Students were sent an email invitation to take an online survey administered by the research team by Qualtrics. Students who completed the survey were entered into a drawing for several $50 Visa gift cards.

This initial data collection effort resulted in a final sample of 718 emerging adults. During this first wave of data collection, the average

age was 20.82 (standard deviation [SD] = 3.53). The sample had a higher proportion of women (75%) than men (25%) and was predominately white (95%). Ninety percent of the sample labeled themselves as heterosexual. Most of the sample (69%) reported a total parental income of more than $50,000, with 23.5% reporting a parental income of more than $100,000. Most (68%) reported that their biological parents were still married. A little more than half (55%) of the sample reported currently working in paid employment. The most commonly reported religious affiliation was conservative Christian (25.5%) followed by liberal Christian (24%) and Roman Catholic (14.3%). Seven percent of the sample reported having at least one biological child. Overall demographics of the sample generally mirrored those of the university population.

The survey assessment itself was divided into five main assessment categories. The first section assessed basic demographic information such as educational status, work status, and relationship status. The second and main component of the survey included a battery of items addressing all six dimensions of Marital Paradigm Theory. The third section of the survey assessed behavioral outcomes including risk-taking, pro-social behaviors, and academic outcomes (for those still in school in later waves). Assessments of religious behavior were also included. The fourth section of the survey addressed relational outcomes including items assessing current relational and sexual behavior. The final and fifth section of the survey included value and belief items regarding non–marriage-related domains such as parenting, employment, and emerging adulthood in general.

As a part of the initial survey, participants were asked to supply several pieces of contact information for potential follow-up surveys. This information included their full name, a current email address, a primary and secondary mailing address, and the name and address of two additional contact people who would know their location. For the second year of the study, this information was used to invite participants to complete a follow-up assessment 1 year later. The year 2 sample consisted of 134 unmarried emerging adults. To attempt to maintain gender balance in the sample, all men from wave 1 were contacted, but only a random sample of 150 unmarried women were contacted. Overall, 25% of the contacted sample agreed to participate. Participants who elected to participate at wave 2 did not differ from nonparticipants in terms of age, educational level, parental income, hours of employment, number of children, grade point average, ideal timing of marriage, or general importance of marriage. Participants who completed wave 2 also did not differ from nonparticipants in terms of race or sexual orientation but did differ on gender. Participants at wave 2 were more likely to be female ($\chi^2(2) = 9.91$, $p < .01$). At wave 2, 72% of the sample reported they were currently full-time students, and 20% reported they were not currently enrolled in any schooling. A majority of the sample reported they were working one job part-time (36%) or one job full-time (26%), and the average number of working hours per week was 8.20 (SD = 11.00). Eighty-seven percent of the sample identified as heterosexual. The most common religious denomination listed was Conservative Christian (21.6%), followed by Liberal Christian (20.9%) and Roman Catholic (20.9%). Most (65.7%) of the sample reported that their parents were married.

For the final year of data collection, participants were again contacted 1 year later for a follow-up survey using the same procedures as year 2. Participants for this final year of data collection were invited to participate in both an online survey and a qualitative interview. All participants who completed the survey and interview received a $50 Visa gift card for compensation. In total, 80 emerging adults completed both portions of the study, representing roughly 60% of the wave 2 sample.

The online survey was again done by Qualtrics. For the qualitative portion, participants were given the option to complete the online interview in one of three ways. Video interviews were conducted by both Skype and ooVoo services. These online tools allow for the video capture and recording of all interviews. Participants who did not have access to a computer had the option to participate by telephone, but no participants used this option. Semi-structured interviews were conducted by a team of trained undergraduate research assistants and the authors. These interviews were based on a standardized set of root questions that all participants were asked during the interview. The interview included questions about the emerging adults' generalized marital beliefs, with a specific focus on marital timing, marital salience, and mate-selection beliefs. Emerging adults were also asked about the development of such beliefs and how various spheres of influence (parents, peers, religion, etc.) contributed to the formation of such beliefs. Finally, emerging adults were asked a series of questions about how their marital beliefs influenced their decision making across multiple domains (relational, risk-taking, etc.).

Once collected, all interviews were transcribed and analyzed by the research team using a thematic analysis technique to understand common patterns in how emerging adults talk about marriage and its influence in their lives. Analytic memos were created for each participant that identified relevant themes and analytical notes. These memos were completed by the authors and trained graduate students and were then double-checked by each author. The research team discussed any disagreements or unclear portions of the memos. The authors followed guidelines for such analyses offered by Braun and Clarke (2006). Coding involved identifying initial codes within the data and then expanding and combining such codes into broader categories and themes. Specifically, two types of thematic coding were utilized: value coding and in vivo coding. Values coding attempts to explore the values, attitudes, and beliefs of the participants, and each transcript was coded across these three categories. Themes were then generated from all three groups and compared across the entire sample. In vivo coding attempts to retain the participants' own language and captures the inherent voices and themes of the individuals as they discussed marriage. Like values coding, each participant's interview was coded, and common themes were identified across the interviews. Coding was also discussed among the authors, and themes were agreed on before finalizing them. The themes generated from both values coding and in vivo coding represent most of the themed subheadings found within the chapters. Illustrative quotes for most sections of the book came from those emerging adults who were coded for each particular theme being discussed.

As a final component of the Marital Paradigm Study, a targeted low-income sample was also acquired to help offset the initial sample that was heavily skewed toward middle-class and educated emerging adults. This targeted sampling occurred in the Mountain West region of the United States and involved posting study flyers at several locations in a large metropolitan area. Locations includes a local food bank, several fast-food restaurants, and employment centers. Inclusion criteria, such as being between the ages of 18 and 30 years, having an annual household income of less than $30,000, and having not attended college. Qualifying participants were put through the same procedure as the wave 3 participants from the larger study. This resulted in a low-income sample of an additional 15 participants. Interviews were also coded in a manner identical to the larger sample. Quotes and information from these low-income participants were utilized across the chapters to help increase the diversity of the perspectives utilized but were not used in any figures or other statistical information from the larger study.

▲ Other Datasets Utilized

The following datasets were utilized at different points in the books. We briefly provide background information for each dataset as well as links for the reader to find more information where applicable.

National Vital Statistics System and National Survey of Family Growth. The National Vital Statistics System (NVCS) and the National Survey of Family Growth (NSFG) are part of the Centers for Disease Control and Prevention. The NVCS studies Public Health through vital events, including marriages, divorces, births, deaths, and fetal deaths. The data for NCVS are collected through vital registration systems and the National Center for Health Statistics (NCHS). The NSFG studies many of the same things but adds information on pregnancy and infertility, contraception, women and men's health, and family life. The NSFG originally studied women until 2002, when information about men was added. Further information on these two datasets can be found at http://www.cdc.gov/nchs/nvss/ and http://www.cdc.gov/nchs/nsfg/.

Current Population Survey. The Current Population Survey (CPS) is a survey for the Bureau of Labor Statistics directed by the Census Bureau. The CPS measures employment, unemployment, labor force, persons not in the labor force, earnings, hours of work, and demographic factors. The CPS surveyed 60,000 households through in-person and telephone interviews. The eligible population for the survey was anyone 16 years or older. Specifically, the CPS splits up the number of persons married by four different races: white, black, Asian, and Hispanic. More information can be found at http://www.census.gov/programs-surveys/cps.html.

Current Employment Statistics. The Current Employment Statistics (CES) is a monthly program that surveys government agencies and businesses. This survey provides information on employment, earnings, and hours of workers. More specifically, the CES looks into the trends in employment over the past. The survey consists of approximately 146,000 businesses, which contain 623,000 individuals. The data cover all fifty states, Puerto Rico, District of Columbia, and the Virgin Islands. More information can be found at http://www.bls.gov/ces/.

Monitoring the Future. Monitoring the Future (MTF) surveyed 50,000 eighth, tenth, and twelfth graders on their attitudes, behaviors, and values. Part of the survey measures alcohol, drug, and cigarette use and the student's attitudes about these behaviors while in twelfth grade. This survey also gives specific data on how important certain milestones are for people, including marriage. The National Institute of Drug Abuse funds this survey, and the data are collected through the Survey Research Center at the University of Michigan. More information can be found at http://www.monitoringthefuture.org/.

The National Survey of Family and Households. The National Survey of Family and Households (NSFH) was a longitudinal survey, and its purpose was to provide information on family life for multiple disciplines. The sample consisted of 13,007 participants from 9,637 households. There was an oversampling of Mexican Americans, Puerto Ricans, African Americans, and nontraditional families. The information that was collected ranged from family living arrangements as children, how often they were in their families' homes, their history of cohabitation, marriage, education, and employment. More information on this dataset can be found at http://www.ssc.wisc.edu/nsfh/.

Millennials and Marriage Message Assessment. The Millennials and Marriage Message Assessment was a nationally representative APCO survey consisting of 1,200 participants between the ages of 18 and 33 years, with a specific target toward low-income emerging adults. The sample was nationally representative of emerging adults with some college education, with participants from urban cities, suburbs, smaller towns, and rural areas of the United States. Of the sample, 300 were married, 200 were cohabitating, and 600 were unmarried.

Living Arrangements of Children. Living Arrangements of Children (LAC): 2009 used data from three different surveys, the Annual Social and Economic Supplement (ASEC), the Current Population Survey (CPS), and the American Community Survey (ACS). The report focused on the living arrangements of families, adults, partners, spouses, and couples. Specifically, the LAC collects data on whom children are living with. It also collected data on the economic status of the families from before and after the 2007 recession.

More information can be found at the following website: https://www.census.gov/prod/2011pubs/p70-126.pdf.

Pew Research Center. The Pew Research Center studies US journalism, media, politics and policy, religion and public life, and demographic and social trends. These studies are done through public polling, content analysis, demographic research, and other types of research. One major branch of the Pew Research Center is the Internet and

Technology Department. Examples of studies done in this department include what percentage of people own technological devices, the availability of the Internet in homes, and social media use. More information can be found at the following website: http://www.pewresearch.org/data-trend/media-and-technology/social-networking-use/.

Notes on Specific Figures

Figure 1.1   **Centers for Disease Control and Prevention marriage and divorce rates from 1900 to 2012.** The eligible population for the marriage rate data included individuals older than 15 years. Since 1900, the number of marriages in the US population has decreased from about 9 per 1,000 to less than 7 per 1,000. The number of divorces has risen since 1900, with a peak of about 5 divorces per 1,000 people in the 1980s.

Figure 1.2   **US Census Bureau current population survey data on educational attainment from 1940 to 2014.** Most adults surveyed had less than a high school (H.S.) education until the 1970s. After that time, people with a high school degree became the largest portion of Americans adults until 2012. In 2012, most adults surveyed had a bachelor's degree, mainly because the different levels of education became more evenly distributed.

Figure 1.3   **Bureau of Labor Statistics data on the US labor force from 1950 to 2015.** The Bureau of Labor Statistics measured multiple forms of labor, including retail, government, education and health, trade and transportation, private sector, and manufacturing. The private sector has been the largest employer since the 1950s and has continually increased until 2015. The largest labor force decrease in the United States occurred in manufacturing, which represented about 25% of the labor force in 1950 but less than 10% in 2015.

Figure 2.1   **US Census Bureau current population survey data on age at first marriage.** The Census Bureau measured the age at first marriage for adults in the United States. The age of marriage steadily decreased for males from 1890 until the 1950s and 1960s. For females, there was a small decrease from 1890 until 1940, then a large decrease until 1960. For both males and females, the age of marriage has increased from the 1960s at a very fast rate. The average age of marriage for males increased from 22.8 in 1960 to 29.3 in 2014. For females, the average age rose from 20.3 to 27 in that same time period.

Figure 2.2   **US Census Bureau current population survey data on the numbers of cohabitating couples.** The number of cohabitating couples continually increased from the 1960s, at 0.44 million, to 2014, at 7.9 million. The largest increase in a 10-year period was between the years 2000 and 2010, with an increase of almost 4 million couples.

Figure 3.1   **Monitoring the Future Survey: good marriage is "very important."** The Monitoring the Future Survey asked high school seniors from 1976 to 2014 if having a good marriage was very important to them and if they planned to get married in the next 3 years. Although having a good marriage stayed consistent, above 70%, the percentage of high school seniors who planned to get married in the next 3 years decreased from 34% in 1976 to 11% in 2014.

Figure 4.1   **Current population survey data on the numbers of married people by race.** In this survey, the numbers of white participants who are getting married steadily increased from 1950 to 2015. The number of black participants who were married barely increased during that time.

Figure 4.2   **Current population survey data on income and gender of married people, with spouse present.** About 40% of the participants who had no income were married. Both males and females were more likely to be married if they had a higher income. For males, 80% of those with a yearly income of $100,000 or more were married. Between 60% and 70% of females who made the same amount were married.

Figure 6.1   **Millennials and Marriage Message Assessment results on the importance of finding one's soul mate to getting married.** Almost two thirds of the participants said it was a very good idea to get married, whereas only 2% of the participants said it was a very bad idea.

Figure 7.1   **Millennials and Marriage Message Assessment results on parents' influence on impressions of marriage.** Parents influence on emerging adults' impressions of marriage was measured on a four-point scale from "not at all influential" to "very influential." The highest percent of participants (38%) said their parents were "somewhat influential," whereas 31% of participants said their parents were "very influential." Only 11% of the participants said they parents were "not at all influential."

Figure 7.4   **Living Arrangements of Children report over time.** The report separated households into those including children living with two parents, children living with one parent, and children living with no parents. When comparing households in 2015 to households in 1996, there were not many changes. In both 1996 and 2015, the majority of children who were white and Hispanic lived with two parents, and the majority of black children lived with only one parent.

Figure 8.1   **Pew Research Center data on social networking use by age.** The percentage of people who use social media has continually risen since 2005. According to the Pew Research Center, the largest percentage of users (92%) were between the ages of 18 and 29 years. When polling all participants between the ages of 18 and 65+ years, the number of participants who use social media rose from 8% in 2005 to 81% in 2015.

Figure 8.2   **Millennials and Marriage Message Assessment of different types of social networking.** Emerging adults were asked which social networking sites they used and how often they used them. The answers ranged from "never" to "every day." The least used form of social media was MySpace, whereas 58% of the participants said they used Facebook "every day."

Figure 8.3   **Millennials and Marriage Message Assessment results on how religious emerging adults are.** Emerging adults were asked two different questions about religion: "How frequently do you attend religious services?" and "How important is religion in your everyday life?" The largest percentage of emerging adults (33%) reported that they never attend services, whereas the smallest percentage (17%) said they attend frequently. An interesting finding was that even though the lowest percentage of people said they attended frequently, the second largest percentage of people (29%) said religion was "very important" in their everyday life. The lowest percentage of participants (14%) said religion was "not very important."

References ⚠

Adams, M., & Coltrane, S. (2007). Framing divorce reform: Media, morality, and the politics of family. *Family Process*, *46*(1), 17–34.

Ahrons, C. (1994). *The good divorce*. New York, NY: HarperCollins.

Allan, G. (2008). Flexibility, friendship, and family. *Personal Relationships*, *15*(1), 1–16.

Amato, P. R., & Cheadle, J. (2005). The long reach of divorce: Divorce and child well-being across three generations. *Journal of Marriage and Family*, *67*(1), 191–206.

Amato, P. R., Kane, J. B., & James, S. (2011). Reconsidering the "good divorce." *Family Relations*, *60*(5), 511–524.

Amato, P. R., & Sobolewski, J. M. (2001). The effects of divorce and marital discord on adult children's psychological well-being. *American Sociological Review*, *66*(6), 900–921. Retrieved from http://www.jstor.org/stable/3088878.

Anderson, C. A., & Bushman, B. J. (2002). The effects of media violence on society. *Science*, *295*(5564), 2377–2379.

Andersson, C. (2015). A genealogy of serial monogamy: Shifting regulations of intimacy in twentieth-century Sweden. *Journal of Family History*, *40*(2), 195–207.

Ajzen, I. (1991). The theory of planned behavior. *Organizational Behavior and Human Decision Processes*, *50*, 179–211.

Arnett, J. J. (2000). Emerging adulthood: A theory of development from the late teens through the twenties. *The American Psychologist*, *55*(5), 469–480.

Arnett, J. J. (2004). *Emerging adulthood: The winding road from the late teens through the twenties*. New York, NY: Oxford University Press.

Arnett, J. J. (2007). Emerging adulthood: What is it, and what is it good for? *Child Development Perspectives*, *1*(2), 68–73.

Arnett, J. J. (2014). *Emerging adulthood: The winding road from the late teens through the twenties* (2nd ed.). New York, NY: Oxford University Press.

Arnett, J. J. (Ed.). (2016). *The Oxford handbook of emerging adulthood*. Oxford, New York, NY: Oxford University Press.

Arnett, J. J., Kloep, M., Hendry, L. B., & Tanner, J. L. (2010). *Debating emerging adulthood: Stage or process?* New York, NY: Oxford University Press.

Arnett, J. J., Kloep, M., Hendry, L., & Tanner, J. (2011). The curtain rises: A brief overview of the book. In *Debating emerging adulthood: Stage or process?* (pp. 3–12). New York, NY: Oxford University Press.

Arnett, J. J., & Schwab, J. (2013). *The Clark University poll of emerging adults, 2012: Thriving, struggling, and hopeful*. Worcester, MA: Clark University.

Arnett, J. J., & Schwab, J. (2014). *The Clark University poll of established adults ages 25–39*. Retrieved from http://www.clarku.edu/clark-poll-emerging-adults/pdfs/Clark_Poll_2014_Hires_web.pdf.

Bandura A. (1977). *Social learning theory*. Englewood Cliffs, NJ: Prentice Hall.

Bandura, A. (1986). *Social foundations of thought and action: A social cognitive theory*. Englewood Cliffs, NJ: Prentice-Hall.

Barry, C. M., & Abo-Zena, M. M. (Eds.). (2014). *Emerging adults' religiousness and spirituality: Meaning-making in an age of transition*. New York, NY: Oxford University Press.

Baucom, D. H., & Epstein, N. (1990). *Cognitive behavioral marital therapy*. New York, NY: Brunner/Mazel.

Baxter, J., Hewitt, B., & Haynes, M. (2008). Life course transitions and housework: Marriage, parenthood, and time on housework. *Journal of Marriage and Family, 70*(2), 259–272.

Beck, L. A., & Clark, M. S. (2010). What constitutes a healthy communal marriage and why relationship stage matters. *Journal of Family Theory and Review, 2*, 299–315.

Bernard, J. (1982). *The future of marriage*. Yale University Press.

Brody, G. H., Moore, K., & Glei, D. (1994). Family processes during adolescence as predictors of parent-young adult attitude similarity: A six-year longitudinal analysis. *Family Relations, 43*(4), 369–373.

Bronfenbrenner, U. (1975). Is early intervention effective? *Teachers College Record 76*(2), 279–303.

Bryant, J., & Oliver, M. B. (Eds.). (2009). *Media effects: Advances in theory and research*. New York, NY: Routledge.

Bubolz, M., & Sontag, M. (1993). Human ecology theory. In P. Boss, W. Doherty, R. LaRossa, W. Schumm, & S. Steinmetz (Eds.), *Sourcebook of family theories and methods: A contextual approach* (pp. 419–448). New York, NY: Plenum Press.

Burnette, J. L., & Franiuk, R. (2010). Individual differences in implicit theories of relationships and partner fit: Predicting forgiveness in developing relationships. *Personality and Individual Differences, 48*(2), 144–148.

Busby, D. M., Willoughby, B. J., & Carroll, J. S. (2013). Sowing wild oats: Valuable experience or a field full of weeds? *Personal Relationships, 20*(4), 706–718.

Buss, D. M. (1989). Sex differences in human mate preferences: Evolutionary hypotheses tested in 37 cultures. *Behavioral and Brain Sciences, 12*(1), 1–14.

Buss, D. M. (2006). Strategies of human mating. *Psihologijske Teme, 15*(2), 239–260.

Buss, D. M., & Schmitt, D. P. (1993). Sexual strategies theory: An evolutionary perspective on human mating. *Psychological Review, 100*(2), 204–232.

Retrieved from https://www.researchgate.net/profile/David_Buss/publication/14715297_Sexual_Strategy_Theory_An_evolutionary_perspective_on_human_mating/links/0deec5181791b73d35000000.pdf.

Buss, D. M., Shackelford, T. K., Kirkpatrick, L. A., & Larsen, R. J. (2001). A half century of mate preferences: The cultural evolution of values. *Journal of Marriage and Family, 63*(2), 491–503.

Byrne, D. (1997). An overview (and underview) of research and theory within the attraction paradigm. *Journal of Social and Personal Relationships, 14*(3), 417–431.

Carr, D., & Springer, K. W. (2010). Advances in families and health research in the 21st century. *Journal of Marriage & Family, 72*(3), 743–761.

Carroll, J. S., Badger, S., Willoughby, B. J., Nelson, L. J., Madsen, S. D., & Barry, C. M. (2009). Ready or not? Criteria for marriage readiness among emerging adults. *Journal of adolescent research, 24*(3), 349–375.

Carroll, J. S., Willoughby, B., Badger, S., Nelson, L. J., Barry, C. M., & Madsen, S. D. (2007). So close, yet so far away: The impact of varying marital horizons on emerging adulthood. *Journal of Adolescent Research, 22*(3), 219–247.

Cartwright, C. (2006). You want to know how it affected me? Young adults' perceptions of the impact of parental divorce. *Journal of Divorce & Remarriage, 44*(3–4), 125–143.

Centers for Disease Control and Prevention (CDC). (2013). *Key statistics from the national survey of family growth*. Retrieved from http://www.cdc.gov/nchs/nsfg/key_statistics/s.htm.

Cheng, D., & Reed, M. (2010). *The project on student debt: Student debt and the class of 2009*. Oakland, CA: Institute for College Access and Success.

Cherlin, A. J. (2004). The deinstitutionalization of American marriage. *Journal of Marriage and Family, 66*(4), 848–861.

Cherlin, A. J. (2009). *The marriage-go-round: The state of marriage and the family in America today*. New York, NY: Alfred Knopf.

Cherlin, A. J. (2010). Demographic trends in the United States: A review of research in the 2000s. *Journal of Marriage and Family, 72*(3), 403–419.

Christensen, T. M., & Brooks, M. C. (2001). Adult children of divorce and intimate relationships: A review of the literature. *The Family Journal, 9*(3), 289–294. Retrieved from http://tfj.sagepub.com/content/9/3/289.full.pdf.

Civic, D. (1999). The association between characteristics of dating relationships and condom use among heterosexual young adults. *AIDS Education and Prevention, 11*(4), 343–352.

Clark, M. S., & Beck, L. A. (2010). Initiating and evaluating close relationships: A task central to emerging adults. In F. D. Fincham & M. Cui (Eds.). (2010). *Romantic relationships in emerging adulthood*. New York, NY: Cambridge University Press.

Braun, V., & Clarke, V. (2006). Using thematic analysis in psychology. *Qualitative research in psychology, 3*(2), 77–101.

Claxton, S. E., & van Dulmen, M. H. (2013). Casual sexual relationships and experiences in emerging adulthood. *Emerging Adulthood, 1*(2), 138–150.

Coontz, S. (2005). *Marriage, a history: From obedience to intimacy or how love conquered marriage*. New York, NY: Viking Adult.

Copen, C. E., Daniels, K., Vespa, J., & Mosher, W. D. (2012). *National health statistics reports: First marriages in the United States—Data from the 2006–2010 National Survey of Family Growth.* (Report No. 49). Retrieved from http://www.cdc.gov/nchs/data/nhsr/nhsr049.pdf.

Cote, J. E. (2000). *Arrested adulthood: The changing nature of maturity and identity.* New York, NY: New York University Press.

Coyne, S. M., Padilla-Walker, L. M., & Howard, E. (2013). Emerging in a digital world a decade review of media use, effects, and gratifications in emerging adulthood. *Emerging Adulthood, 1*(2), 125–137.

Cui, M., Fincham, F. D., & Durtschi, J. A. (2011). The effect of parental divorce on young adults' romantic relationship dissolution: What makes a difference? *Personal Relationships, 18*(3), 410–426.

Critelli, J. W., & Suire, D. M. (1998). Obstacles to condom use: The combination of other forms of birth control and short-term monogamy. *Journal of American College Health, 46*(5), 215–219.

Dadds, M. R., Holland, D. E., Laurens, K. R., Mullins, M., Barrett, P. M., & Spence, S. H. (1999). Early intervention and prevention of anxiety disorders in children: Results at 2-year follow-up. *Journal of Consulting and Clinical Psychology, 67*(1), 145. Retrieved from http://dx.doi.org/10.1037/0022-006X.67.1.145.

Dailey, R. M., Pfiester, A., Jin, B., Beck, G., & Clark, G. (2009). On-again/off-again dating relationships: How are they different from other dating relationships? *Personal Relationships, 16*(1), 23–47.

Dawson, L. H., Shih, M. C., de Moor, C., & Shrier, L. (2008). Reasons why adolescents and young adults have sex: Associations with psychological characteristics and sexual behavior. *Journal of Sex Research, 45*(3), 225–232.

de la Croix, D., & Mariani, F. (2015). From polygyny to serial monogamy: A unified theory of marriage institutions. *Review of Economic Studies, 82*(2), 565–607.

DeMaris, A., Mahoney, A., & Pargament, K. I. (2010). Sanctification of marriage and general religiousness as buffers of the effects of marital inequity. *Journal of Family Issues, 31*, 1255–1278.

Dennison, R. P., & Koerner, S. S. (2006). Post-divorce interparental conflict and adolescents' attitudes about marriage: The influence of maternal disclosures and adolescent gender. *Journal of Divorce & Remarriage, 45*(1–2), 31–49.

Dennison, R. P., & Koerner, S. S. (2008). A look at hopes and worries about marriage: The views of adolescents following a parental divorce. *Journal of Divorce & Remarriage, 48*(3–4), 91–107. Retrieved from http://dx.doi.org/10.1300/J087v48n03_06.

De Valk, H. A., & Liefbroer, A. C. (2007). Timing preferences for women's family-life transitions: Intergenerational transmission among migrants and Dutch. *Journal of Marriage and Family, 69*(1), 190–206.

Diekmann, A., & Schmidheiny, K. (2013). The intergenerational transmission of divorce: A fifteen-country study with the fertility and family survey*. *Comparative Sociology, 12*(2), 211–235.

Dronkers, J., & Härkönen, J. (2008). The intergenerational transmission of divorce in cross-national perspective: Results from the Fertility and Family Surveys. *Population Studies, 62*(3), 273–288.

The Economy in the 1980s and 1990s. (2012). Retrieved from http://www. let.rug.nl/usa/outlines/economy-1991/a-historical-perspective-on-the-american-economy/the-economy-in-the-1980s-and-1990s.php.

Edin, K., & Kefalas, M. (2005). *Promises I can keep: Why poor women put motherhood before marriage*. Berkeley, CA: University of California Press.

Fauth, K., & Marganski, A. (2013). Socially interactive technology and contemporary dating: A cross-cultural exploration of deviant behaviors among young adults in the modern, evolving technological world. *International Criminal Justice Review, 23*(4), 357–377.

Feng, D., Giarrusso, R., Bengtson, V. L., & Frye, N. (1999). Intergenerational transmission of marital quality and marital instability. *Journal of Marriage and the Family, 61*(2), 451–463.

Ferris, A. L., Smith, S. W., Greenberg, B. S., & Smith, S. L. (2007). The content of reality dating shows and viewer perceptions of dating. *Journal of Communication, 57*(3), 490–510.

Fincham, F. D., & Cui, M. (2011). *Romantic relationships in emerging adulthood*. Cambridge, UK: Cambridge University Press.

Fincham, F. D., Stanley, S. M., & Beach, S. R. (2007). Transformative processes in marriage: An analysis of emerging trends. *Journal of Marriage and Family, 69*, 275–292.

Finer, L. (2007). Trends in premarital sex in the United States, 1954–2003. *Public Health Report, 122*(1), 73–78.

Flanagan, C. (2009, July 2). Is there hope for the American marriage? *TIME Magazine*. Retrieved from http://content.time.com/time/magazine/article/0,9171,1908434,00.html.

Fogel, J., & Kovalenko, L. (2013). Reality television shows focusing on sexual relationships are associated with college students engaging in one-night stands. *Journal of Cognitive and Behavioral Psychotherapies, 13*(2), 321–331.

Franiuk, R., Cohen, D., & Pomerantz, E. M. (2002). Implicit theories of relationships: Implications for relationship satisfaction and longevity. *Personal Relationships, 9*, 345–367.

Franiuk, R., Shain, E. A., Bieritz, L., & Murray, C. (2012). Relationship theories and relationship violence: Is it beneficial to believe in soulmates? *Journal of Social and Personal Relationships, 29*(6), 820–838.

Garcia, L. T., & Markey, C. N. (2007). Matching in sexual experience for married, cohabiting, and dating couples. *The Journal of Sex Research, 44*(3), 250–255.

Garcia, J. R., Reiber, C., Massey, S. G., & Merriwether, A. M. (2012). Sexual hookup culture: A review. *Review of General Psychology, 16*(2), 161–176.

Glenn, N. D. (1991). The recent trend in marital success in the United States. *Journal of Marriage and the Family*, 261–270.

Glenn, N. D., Uecker, J. E., & Love, R. W. (2010). Later first marriage and marital success. *Social Science Research, 39*(5), 787–800.

Gibson-Davis, C. M., Edin, K., & McLanahan, S. (2005). High hopes but even higher expectations: The retreat from marriage among low-income couples. *Journal of Marriage and Family, 67*(5), 1301–1312.

Goodsell, T. L., James, S. L., Yorgason, J. B., & Call, V. R. A. (2015). Intergenerational assistance to adult children: Gender and number of sisters and brothers. *Journal of Family Issues, 36*(8): 979–1000.

Grabe, S., Ward, L. M., & Hyde, J. S. (2008). The role of the media in body image concerns among women: A meta-analysis of experimental and correlational studies. *Psychological Bulletin, 134*(3), 460–476.

Hall, A. (1997). Cohabitation and the risk of divorce: An empirical study. *Zeitschrift Fur Soziologie, 26*(4), 275–295.

Hall, D. R., & Zhao, J. Z. (1995). Cohabitation and divorce in Canada: Testing the selectivity hypothesis. *Journal of Marriage and Family, 57*(2), 421–427.

Halpern-Meekin, S., Manning, W. D., Giordano, P. C., & Longmore, M. A. (2012). Relationship churning in emerging adulthood: On/off relationships and sex with an ex. *Journal of Adolescent Research, 28*(2), 166–188.

Hamilton, B. E., Martin, J. A., Osterman, M. K., & Curtin, S. C. (2014). Births: Preliminary data for 2013. *The National Vital Statistics Reports, 63*(2). Retrieved from http://www.cdc.gov/nchs/data/nvsr/nvsr63/nvsr63_02.pdf.

Hanson, T., McLanahan, S., & Thomson, E. (1994). Family structure and child well-being: Economic resources vs. parental behaviors. *Social Forces, 73*(1), 221–242.

Harris, K. M., Halpern, C. T., Whitsel, E., Hussey, J., Tabor, J., Entzel, P., & Udry, J. R. (2009). The national longitudinal study of adolescent health: Retrieved from http://www.cpc.unc.edu/projects/addhealth/design.

Hartford Courant. (1975a, February 20). Broken marriages on rise, p. 48.

Hartford Courant. (1975b, December 31). Marriage and family face stormy future, p. 8.

Hawley, D. R., & DeHaan, L. (1996). Toward a definition of family resilience: Integrating life-span and family perspectives. *Family Process, 35*(3), 283–298.

Heaton, T. B. (2002). Factors contributing to increasing marital stability in the United States. *Journal of Family Issues, 23*(3), 392–409.

Heuveline, P., & Timberlake, J. M. (2004). The role of cohabitation in family formation: The United States in comparative perspective. *Journal of Marriage and Family, 66*(5), 1214–1230.

Hochschild, A. R. (1989). *The second shift.* New York, NY: Avon Books.

Hymowitz, K., Carroll, J., Wilcox, W. B., & Kaye, K. (2013). Knot yet: The benefits and costs of delayed marriage in America. *The National Marriage Project at the University of Virginia, 20*, 103–107.

Jacobs, J. A., & Gerson, K. (2004). *The time divide.* Cambridge, MA: Harvard University Press.

Jacobson, I. (2016). *The national average cost of a wedding is $32,641.* Retrieved from https://www.theknot.com/content/average-wedding-cost-2015.

Janz, P., Pepping, C. A., & Halford, W. K. (2015). Individual differences in dispositional mindfulness and initial romantic attraction: A speed dating experiment. *Personality and Individual Differences, 82*, 14–19.

Jose, A., O'Leary, K. D., & Moyer, A. (2010). Does premarital cohabitation predict subsequent marital stability and marital quality? A meta-analysis. *Journal of Marriage and Family, 72*(1), 105–116.

Kaestle, C. E., & Halpern, C. T. (2007). What's love got to do with it? Sexual behaviors of opposite-sex couples through emerging adulthood. *Perspectives on Sexual and Reproductive Health, 39*(3), 134–140.

Kalkan, M., & Odaci, H. (2010). Problematic internet use, loneliness and dating anxiety among young adult university students. *Computers and Education, 55,* 1091–1097.

Kapinus, C. A., & Pellerin, L. A. (2008). The influence of parents' religious practices on young adults' divorce attitudes. *Social Science Research, 37*(3), 801–814. Retrieved from http://www.sciencedirect.com/science/article/pii/S0049089X08000227.

Kreider, R.M. (2005). *Number, timing, and duration of marriages and divorces: 2001.* Current Population Reports, P70–P97. U.S. Census Bureau, Washington, DC.

Kreider, R. M., & Ellis, R. (2011). Number, timing, and duration of marriages and divorces: 2009. *US Census Bureau,* Washington, DC. Retrieved from https://www.census.gov/prod/2011pubs/p70-125.pdf.

Lee, L., Loewenstein, G., Ariely, D., Hong, J., & Young, J. (2008). If I'm not hot, are you hot or not? Physical-attractiveness evaluations and dating preferences as a function of one's own attractiveness. *Psychological Science, 19*(7), 669–677.

Lehrer, E. L. (2008). Age at marriage and marital instability: Revisiting the Becker–Landes–Michael hypothesis. *Journal of Population Economics, 21*(2), 463–484.

Li, N. P., Yong, J. C., Tov, W., Sng, O., Fletcher, G. J. O., Valentine, K. A., . . . Balliet, D. (2013). Mate preferences do predict attraction and choices in the early stages of mate selection. *Journal of Personality and Social Psychology, 105*(5), 757–776.

Lichter, E. L., & McCloskey, L. A. (2004). The effects of childhood exposure to marital violence on adolescent gender-role beliefs and dating violence. *Psychology of Women Quarterly, 28*(4), 344–357.

Long, B. H. (1987). Perceptions of parental discord and parental separations in the United States: Effects on daughters' attitudes toward marriage and courtship progress. *The Journal of Social Psychology, 127*(6), 573–582.

Mahoney, A., Pargament, K. I., Murray-Swank, A., & Murray-Swank, N. (2003). Religion and the sanctification of family relationships. *Review of Religious Research, 44*(3), 220–236.

Manning, W. D., & Cohen, J. A. (2012). Premarital cohabitation and marital dissolution: An examination of recent marriages. *Journal of Marriage and Family, 74*(2), 377–387.

Manning, W. D., & Smock, P. J. (2005). Measuring and modeling cohabitation: New perspectives from qualitative data. *Journal of Marriage and Family, 67*(4), 989–1002.

Manning, W. D., & Stykes, B. (2015). Twenty-five years of change in cohabitation in the U.S., 1987–2013 (NCFMR Family Profiles Series FP-15-01). *National Center for Family and Marriage Research,* Bowling Green State University. Retrieved from https://www.bgsu.edu/content/dam/BGSU/college-of-arts-and-sciences/NCFMR/documents/FP/FP-15-01-twenty-five-yrs-cohab-us.pdf.

Marquardt, E. (2005). *Between two worlds: The inner lives of children of divorce.* New York, NY: Crown.

Martin, J. A., Hamilton, B.E., Osterman, M.J., Curtin, S.C., & Mathews, T.J. (2015). Births: Final data for 2013. *National Vital Statistics Report, 64*(1). Hyattsville, MD: National Center for Health Statistics. 2015.

Masten, A. S., Burt, K. B., Roisman, G. I., Obradovic, J., Long, J. D., & Tellegen, A. (2004). Resources and resilience in the transition to adulthood: Continuity and change. *Development and Psychopathology, 16*(4), 1071–1094.

Matamela, N. A., Bello, N. U., & Idemudia, E. S. (2014). Sexual attitudes, marriage attitudes and sexual behaviours of females raised by single mothers and both parents: A comparative study. *Gender & Behaviour, 12*(3), 5911.

McCubbin, H. I., & Patterson, J. M. (1983). The family stress process: The double ABCX model of adjustment and adaptation. *Marriage & Family Review, 6*(1–2), 7–37.

McLanahan, S. (2004). Diverging destinies: How children are faring under the second demographic transition. *Demography, 41*(4), 607–627. Retrieved from http://prelim2009.filmbulletin.org/readings/04-Population/McLanahan.pdf.

Michaelides, M. & Mueser, P. (2012). Recent trends in the characteristics of unemployment insurance recipients. *Monthly Labor Review, 135*(7), 28–47.

Miller, S. L., & Maner, J. K. (2011). Ovulation as a male mating prime: Subtle signs of women's fertility influence men's mating cognition and behavior. *Journal of Personality and Social Psychology, 100*(2), 295–308.

Mintz, S., & Kellogg, S. (1989). *Domestic revolutions: A social history of American family life.* New York, NY: Free Press.

Monahan, K. C., Steinberg, L., Cauffman, E., & Mulvey, E. P. (2013). Psychosocial (im)maturity from adolescence to early adulthood: Distinguishing between adolescence-limited and persisting antisocial behavior. *Development and Psychopathology, 25*(4.1), 1093–105.

Montgomery, M. J. (2005). Psychosocial intimacy and identity: From early adolescence to emerging adulthood. *Journal of Adolescent Research, 20*(3), 346–374.

Mulder, M. (2009). Serial monogamy as polygyny or polyandry? Marriage in the Tanzanian Pimbwe. *Human Nature: An Interdisciplinary Biosocial Perspective, 20*(2), 130–150.

National Center for Health Statistics (NCHS). (2016, February). Table I–7. Number of deaths, death rates, and age-adjusted death rates for ages 15 and over, by marital status and sex: United States, 2013. *National Vital Statistics Reports, 64*(2). Retrieved from U.S. Department of Health & Human Services, Centers for Disease Control and Prevention website: http://www.cdc.gov/nchs/data/nvsr/nvsr64/nvsr64_02_tables.pdf#I07.

National Marriage Project. (2012). *The state of our unions—marriage in America 2012.* Retrieved from University of Virginia, National Marriage Project website: http://www.stateofourunions.org/2012/SOOU2012.pdf.

Nelson, L. J., & Padilla-Walker, L. M. (2013). Flourishing and floundering in emerging adult college students. *Emerging Adulthood, 1*(1), 67–78.

Oppenheimer, V. K. (1997). Women's employment and the gain to marriage: The specialization and trading model. *Annual Review of Sociology, 23*, 431–453.

O'Sullivan, L. F. (1995). Less is more: The effects of sexual experience on judgments of men's and women's personality characteristics and relationship desirability. *Sex Roles, 33*(3–4), 159–181.

Owen, J., Fincham, F. D., & Moore, J. (2011). Short-term prospective study of hooking up among college students. *Archives of Sexual Behavior, 40*(2), 331–341.

Owen, J., Rhoades, G. K., & Stanley, S. M. (2013). Sliding versus deciding in relationships: Associations with relationship quality, commitment, and infidelity. *Journal of Couple and Relationship Therapy, 12*(2), 135–149.

Paul, E. L., McManus, B., & Hayes, A. (2000). "Hookups": Characteristics and correlates of college students' spontaneous and anonymous sexual experiences. *Journal of Sex Research, 37*(1), 76–88.

Perrin, A. (2015). *Social media usage: 2005–2015.* Washington, DC: Pew Research Center.

Pew Research Center. (2009). *College enrollment hits all-time high, fueled by community college surge.* Retrieved from http://www.pewsocialtrends.org/2009/10/29/college-enrollment-hits-all-time-high-fueled-by-community-college-surge/.

Phillips, J. C. (2007, February 5). The death of marriage. *Chicago Defender.*

Pulakos, J. (2001). Young adult relationships: Siblings and friends. *Journal of Psychology, 123,* 237–244.

Ravert, R. D. (2009). "You're only young once" Things college students report doing now before it is too late. *Journal of Adolescent Research, 24,* 376–396.

Regnerus, M., & Uecker, J. (2010). *Premarital sex in America: How young Americans meet, mate, and think about marrying.* New York, NY: Oxford University Press.

Riggio, H. R., & Weiser, D. A. (2008). Attitudes toward marriage: Embeddedness and outcomes in personal relationships. *Personal Relationships, 15*(1), 123–140.

Rindfuss, R. R., & VandenHeuvel, A. (1990). Cohabitation: A precursor to marriage or an alternative to being single? *Population and Development Review, 16*(4), 703–726.

Roberts, S. (2006, October 15). It's official: To be married means to be outnumbered. *The New York Times.*

Rodrigues, L. N., & Kitzmann, K. M. (2007). Coping as a mediator between interparental conflict and adolescents' romantic attachment. *Journal of Social and Personal Relationships, 24*(3), 423–439.

Rosenfeld, M. J. (2007). *The age of independence: Interracial unions, same-sex unions, and the changing American family.* Cambridge, MA: Harvard University Press.

Ryan, R. M., & Claessens, A. (2013). Associations between family structure changes and children's behavior problems: The moderating effects of timing and marital birth. *Developmental Psychology, 49*(7), 1219–1231.

Saad, L. (2015, June 8). Fewer young people say I do—to any relationship. *Gallup.* Retrieved from http://www.gallup.com/poll/183515/fewer-young-people-say-relationship.aspx.

Sales, N. J. (2015, August 31). Tinder and the dawn of the "dating apocalypse." *Vanity Fair.* Retrieved from http://www.vanityfair.com/culture/2015/08/tinder-hook-up-culture-end-of-dating.

Schulenberg, J. E., Sameroff, A. J., & Cicchetti, D. (2004). The transition to adulthood as a critical juncture in the course of psychopathology and mental health. *Development and Psychopathology, 16,* 799–806

Seltzer, J. A. (2000). Families formed outside of marriage. *Journal of Marriage and Family, 62*(4), 1247–1268.

Shafer, K., & James, S. L. (2013). Gender and socioeconomic status differences in first and second marriage formation. *Journal of Marriage and Family, 75*(3), 544–564.

Shulman, S., & Connolly, J. (2013). The challenge of romantic relationships in emerging adulthood reconceptualization of the field. *Emerging Adulthood, 1*(1), 27–39.

Simons, L. G., Burt, C. H., & Tambling, R. B. (2013). Identifying mediators of the influence of family factors on risky sexual behavior. *Journal of Child and Family Studies, 22*(4), 460–470.

Smith, C., & Snell, P. (2009). *Souls in transition: The religious and spiritual lives of emerging adults.* New York, NY: Oxford University Press.

Smith, G. (2015). *America's changing religious landscape.* Washington, DC: Pew Research Center.

Smock, P. J. (2000). Cohabitation in the United States: An appraisal of research themes, findings, and implications. *Annual Review of Sociology, 26,* 1–20.

Smock, P. J., Manning, W. D., & Porter, M. (2005). "Everything's there except money": How money shapes decisions to marry among cohabitors. *Journal of Marriage and Family, 67*(3), 680–696.

Snyder, A. R. (2006). Risky and casual sexual relationships among teens. *Romance and sex in adolescence and emerging adulthood: Risks and opportunities,* 161–169.

Solomon-Fears, C. (2014). Teenage pregnancy prevention: statistics and programs. Retrieved from www.fas.org/sgp/crs/misc/RS20301.pdf.

Spanier, G. B. (1972). Romanticism and marital adjustment. *Journal of Marriage and the Family,* 481–487.

Staff, J. (2013). Coming of age in America: The transition to adulthood in the twenty-first century. *Contemporary Sociology, 42*(1), 117–118. Retrieved from http://search.proquest.com/docview/1464870646/abstract/EA4983B63 E564A30PQ/2.

Stanley, S. M., Whitton, S. W., & Markman, H. J. (2004). Maybe I do: Interpersonal commitment and premarital or nonmarital cohabitation. *Journal of Family Issues, 25*(4), 496–519.

Stevenson, B., & Wolfers, J. (2007). Marriage and divorce: Changes and their driving forces. *The Journal of Economic Perspectives, 21*(2), 27–52.

Strohschein, L. (2012). Parental divorce and child mental health: Accounting for predisruption differences. *Journal of Divorce & Remarriage, 53*(6), 489–502.

Sun, Y., & Li, Y. (2011). Effects of family structure type and stability on children's academic performance trajectories. *Journal of Marriage and Family, 73*(3), 541–556.

Sweeney, M. M. (2002). Two decades of family change: The shifting economic foundations of marriage. *American Sociological Review, 67*(1), 132–147.

Sylwester, K., & Pawlowski, B. (2010). Daring to be darling: Attractiveness of risk takers as partners in long- and short-term sexual relationships. *Sex Roles, 64*(9–10), 695–706.

Taylor, P., & Keeter, S. (2010). *Millennials: A portrait of generation next; confident, connected, open to change.* Washington, DC: Pew Research Center.

Thornton, A., Axinn, W. G., & Xie, Y. (2008). *Marriage and cohabitation.* Chicago, IL: University of Chicago Press.

Ugoji, F. N. (2011). Romanticism and gender identity as predictors of sexual behaviours among undergraduate students in a Nigerian university. *Journal of Social Sciences, 26,* 147–152. Retrieved from http://www.krepublishers. com/02-Journals/JSS/JSS-26-0-000-11-Web/JSS-26-2-000-11-Abst-PDF/ JSS-26-2-147-11-990-Ugoji-F-N/JSS-26-2-147-11-990-Ugoji-F-N-Tt.pdf.

U.S. Bureau of Labor Statistics. (2009, November). *Monthly labor review. 132*(11), 1–207.

U.S. Census Bureau. (2014). *Marital status.* Retrieved from https://www.census. gov/hhes/families/files/ms2.csv.

U.S. Census Bureau. (2015a) *Unmarried couples of the opposite sex, by presence of child: 1960 to present.* Retrieved from http://www.census.gov/hhes/families/data/adults.html.

U.S. Census Bureau (2015b). Current Population Survey and Annual Social and Economic Supplements. *Estimated median age at first marriage: 1890 to present.* Retrieved from http://www.census.gov/hhes/families/data/marital. html.

U.S. Census Bureau, American Community Survey (2010). Household Income and Income per Household Member among Women with a Birth in the Past year, by Marital Status: 2006–2014. Retrieved from http://www.census. gov/hhes/fertility/.

U.S. Census Bureau, Housing and Household Economic Statistics Division, Fertility & Family Statistics Branch (2011). Marital status of people 15 years and over, by age, sex, personal earnings, race, and Hispanic origin, 2011. *America's families and living arrangements: 2011.* Retrieved from http:// www.census.gov/population/www/socdemo/hh-fam/cps2011.htm.l.

U.S. Department of Education, National Center for Education Statistics. (2015). *Digest of Education Statistics, 2013.* Retrieved from http://nces.ed.gov/fastfacts/display.asp?id=98.

Valkenburg, P., Peter, J., Schouten, A. P. (2006). Friend networking sites and their relationship to adolescents' well-being and social self-esteem. *CyberPsychology & Behavior, 9,* 584–590.

VanderValk, I., Spruijt, E., de Goede, M., Maas, C., & Meeus, W. (2005). Family structure and problem behavior of adolescents and young adults: A growth-curve study. *Journal of Youth and Adolescence, 34*(6), 533–546.

Veblen, T. (1899). *The theory of the leisure class: An economic study in the evolution of institutions.* Oxford University Press, Oxford.

Ventura, S. J., & Bachrach, C. A. (2000). Nonmarital childbearing in the United States, 1940–99. *National vital statistics reports, 48*(16), n16. Retrieved from http://files.eric.ed.gov/fulltext/ED446210.pdf.

Waite, L. J., & Gallagher, M. (2000). *The case for marriage: Why married people are happier, healthier, and better off financially.* New York, NY: Doubleday.

Wang, W., & Parker, K. (2014, September). *Record share of Americans have never married: As values, economics and gender patterns change.* Washington, DC: Pew Research Center's Social & Demographic Trends project.

Weigel, D. J., Bennett, K. K., & Ballard–Reisch, D. S. (2003). Family influences on commitment: Examining the family of origin correlates of relationship commitment attitudes. *Personal Relationships, 10*(4), 453–474.

Whitton, S. W., Rhoades, G. K., Stanley, S. M., & Markman, H. J. (2008). Effects of parental divorce on marital commitment and confidence. *Journal of Family Psychology, 22*(5), 789.

Williams, J. D., & Jacoby, A. P. (1989). The effects of premarital heterosexual and homosexual experience on dating and marriage desirability. *Journal of Marriage and Family, 51*(2), 489–497.

Willoughby, B. J. (2012). Using marital attitudes in late adolescence to predict later union transitions. *Youth & Society, 46*(3), 425–440.

Willoughby, B. J., & Carroll, J. S. (2012). Correlates of attitudes toward cohabitation: Looking at the associations with demographics, relational attitudes and dating behavior. *Journal of Family Issues, 33*, 1450–1476.

Willoughby, B. J., & Carroll, J. S. (2015). On the horizon: Marriage timing, beliefs, and consequences in emerging adulthood. In J. J. Arnett (Ed.), *The Oxford handbook of emerging adulthood* (pp. 280–295). New York, NY: Oxford University Press.

Willoughby, B. J., Carroll, J. S., Vitas, J. M., & Hill, L. M. (2011). "When are you getting married?": The intergenerational transmission of attitudes regarding marital timing and marital importance. *Journal of Family Issues. 33*(2).

Willoughby, B. J., & Dworkin, J. (2009). The relationships between emerging adults' expressed desire to marry and frequency of participation in risk-taking behaviors. *Youth & Society, 40*(3), 426–450.

Willoughby, B. J., & Hall, S. (2015). Enthusiasts, delayers, and the ambiguous middle: Marital paradigms among emerging adults. *Emerging Adulthood, 3*, 123–135.

Willoughby, B. J., Hall, S. S., & Goff, S. (2015). Marriage matters but how much? Marital centrality among young adults. *Journal of Psychology, 149*, 796–817.

Willoughby, B. J., Hall, S. S., & Luczak, H. P. (2015). Marital paradigms: A conceptual framework for marital attitudes, values, and beliefs. *Journal of Family Issues, 36*(2), 188–211.

Willoughby, B. J., Medaris, M., James, S., & Bartholomew, K. (2015). Changes in marital beliefs among emerging adults examining marital paradigms over time. *Emerging Adulthood, 3*, 219–228.

Willoughby, B. J., Olson, C. D., Carroll, J. S., Nelson, L. J., & Miller, R. B. (2012). Sooner or later? The marital horizons of parents and their emerging adult children. *Journal of Social and Personal Relationships, 29*(7), 967–981.

Wrzus, C., Hänel, M., Wagner, J., & Neyer, F. J. (2013). Social network changes and life events across the life span: A meta-analysis. *Psychological Bulletin, 139*(1), 53–80.

Zimmer-Gembeck, M. J., & Petherick, J. (2006). Intimacy dating goals and relationship satisfaction during adolescence and emerging adulthood: Identity formation, age and sex as moderators. *International Journal of Behavioral Development, 30*(2), 167–177.

Zurbriggen, E. L., & Morgan, E. M. (2006). Who wants to marry a millionaire? Reality dating television programs, attitudes toward sex, and sexual behaviors. *Sex Roles, 54*(1), 1–17.

ABOUT THE AUTHORS ▲

Brian J. Willoughby, Ph.D., is an associate professor in the School of Family Life at Brigham Young University. Dr. Willoughby is considered an international expert in the field of couple and marital relationships, sexuality, and emerging adult development. His research generally focuses on how adolescents, young adults, and adults move toward and form long-term committed relationships.

Spencer L. James, Ph.D., is an assistant professor in the School of Family Life at Brigham Young University. As a family demographer, Dr. James is interested in the ways people form, maintain, and dissolve long-term romantic relationships, especially during emerging adulthood. He draws primarily on nationally representative longitudinal datasets and advanced statistical methods to answer questions about contemporary trends in marital and cohabiting relationships.

Index ▲

Note: Page numbers followed by *f* indicate a figure

substance use, 30, 105

teenage marriages, 48
television
    depiction of "love conquers all"
      theme, 42
    reality television, 150–152, 154
theories
    family ecological theory, 108
    Marital Horizon Theory, 31–33, 70
    Marital Paradigm Theory, 28–33,
      45, 70, 99, 208
    stress theory, 200
Tinder, 11
traditional ideals, 55, 57
traditional marriage, 73, 74, 75, 96, 168
traditional patterns in gender roles,
    157, 159, 162–168, 174, 182
Twitter, 137*f*
two-parent families, 73–76, 119, 120*f*

Uecker, J. E., 48
uncertainty
    about career, 63–65
    economic, 6
    emotional impact of, 9, 13, 50, 195
    about life transitions, 61, 68
    residential mobility and, 97
unemployment, 5, 211
unhealthy parental examples,
    115–124, 171

values
    reinforcing by peers, 138–140
    religious, 142–144
    similarity in, 90–92
values coding, 210
Veblen, Thorstein, 156

weddings
    delaying for education, 67
    idealization of, 53
    media depictions, 151–153
    planning, 31, 116–117
    social media and, 153–154
    thinking about, 29
Willoughby, B. J., 28, 29, 77–78
women's rights movement, 22, 166

Zimmer-Gembeck, M. J., 16